FROM

HEART OF TIBET

FROM THE

HEART

— OF —

TIBET

The Biography of
Drikung Chetsang Rinpoche,
the Holder of the
Drikung Kagyu Lineage

ELMAR R. GRUBER

Forewords by the Fourteenth Dalai Lama,
the Gyalwang Drukpa, and Garchen Rinpoche

SHAMBHALA
Boston & London
2010

SHAMBHALA PUBLICATIONS, INC.
Horticultural Hall
300 Massachusetts Avenue
Boston, Massachusetts 02115
www.shambhala.com

9 8 7 6 5 4 3 2 1

FIRST EDITION
Printed in the United States of America

♾ This edition is printed on acid-free paper that meets the
American National Standards Institute z39.48 Standard.
♻ This book was printed on 30% postconsumer recycled paper.
For more information please visit www.shambhala.com.
Distributed in the United States by Random House, Inc.,
and in Canada by Random House of Canada Ltd

Designed by Steve Dyer

LIBRARY OF CONGRESS CATALOGING-IN-PUBLICATION DATA
Gruber, Elmar, 1955–
[Aus dem Herzen Tibets. English]
From the heart of Tibet: the biography of Drikung Chetsang Rinpoche,
the holder of the Drikung Kagyu lineage / Elmar R. Gruber; forewords by
the Fourteenth Dalai Lama, the Gyalwang Drukpa, and Garchen Rinpoche.
p.   cm.
Includes bibliographical references and index.
ISBN 978-1-59030-765-6 (pbk.: alk. paper)
1. Chetsang, Rinpoche. 2. Dkon-mchog-bstan-’dzin-’phrin-las-lhun-’grub,
’Bri-gun Skyabs-mgon Che-tshan VII. 3. ’Bri-gun-pa lamas—Biography.
4. ’Bri-gun-pa lamas—China—Tibet—Biography. 5. ’Bri-gun-pa
(Sect)—History. 6. Tibet (China)—Biography. I. Title.
BQ946.E494G7813 2010
[B]
2010006463

CONTENTS

THE DALAI LAMA

FOREWORD

THE STORY OF Drikung Chetsang Rinpoche's life encompasses a remarkably broad range of Tibetan experience spanning the past fifty years. Born into a prominent aristocratic family and then recognized as an important reincarnate lama, he might have been expected to lead a life of privilege and esteem, in addition to the responsibilities he had to bear. However, the changes that overwhelmed Tibet in the middle of the twentieth century affected everyone. Following the Lhasa uprising of 1959, after which I and many other Tibetans escaped from Tibet, Rinpoche found himself left behind. Other aristocrats and lamas were punished by the Communist authorities with long terms of harsh imprisonment, but as luck would have it, Chetsang Rinpoche was deemed too young for such treatment and was sent to school instead. There, at least, he was introduced to socialist ideals and modern ways of thinking. He studied hard and was a model student until he was sent to do manual labor in the countryside.

The sixties and seventies were difficult times for everyone in Tibet, but Rinpoche did not despair or become complacent. When the opportunity arose he made his escape, crossing the Tibetan border into Nepal and making his way to India, where he encountered an atmosphere of freedom he had not experienced since his childhood. After many years of being unable to communicate with any member of his family, he was surprised to find that nearly all of them had moved to the United States. Arrangements were made for him to join them, and so he began a new life in a foreign land, struggling to come to terms with a new language and many new customs and attitudes. He even took a job while he learned to speak English.

Rinpoche must have been very tempted to relax and accept the circumstances in which found himself, particularly after the hardships of life in Tibet under Chinese rule. There he was, reunited with his family, faced with the prospect of a comfortable life, and yet, all the while, he had remained a monk. Reading a history of the Drikung Kagyu tradition to which he belonged, his interest in his religious heritage, and his sense of responsibility for the lineage of which he was the head, were reawakened once more. He returned to India and began the task of reviving his tradition. This involved a great deal of work on his part in terms of receiving teachings, transmissions, and empowerments and consolidating their practice in meditative retreat, as well as visiting his various monasteries and organizing their more mundane affairs.

His efforts have borne ample fruit; the Drikung Kagyu tradition has been revived not only in the Tibetan community in exile, but also in its monasteries in Ladakh and elsewhere. Rinpoche has established an excellent centre for the study and practice of the Drikung Kagyu tradition called Jangchubling in Dehra Dun, North India, which functions as the tradition's headquarters outside Tibet. In response to many requests, he has also founded meditation and study centers abroad. He himself teaches and passes on his tradition. It gives me great pleasure to know that with the publication of this book readers in the wider world will be able to learn for themselves about Drikung Chetsang Rinpoche's unusual life, which, as I said at the beginning, covers such a range of experience, from the ways of life of old Tibet, through the hardships that followed, to his successful efforts here in exile to preserve and promote the values that all Tibetans hold dear. Therefore, while I pray that Rinpoche may live a long and healthy life, I trust that others will take hope and inspiration from what he has achieved so far.

THE DALAI LAMA

FOREWORD

His Holiness Kyabgon Drikung Chetsang Rinpoche, my best friend and vajra brother, is one of the most accomplished spiritual masters in our time. His experiences in life and spiritual practice are rich and encouraging for anyone who has heard about them. His positive attitude toward life, despite facing many difficulties at a young age and challenges at other times, is something all of us should be following as a great example.

I am very happy that Dr. Elmar R. Gruber is offering the biography of His Holiness as an inspiration to the present world and beyond. His life story will definitely encourage countless spiritual practitioners to take challenges as a form of spiritual practice so that the strength of spirituality will grow within their mind as a positive development for the long run.

From the depth of my heart, I pray for the longevity and happiness of His Holiness. May all that he wishes be effortlessly accomplished!

THE GYALWANG DRUKPA
November 2009

ༀ། །མགར་ཆེན་ཁྲི་སྤྲུལ།

GARCHEN TRIPTRÜL,
KÖNCHOG GYALTSEN

FOREWORD

A S STUDENTS OF DHARMA, we turn to the life and liberation stories of the great masters to strengthen our faith and devotion and to gain inspiration for our practice of the path. The true Dharma taught by Lord Buddha has been passed down by an unbroken line of realized masters, from generation to generation, until the present day. By reading about such masters' lives, we gain confidence in the authenticity of the teachings they have transmitted, develop gratitude for the hardships they endured to ensure that transmission, and generate faith in their qualities as objects of refuge. Because such stories are unfailing sources of inspiration and guidance, it brings me great joy that this biography of Drikung Kyabgön Chetsang Rinpoche will now be available to a wide audience.

The Drikung Kagyu lineage is often described as a golden rosary. Each lineage master is like a bead of gold on an unbroken strand, ultimately linking us, through our root teacher (the bead nearest us), to the Buddha. *Bodhicitta,* the altruistic mind of enlightenment, is like the single thread running through all the beads. So while it is possible to count the individual beads, their essence is one—it is that of all the buddhas. The present Kyabgön Chetsang Rinpoche, Tenzin Trinle Lhundrub, as the thirty-seventh head of the Drikung lineage of Tibetan Buddhism that was founded in the twelfth century by Lord Jigten Sumgön, is one such master.

Due to the difficulties of the period in which we came of age, I was not able to meet Kyabgön Chetsang Rinpoche until later in my life.

From the time I was a small boy, I had great faith in Jigten Sumgön and, therefore, in his emanation, Kyabgön Chetsang Rinpoche. But when I went to Nepal and India in 1993 and was finally able to meet him and hear his story, even more faith and confidence arose within me. Now, seeing him as a buddha, I have unshakeable faith in him.

Kyabgön Chetsang Rinpoche's story is one of wholehearted dedication to the Buddhadharma. Throughout the turmoil of his youth, he maintained his monastic vows in a hostile, anti-religious environment, finally managing a miraculous escape from Tibet. After all the hardships he had suffered, he went to India to take up the heavy responsibility of leading and revitalizing the Drikung Kagyu lineage, still finding time for his own practice, study, and retreat. I am amazed at how much a single person has accomplished in such a short time. When I witnessed how hard Kyabgön Chetsang Rinpoche works, I thought, "I really should work like that, too."

Now, as the Buddhadharma in general and the Drikung teachings in particular take root in the West, I pray that Drikung Kyabgön Rinpoche's example may inspire many others in the same way. I am confident that this book will play a role in that process.

KYABJE GARCHEN TRIPTRUL RINPOCHE

FROM THE
HEART OF TIBET

View from Drikung Dzong to the south.

Prologue

WHERE THE LUNGSHÖ RIVER enters from the northwest and meets the Shorong and the Mangra, they form the Kyichu, which flows in a sharp bend toward Lhasa in the southwest. The streams converge here like the spokes of a wheel at the hub. The stronghold of Drikung Dzong is enthroned on the majestic mountain ridge north of the triangle formed by these river valleys. "Dzong" means stronghold, and Tibetan monasteries often provided not only spiritual but also physical refuge, offering protection from marauding bandits or armies. Its buildings, with steep stairways clinging to the slope and mighty whitewashed walls, are reminiscent of the Potala Palace in Lhasa. The administrative center and monastery complex of the district government of Drikung has inspired reverence and envy throughout the centuries, and was often threatened by hostile encroachment. Swift reconstruction, often more imposing and resplendent than before, always followed its destruction.

It is 1959. Drikung Dzong has lost none of its splendor and magnificent appearance. From this strategic location one can survey the main roads running beside the rivers far into the distance. On the high terraced roof of the building, where victory banners wave, symbolic of the Buddha's triumph over the four Maras,[1] and eagles circle in the winds, young Chetsang Rinpoche runs about excitedly, his eyes firmly pressed into a pair of field glasses. Far away to the south he sees a dust cloud shimmering in the light along the Kyichu. The boy is uneasy and fascinated at the same time. He has thoroughly explored this familiar landscape with his binoculars, a gift from his grandfather: the bare slopes to his right; the mountain flank directly across from him with the eroded and overgrown ruins of Namgyal Chödzong, the area's oldest

1

stronghold; the daunting suspension bridge built by his grandfather; and the houses of Dzongshol, with nomads in their fur cloaks, girls drawing water and spreading laundry to dry along the river bank, and boys with slingshots skillfully driving stray sheep back to the herd. Now and then he has watched the nomads' small trade caravans traveling to Lhasa to sell their butter and dried cheese. But most of all he enjoys observing animals. He never tires of watching the graceful horses or the contented, dignified yaks. His heart leaps with the gazelles that come down from the mountains in the evenings to drink from the river and then suddenly spring away as if at a secret command. There is consummate beauty in all of nature. But now, as he stands on the roof and looks through his field glasses, nature seems disturbed, as if something has been thrown off balance. A dull confusion of angry voices rises from the abbot's chambers below. Dark storm clouds gather in the east beyond the mountains, and as the sun's rays pierce the clouds they ignite fireworks of dancing light particles in the dust cloud far to the south.

His field glasses seem to make the invisible appear, and he sometimes imagines that they can also draw a long-vanished past back into the present. As he looks and dreams into the distance, his mother's face appears in his mind, dim but no less real than the yakskin boat the ferryman steers to the far bank of the Kyichu. He sees the stocky form of his grandfather in the light of the evening sun. The boy sees himself in the lush garden of his parents' house, hiding in the greenhouse, or petting his white rabbits, peacefully absorbed in play, all sense of self forgotten.

Is he looking out or looking in? The view through the binoculars is like a glimpse into a hidden reality. It is like looking into a glass case through which one can discover further glass cases, on and on until the field glasses' limit is reached. Things look as if they would in fact be empty, if only he could look at them closely enough, as the lamas have been teaching him.[2] The forms emerging from the dust cloud are disquieting. At first he makes out the tall, proud steeds, and he is thrilled by their powerful tread and the strong sweep of their necks. They are much taller and more elegant than Tibetan horses. Their riders are in uniform, and behind them are countless soldiers, marching in step like rows of beads strung one after another on a cord.

His heart beats faster, but he cannot pull himself away from the vision, at once frightening and alluring, of so many armed men. He thinks he can almost hear them singing, although they are too far away. All he really hears is the rustling of the bushes and the occasional gloomy cawing of a bird above him. Steadying his elbows on top of the wall, he now notices someone at the head of the column who, like himself, is looking through field glasses, focusing them directly at Drikung Dzong. Directly at him. Startled, he jerks the binoculars away from his eyes as if this will make him invisible, and rushes to hide behind one of the long, cylindrical banners on the monastery roof. Made of black yak hair, they represent the wrathful protectors of Buddhism, but these protectors seem to have lost their power in Tibet. Countless monasteries have already fallen to the aggressors, but the boy knows nothing of all this. He lives surrounded by devoted servants and teachers who speak only of the sacred world and insulate him from the violence of the real world. Incorrigibly adventurous, the boy cautiously raises his field glasses again and observes the foreign scout as the scout observes him through his binoculars. They are locked together in a reciprocal gaze in which both have emerged from invisibility.

1

In Search of the Precious Jewel

KONCHOG SAMTEN and his companions were searching for the most precious thing known to them. Disguised as traders with pack animals and wearing the traditional clothing of their regional homeland they traveled in inconspicuous groups of two or three, visiting villages and nomads' camps. The travelers sat by flickering stove fires in houses or in nomads' tents made of dark yak hair and listened attentively to the stories their hosts told them of the daily lives of the local families while sharing salty butter tea, *tsampa,* and *chang.*[1]

Disguised as casual travelers, they bore a heavy responsibility; they were actually monks in search of the reincarnation of a high lama. As similar delegations had for centuries, they traveled incognito in the areas indicated through visions, prophecies, or oracles, cautiously approaching families in which a possible candidate had been born. When they found one, they observed his behavior and that of his parents very closely, playing with the child and showing him objects that had belonged to the deceased lama to see how he responded. They did not reveal their mission even when they felt certain that the boy should be included in the group of candidates, because everything had to be discussed with other lamas and dignitaries before the process of recognition could take its course. This secrecy was necessary since many parents coveted the elevated social position that went with having a son recognized as a *tulku,* a reincarnated lama. The birth of a *rinpoche* ("Precious One") or tulku is always a sign that the parents have accumulated great merit, and it was by no means unusual for Tibetans to try to boost a son into this position with fictitious tales of miraculous events during the mother's pregnancy and the child's birth, and in the child's early years.[2]

H. H. Tenzin Shiwe Lodrö, the Sixth Chetsang Rinpoche, ca. 1940.

This was without a doubt the easiest way to move up in the political and economic hierarchy of tradition-bound Tibet, not only for the child, but for the whole clan.

During a journey to eastern Tibet, His Holiness Tenzin Shiwe Lodrö, the throne holder of the Drikung Kagyu lineage of Tibetan Buddhism, suffered a stroke, thereafter speaking only with difficulty, and spending most of his time in meditation. He failed to recover and died on a frosty December day in 1943. While yogis and high lamas prepared for the death rites, the body of Shiwe Lodrö remained in meditation posture for a whole week, until some blood and a white substance (the "red and white *bodhicitta*," a manifestation of the mind of enlightenment) flowed out of his nose.[3] The precious substances were mixed with tsampa and made into pills to be put in reliquaries, stupas, and hollow statues.[4] Only then was the Kyabgön Rinpoche—"Refuge and Protector"—pronounced dead. Threatening dark clouds hung low over Drikung and it seemed that the sun and moon would never shine again. As diseases raced through the land, a fever took the lives of many monks. Drikung's disciples yearned for the day when their Kyabgön's reincarnation would return.

The search for the reincarnation of Shiwe Lodrö began a few years after his death. A commission of leading lamas selected the monks who were to search in different locations and the responsibility for the search parties lay in the hands of the *chagdzö*, Döndrup Khangsar.[5] Shiwe Lodrö himself had left no indications during his lifetime as to where he would be reborn. A few witnesses had noticed how his cremation smoke had drifted southwest, toward Lhasa, but this was too vague to be considered a significant indication. And so two groups were sent out to search for the new incarnation of the deceased Drikung Kyabgön, also known as Chetsang Rinpoche, one group to the south and the other to the north. Among them was Konchog Samten, who had been a close attendant to the deceased Chetsang Rinpoche.

These were troubling times. In China a civil war raged between the Nationalists and the Communists, and the danger of the upheaval spilling into Tibet was growing daily. This political uncertainty added urgency to the search for the Drikung Kyabgön's reincarnation. Without a throne holder, the continuity of the Drikung order was not assured. The interim regent in Drikung, Tritsab Gyabra (1924–1979), was responsible for the fate and fortune of the lineage until the new throne holder reached an age when he could assume leadership. The regent knew that no matter how honorably and diligently he dedicated himself to his task, he would never have the unquestioned authority of a Kyabgön.

The monks of Drikung Thil, the main Drikung Kagyu monastery, traveled throughout the countryside for months, carefully investigating any unusual events that might indicate the birth of a candidate. A long list of candidates was compiled and discussed with yogis, tulkus, and oracles. After a series of divinations, they came up with a short list through *senryl*, a divination by lottery. After hours of prayers recited before the statue of the lineage founder, Jigten Sumgön, and inside the shrine of the protector deity Achi Chökyi Dolma, two identical balls of dough were placed in a large silver bowl that a high lama slowly shook. One contained a slip of paper that said "yes," in the other, "no." The name of one candidate from the list was read aloud and the first ball of dough to roll out was opened. If the paper said "no" the candidate was eliminated; if "yes," he stayed in the running. After this procedure six candidates remained under provisional consideration as the new incarnation of Chetsang Rinpoche.

Regent Tritsab Gyabra decided to go, with a handful of lineage dignitaries and a small following of monks, on a pilgrimage to southern Tibet to consult the sacred oracle lake Lhamo Latso. This lake has played a significant role in the search for important incarnations, and numerous rinpoches have received decisive visionary indications while meditating there.

As the pilgrims from Drikung made their arduous way over high passes and through wind-whipped valleys they took care not to cast even a glance at the rivers and lakes they passed because it was said that if one saw an image in another body of water, one would no longer have a vision at Lhamo Latso. They finally arrived and made camp on a hill above the lake shimmering far below. Tents were raised, ritual instruments unpacked, and a purification offering of fragrant juniper made. Prayers and ritual chants were performed for days until Tritsab Gyabra at last went down to the mirror-like lake to meditate in solitude and pray for an oracular vision. A fog soon veiled the water's surface, and as shapes and shadows superimposed themselves upon one another, images began to emerge, at first indistinct, then with increasing clarity. He saw a beautiful, wide valley and a stately two-story house with a staircase outside. The main entrance faced east, and surrounding the house was a magnificent garden enclosed by a wall, with silvery eucalyptus trees, unusual for Tibetan homes. On the roof he recognized a victory banner on a mast with an arrowhead and a five-colored flag symbolizing the five buddha families. A small red dog was tied to it. Tritsab Gyabra knew this image meant Chetsang Rinpoche's reincarnation had been born in the year of the Fire Dog. He prayed for greater clarity regarding the location of the house and intuitively knew it was in Lhasa. The vision dissolved in an instant, and once again the surface of the lake reflected only the panorama of the mountains around it.

Tritsab Gyabra was pleased by the clear visionary impressions, but they still needed further verification. Back in Drikung Thil there was another divination with the balls of dough, and Khenpo Tseten Sangpo performed a *trabab,* divination with mirrors. Children are usually called on for this type of divination, because they more easily perceive vision-

Drikung regent Tritsab Gyabra in the shrine room at Tsarong House.

ary images in reflective surfaces. Few adults possess these special visionary abilities, but Tseten Sangpo was a master of them. A mirror was placed in a container filled with grain and sprinkled with a sacred yellow powder. In front of the mirror was a crystal, and behind it an arrow with ribbons in five colors; offering cakes with butter ornaments and ritual libations surrounded everything. Tseten Sangpo invoked the power of the oracle deity by reciting a mantra, and in the mirror he verified the accuracy of Tritsab Gyabra's vision. Taklung Matrul and the Sixteenth Karmapa Rangjung Dorje (1924–1981) also subsequently confirmed the result.

Tritsab Gyabra dispatched a delegation to Lhasa to search for the boy. A brother of the Dalai Lama matched some of the visionary indications, as he had been born in the Fire Dog Year in a manorial house in Lhasa. The Drikung lamas petitioned Taktra Rinpoche (1874–1952), the regent of Tibet, with their indications that he may be their Kyabgön, but Taktra was not convinced. He recommended that the monks hold large-scale prayer ceremonies, and soon afterward, the Dalai Lama's young brother was recognized as the Fifteenth Ngari Rinpoche.

Konchog Samten, one of the managers of Drikung Labrang,[6] had been ordered to Lhasa as the leader of a search party. He discovered another candidate through the prophecy of a local deity, which directed him to Gyume Dratsang, the famous school of higher tantric studies. Behind the venerable building he encountered a very poor family with a three-year-old son, and when he sat down with them the young boy immediately jumped onto his lap and the parents related several remarkable events in connection with his birth. They also had some documents written by lamas that testified to their son's exceptional qualities. When Samten rose to leave with his companions, the child tried to hold him back.

At the same time some Drikung managers and officials traveled to Lhasa to settle a dispute about some taxes to be paid to the government. As usual in such matters, they sought the advice of old Dasang Damdul Tsarong, one of the country's most influential politicians and a successful businessman with many ties to Drikung. He had known the deceased throne holder Shiwe Lodrö and was responsible for building the suspension bridge below Drikung Dzong.

A delegation of Drikung monastic officials was nothing out of the ordinary for Tsarong, but as soon as the two monks entered the gate, the grandson of the great Tsarong, a little boy named Tseten Gyurme, started to cry and cling to one of the monks. Nothing could quiet the child. His nanny had to remove the weeping child from the monks so they could go in to their conference. After they finished and came out of the house, the boy ran to them and accompanied them to the main gate. A monk bent down to ask where he wished to go, and the young boy stretched out his arm to the east. Once again, he refused to part with them until the monks reluctantly frightened him into letting them go. Their eyes filled with tears. They were profoundly moved, convinced that this boy must be the reincarnation of Kyabgön Chetsang Rinpoche.

Excitedly they told Tritsab Rinpoche about their experience in the stately home of the Tsarong family, which corresponded exactly to the one in his vision. There was a spacious, lovely garden with beautiful shrubs, fruit trees, and even eucalyptus trees, the main entrance faced east, and an auspicious victory banner rose from the roof of the house.

Tritsab Rinpoche sent the monks back to investigate further, and from time to time they returned to Lhasa to see the boy without informing his parents. The boy's nannies suspected nothing and were happy to let the monks play with Tseten Gyurme, who obviously enjoyed their visits. One day they brought some religious objects: a *vajra*, bell, *mala* (prayer beads), hand drum, and ritual dagger, some of which had been owned by Chetsang Rinpoche's previous incarnation.[7] The monks watched closely to see which objects the boy preferred. Without hesitation he reached for a simple string of prayer beads, although magnificent ones made of precious stones with silver counters were laid out next to them. With unwavering confidence he played only with the objects that had belonged to Shiwe Lodrö, the deceased Drikung Chetsang Rinpoche.

A tulku is the reincarnation of a master on the spiritual path who has attained liberation from the cycle of existence but consciously decides to be reborn as a human being in order to help all other beings attain liberation. Tulku reincarnation in Tibetan Buddhism is very complex. It is based on the three "bodies" of a buddha, which are more accurately conceived of as three dimensions of expression or embodiment: *nirmanakaya, sambhogakaya,* and *dharmakaya.*[8] They correspond to the three levels of experience—concrete, subtle, and mental, respectively—as well as to the body, speech, and mind. Sometimes a tulku embodies himself in different persons simultaneously, who are then regarded as emanations of diverse aspects of one single former incarnation. In addition, incarnations can be emanations of important masters, bodhisattvas, or divine beings. The Nyingma and Kagyu have occasionally recognized up to five incarnations of a single lama.[9]

The two children from Lhasa expanded the circle of candidates for the reincarnation of Chetsang Rinpoche to eight. The oracle of Gaden Chökor Monastery announced that three incarnations of the previous Chetsang Rinpoche had been born, one of the body, one of speech, and one of mind, but that the incarnation of his speech aspect had died. (The common explanation for the early death of the incarnation of a high spiritual master was that their disciples and other people close to them had not accumulated enough merit.) The boy from the poor family behind Gyume Dratsang was identified as the rebirth of the body aspect, and the mind aspect had incarnated as the grandson of the great Tsarong. He was therefore to be entrusted with the responsibility of leading the Drikung Kagyu lineage as its throne holder. The final selection of Tseten Gyurme Tsarong was also confirmed by the Dalai Lama's tutors, Trijang Rinpoche and Ling Rinpoche, by the state oracles of Nechung and Gadong, and by many high lamas in the Kagyu tradition.

The procedure was entering its final phase. A great prayer ceremony was held in Drikung Thil's temple of Achi Chökyi Dolma for seven days, after which Tritsab Gyabra used dough balls to question the oracle yet again. Was the reincarnation of Shiwe Lodrö definitely among the eight remaining candidates? Accompanied by the murmur of prayers, he rocked the bowl and the dough ball with the affirmative answer sprang out. Then eight dough balls with the candidates' names were placed in the bowl, and tension mounted as the bowl was rocked again. The first ball to spring out contained the name of Tseten Gyurme, the scion of the Tsarong family. The result could not be more conclusive. A delegation was immediately dispatched to the regent of Tibet, Taktra Rinpoche, in Lhasa to present him with the extensive report on their long search. He was to authenticate the outcome, since the Dalai Lama was still too young to do it himself. After studying all the documents carefully and meditating on them, Taktra Rinpoche officially confirmed that the indisputable incarnation of Drikung Kyabgön Chetsang Rinpoche had been identified. He found the details of the oracle lake vision to be especially conclusive.

The people of Drikung were overjoyed to have found their precious lineage holder again. An auspicious day was determined for the official recognition ceremony and presentation of monastic robes. A delegation of high-ranking Drikung dignitaries was sent to Lhasa since neither the candidate's parents nor the elder Tsarong knew of the selection, and their agreement was a potential hurdle. Men in the Tsarong family traditionally held high positions in the Tibetan government and it could not be taken for granted that Tsarong would accept the selection. It was not uncommon for some monasteries and lineages to bias the selection process for high tulkus by preferring children from prominent aristocratic families, since such a connection to an influential noble family brought legal and financial advantages for a monastery.[10]

2

Family and Childhood in Lhasa

THE HOUSE OF TSARONG was one of Tibet's most prominent aristocratic families. Their ancestral estate, from which the family name was derived, was a twelve-day journey on horseback from Lhasa. They claimed descent from a legendary eighth-century physician, Yuthog Yonten Gonpo, whose statue and skull were kept in a temple dedicated to healing on the estate. The Tsarongs settled in Lhasa when the male descendants became active in various government offices.

A few family members are recorded as having prominent political positions in the seventeenth and eighteenth centuries, including a high ranking monastic official, a head of the renowned Chakpori medical college and physician to the Eighth Dalai Lama, and a district governor. In the middle of the nineteenth century Kelsang Damdul Tsarong gained prominence as governor of Tsaparang. In the late nineteenth century, Tibet was mostly closed to outsiders except the Chinese, although the Qing Dynasty, which had ruled in China since the seventeenth century, was in decline and its influence in Tibet was fading. In 1885 a British incursion under Colman Macauley was thwarted and the Tibetans sent a delegation headed by Dorje Rigzin Tsarong, a treasury officer of the Lhasa government, to demarcate the border with Sikkim and thus block any potential British claims. Through the course of his career Dorje Rigzin Tsarong held various influential positions and was eventually appointed a *kalön,* one of the four ministers in the *Kashag,* the Council of Ministers or cabinet.[1] Dorje Rigzin's son Wangchug Gyalpo Tsarong (1866–1912) became the district commander of central Tibet. He was the leader of a delegation sent to negotiate with Francis Edward Young-husband when the latter crossed into Tibet in July 1903 with an "escort" of two hundred men under the pretext of wishing to open up trade relations with Tibet. When the negotiations failed, Younghusband sent his troops marching toward Lhasa, which triggered the Thirteenth Dalai Lama's flight into temporary exile in Mongolia.

Among the entourage accompanying the Dalai Lama into exile was Dasang Damdul, later to become the grandfather of Chetsang Rinpoche but then just a sixteen-year-old boy of unconditional loyalty, decisiveness, and swift comprehension. Called Namgang in his youth, he was born in Phenpo in 1888, the son of a farmer and bow maker. Despite the boy's humble origins the Dalai Lama recognized his potential and began to foster and promote him, giving him the name Dasang Damdul. On the arduous journey to Mongolia the travelers became uncertain of their route, and Dasang Damdul was selected to take on the role of an oracle to provide guidance. Although he apparently did not enter into a full oracular trance, his right hand, rigidly clasping the oracle staff, was said to have shaken uncontrollably, the movements being enough for the lamas to deduce a direction for the rest of the journey. While in exile, Dasang Damdul received some Russian military training, and, fascinated by the technology unknown in his homeland, he purchased cameras, watches, a protractor, and a theodolite for surveying land.

The Dalai Lama and his entourage returned to Lhasa on December 25, 1909. On the return journey Dasang Damdul was raised to the fifth rank in the Tibetan government.[2] But six weeks later a Chinese army stood before the gates of the city and the Dalai Lama was forced to take flight once again. With a unit of only sixty-seven men, Dasang Damdul confronted the superior Chinese forces with unyielding determination, audacity, and strategic skill, and succeeded in delaying the pursuers long enough to allow the Dalai Lama to reach safety in India. His bravery made him a national hero in Tibet: the man who had saved the Dalai Lama's life.

Soon afterward, nationalist insurgents in China overthrew the Qing Dynasty of the Manchus, and the Dalai Lama saw an opportunity to regain Tibetan independence. He appointed Dasang Damdul commander general of the Tibetan forces, entrusting him with the task of organizing the resistance into an army to drive the Chinese out of Lhasa. The superbly organized Chinese troops, equipped with modern weapons, far outnumbered the Tibetan troops Dasang Damdul was able to enlist.

A Tibetan army as such did not exist, and Dasang Damdul was compelled to recruit volunteers without any training or combat experience, equipped with only swords, bows and arrows, and obsolete muskets. He assembled a ragtag unit with which he conducted a bitter, house-to-house battle with the Chinese in Lhasa, where fortune was with him—when word of the revolution in China reached Lhasa, some of the Chinese troops deserted, and Dasang Damdul was able to persuade many of them to join the Tibetan cause and fight against their own countrymen. The Tibetans emerged victorious, and Dasang Damdul's reputation as a hero again spread throughout the country.

Tibet's hero became the symbol of the country's liberation. The Dalai Lama returned to Lhasa from his second exile in January 1912, and to the jubilant population he proclaimed Tibet an independent state. Dasang Damdul was promoted to a government position ranking directly below a cabinet minister.

During the Dalai Lama's second period of exile, Wangchug Gyalpo Tsarong had become a cabinet minister. In this difficult time Tsarong had tried to secure Tibetan independence under the authority of the Kashag by means of good ties with China—a route which may have seemed the only option in the face of China's military superiority. Using his diplomatic skills, he became an important negotiating partner with the Chinese. After the liberation of Lhasa, opponents of this approach accused Tsarong of high treason and had him dragged down the steps of the Potala palace and summarily beheaded. The monks of Sera showed his severed head to his son, Samdup Tsering Tsarong (1887–1912), who was then executed just as cruelly, together with the secretary and the treasurer of the Kashag, and a general secretary of the clerical council.

These events might have spelled the end of the House of Tsarong, with the confiscation of the family's property and the surviving members' descent into poverty and insignificance. But the Dalai Lama was grieved by the assassination of Wangchug Gyalpo Tsarong, who had been loyal to him, and found a way to help the Tsarong family and to bring his favorite hero into the nobility at the same time. He married Dasang Damdul to the widow of Samdup Tsering Tsarong, the murdered son, and from then on Dasang Damdul bore the Tsarong name as head of his wife's clan. The Dalai Lama also gave his consent to a second marriage, to Pema Dolkar, the daughter of Wangchug Gyalpo Tsarong.

*Dasang Damdul Tsarong with his wife Pema Dolkar at
New Year in their mansion in Lhasa in 1937.*

The second marriage ensured the survival of the family's bloodline, and Dasang Damdul Tsarong later married Pema Dolkar's sister as well. Polygyny and polyandry were both commonly practiced in Tibet at that time, and Dasang Damdul's marriage to Pema Dolkar in particular was said to be a happy one, characterized by mutual love and respect.

The old aristocracy eyed the upstart's rise carefully, looking for an excuse to rid themselves of him, but Dasang Damdul gave them no such opportunity. As commander general he began to build up a modern army, sharing the Dalai Lama's view that the survival of an independent Tibet depended on initiating reforms and modernization without delay, and on forming alliances with other nations interested in limiting China's influence in central Asia. In 1915 he became a cabinet minister, going on to become one of the country's most influential statesmen and steering the course of political developments for a long time. He broke up the clique of established aristocrats, and with his directness and fiery temperament he inspired both fear and respect among his colleagues in the Kashag.

With his business acumen, Dasang Damdul succeeded in recovering and even increasing the family's wealth, and the magnificent manor house he built at the southern edge of the city was said to be Lhasa's most impressive. The house had glass windows, bathrooms, soap, and toothbrushes, and the family slept in beds with white sheets, all of which was unusual in Tibet at that time, even among the wealthy. Dasang Damdul had a total of ten children with his three wives, and sent several of them to English boarding schools in Darjeeling, convinced of the value of a Western education. His son Dundul Namgyal, born in 1920, attended St. Joseph's College (one of these boarding schools in Darjeeling), where he received the English name "George." Dundul Namgyal also shared a passion for photography and filming with his father, whose fascination with modern technology had begun during his exile in Mongolia and Russia with the Dalai Lama.

Meanwhile both change and continuity were at work in Tibet. At the end of 1924, Tsarong's political rivals finally succeeded in contriving an intrigue against him. He lost his high office, but remained very active in the political and economic life of the country. Nine years later, following the death of the Thirteenth Dalai Lama in December 1933, a permanent delegation led by a representative of Chiang Kai-shek's (1887–1975) Nationalist Party took up residence in Lhasa, continuing their imperial predecessors' policies in Tibet. The young Reting Rinpoche (1911–1947), popular but lacking in ethical discipline, was appointed regent, and was to rule until the young Fourteenth Dalai Lama was ready to take his monk's vows in 1941. Intending to return to office after a period of retreat, Reting temporarily elevated the staid and nonpolitical Taktra Rinpoche to the regent's throne. Winds of change blew through the offices and seats of monastic power with Taktra Rinpoche in office. Decadence and corruption in the highest government councils were replaced with ethically impeccable norms. But Taktra was a conservative old lama and his advisors advocated a halt to the process of modernization, apparently wishing to reaffirm the power of the old monastic aristocracy by returning to traditional ways.

In June 1941 a magnificent wedding was celebrated between the noble houses of Tsarong and Ragashar. Descending from the ancient royal dynasty, the Ragashar family was one of the most highly respected and

FRONT: *Chetsang Rinpoche's grandparents, Pema Dolkar and Dasang Damdul Tsarong.* BACK: *Chetsang Rinpoche's parents, Yangchen Dolkar and Dundul Namgyal Tsarong.*

politically powerful in the country. Phuntsok Rabgye Ragashar (1903–1957) held the office of commander general of the army, a position Tsarong had held before him. Tsarong's son Dundul Namgyal, who held a high office of the fourth rank in the Ministry of Finance, married Ragashar's beautiful daughter, Yangchen Dolkar, just fifteen years old at the time. In 1942 the couple had their first child, a girl named Namgyal Lhamo. A year later a sister arrived, Norzin Yangkyi, and in 1944 came Tsewang Jigme, the couple's first son.

In the summer of 1945, Dundul Namgyal supervised the smelting of silver for new coins in Ghelahor, about fifteen kilometers beyond the Drikung Tse monastery. After smelting, the silver was poured into flat bars and taken to the mint in Lhasa. Yangchen Dolkar welcomed the change; she loved the lush meadows and scenic rivers, and the hundreds of little sparrows that nested in the majestic trees surrounding the house they rented. The couple and their children enjoyed their relaxed summer, for the most part released from the duties and obligations of city life. They amused themselves with picnics, target practice, and horseback riding, taking in the countryside like exuberant children.

After their return to Lhasa, Yangchen Dolkar was awakened in the night by a movement at the foot of her bed, where she then saw a life-sized Green Tara. She immediately got up and made three prostrations to the deity and the apparition vanished.[3] A few nights later, Yangchen realized that she was pregnant with their fourth child. She was certain that the apparation had not been a dream, that the figure had really been present in her room. When she told her husband and parents about it they assured her that she should be very happy to have had such an auspicious experience.

At about this time, in January 1946, two strange figures in ragged clothing, with matted hair and infected eyes, reached the Forbidden City. Most Lhasans didn't know what to make of these foreigners, but the elder Tsarong saw them for what they were, human beings in desperate need of a place where they could stay for a while. He reached out to these strangers from the West, and put them up in one of the guest houses on his property. Heinrich Harrer and Peter Aufschnaiter were Austrians who had escaped from the British internment camp in Dehra Dun, India, crossed the Himalayas on foot, and reached Lhasa after an ardous, though adventurous, journey. They became close friends of the family, and Harrer and "George"—Dundul Namgyal—became friends for life.

The Fire Dog Year of 1946 began with an elaborate social obligation for the Tsarong family. The Great Prayer Festival, *Mönlam Chenmo*, always began on the second day of the Tibetan New Year and lasted for the entire first month, and each year one of the wealthy families officially invited the Dalai Lama to the festival. That year Dasang Damdul Tsarong was the Dalai Lama's host. Hundreds of offerings had to be procured: silk brocade from China and India; tiger, leopard, and bear skins; and elephant tusks wound about with embossed silver bands among them. To this list were added ample gifts of money for the monks. Everything was taken to the Tsuglagkhang (or Jokhang), Lhasa's main temple, in a ceremonial procession of 250 monks, whom Tsarong had engaged for the purpose. Two days before the start of the solemnities Tsarong and his son, dressed in ceremonial garb, escorted the eleven-year-old Dalai Lama in a magnificent procession from the Potala Palace to the temple, where more than twenty thousand monks had assembled.

The Tibetans both loved and hated Mönlam Chenmo. They loved it because it was the most important festival of the year, an indispensable part of their religious identity, and people streamed into the capital from all parts of the country. They hated it because the authority of the state was suspended during the festivities and transferred to two monastic disciplinary supervisors (*shelngos*) from the Drepung Monastery who even had the power to order executions. There had always been a great deal of jockeying for the position of shelngo, in part because it brought power and prestige, but above all because it was financially rewarding. The shelngos could confiscate—and keep—the fortunes, houses, and landed estates of alleged criminals that fell into their hands; many Lhasans quietly slipped out of the capital to escape the arbitrary despotism. A shelngo also strictly regulated cleanliness and decency, and not without reason. When the masses had departed at the end of the Mönlam festival, they left behind such immense amounts of garbage and feces that it took another month to clean the city and dispel the unbearable stench.

But the Mönlam had truly magical moments. On the evening of the full moon, one hundred huge wooden scaffolds, some up to three storeys high, bore elaborate sculptures made from immense quantities of colored barley flour mixed with butter. Erected in front of the most impressive sculptures were stages on which the monks provided performances of puppet theatre. They delighted the public as they moved figures mounted on the butter sculptures with hidden wires. Lit by moonlight and the flickering of a sea of butter lamps, the fantastic world of the puppet theater enchanted the city and its visitors.

On the twenty-second day of the first month, military games were opened by a reenactment of the victory parade of the Tibetan and Mongolian cavalries in 1642. The noble houses equipped a number of men who were under the command of two so-called *yar-so* (an old Mongolian title for the commander of the cavalry) generals, with armor and weapons from the seventeenth century for the spectacle. Stemming from the seventeenth century, when the Fifth Dalai Lama united all of Tibet under his rule with the help of the Mongolian monarch Gushri Khan,

the parade, was reenacted every year until the Tibetan national uprising in 1959. Heinrich Harrer photographed this military display with all
its pomp and glory in 1946, when his friend Dundul Namgyal Tsarong
played a role as one of the yar-so generals, wearing brocade garments
from czarist Russia and a broad cap of blue fox fur. After a reception
the generals and several hundred soldiers in historic armor led a festive
procession to the Drapchi plain north of the Potala, where riflery and
archery contests and boisterous horse races were held.

The festival of Drukpa Tseshi, celebrated on the fourth day of the
sixth month, commemorates the beginning of the historical Buddha's
teaching activity. On this day the faithful go on short pilgrimages to
sacred places in Lhasa and the vicinity, and in 1946 the regent wished
to donate costly new ornaments to the Jowo Rinpoche in the Jokhang.
The Jowo Rinpoche, the most highly revered religious image in Tibet,
depicts the historical Buddha Shakyamuni. Regent Taktra knew that
Dasang Damdul Tsarong had brought an 18-carat diamond back from
one of his many journeys to India, and he convinced Tsarong to sell
him the diamond for what it had cost so it could be set in the new headdress of the statue during the festival.

Shortly before the festival began, Yangchen Dolkar went into labor.
Her husband sent for his friend Dr. James Guthrie, a physician of the
British Mission and the only doctor he trusted, but after a while Yang-
chen Dolkar's contractions subsided. The next day began quietly, and
Dr. Guthrie returned home.

Later that evening the contractions began again and lasted throughout the night, while Yangchen Dolkar's mother, her mother-in-law, her
husband's half-sister, and a serving girl recited mantras. Finally, as the
brilliance of the morning sun filled the room, Yangchen Dolkar gave
birth to a son. But the baby was still completely covered by the unbroken amniotic sac; and, contrary to the Tibetan superstition that this is
a lucky omen, he appeared dead, his motionless body completely yellow. The attending family was almost paralyzed with fear, but fortunately
Dr. Guthrie had returned. Without a moment's hesitation he opened the
amniotic sac, stuck his finger in the baby's mouth, and removed something blocking the respiratory tract. When the doctor turned the baby
upside-down and struck his back, the newborn began to wail and the
family was filled with joy and relief.

Chetsang Rinpoche with his mother, Yangchen Dolkar.

Yangchen Dolkar's long labor had lasted until the beginning of Drukpa Tseshi. At the very moment Taktra Rinpoche offered the Tsarong jewel to the Jowo Rinpoche, the second son of Dundul Namgyal and Yangchen Dolkar was born. It was the fourth day of the sixth Tibetan month in the Fire Dog year of the sixteenth *rabjung* cycle, which corresponds to August 1, 1946, in the Gregorian calendar.[4]

Yongzin Ling Rinpoche gave the baby the name Tseten Gyurme. The little boy developed splendidly, and no one failed to notice his swift comprehension, even as a small child. He kept the servants on their toes with his insatiable curiosity. He was said to be like his elder sister Namlha—as Namgyal Lhamo was also known—in this, while sister Norzin and brother Jigme were quieter. The children spent more time with their grandmother and, when time allowed, their grandfather than they did with their busy parents. The elder Tsarong loved playing with the children. He once pretended to have fallen into an oracle's trance of possession, rolling his eyes, stamping his feet, making dreadful noises, and chasing the children though the house. In winter he wore a huge

The Tsarong mansion in Lhasa.

coat lined with camel hair, which he would spread out to wrap his grand-children in while he told them bed-time stories. Their mother strongly disapproved of the stories, which often related the adventures of a racy character known as the notorious "Uncle Tönpa," but she dared not give orders to the head of the family.

The manor house the children grew up in, with its many rooms and beautiful garden with rare plants, fruit trees, vegetable beds, and greenhouses—all cared for by a diligent staff—was like a paradise. In the main building alone there were forty rooms to explore, among them the somber shrine of Palden Lhamo—the protector deity of the Tsarong family—with its terrifying masks; the storage rooms bursting with grain, flour, tea, sugar, oil, salt, and raw wool, where the children were some-times able to sneak a snack of chickpea flour; and the attic, which was a true treasure chamber with tiger skins and whole bear skins complete with heads and claws, rhinoceros horns, elephant tusks, swords, rifles, books, foreign magazines, paintings, maps, photographs, gramophones, watches, and music boxes. The children enjoyed themselves thoroughly, blissfully playing among all the crates and bundles.

They also loved to visit the kitchen, which was housed in its own separate building. There were actually three kitchens: one for the everyday typical Tibetan family meals, one for the exquisite Chinese and Indian dishes the Tsarong's cook prepared for special occasions, and the indispensable tea kitchen, where the beverage was prepared from morning to night. In the middle of this kitchen a kettle with water for butter tea was constantly simmering on a great mud brick stove, and the servants continually bustled around, carrying in firewood and dried animal dung, removing ashes, and chatting while slurping from their cups of tea.

In 1949 Paljor, the youngest son of the family, was born. The five Tsarong children and their cousins played happily together in what seemed a fairy-tale kingdom, oblivious to the dark political clouds that were gathering over the Land of Snows. They had not the slightest inkling that this carefree life of abundance, joy, and freedom would soon come to an abrupt end.

During Taktra Rinpoche's regency, members of Reting Rinpoche's faction as well as the profiteers of the previous regime were gradually driven from power; when Reting tried to reclaim the position in 1946, Taktra had not the slightest intention of returning it to him. Enraged, Reting struck a deal with the Chinese government, allegedly promising the Chinese sovereignty over Tibet if they regained the regency for him. Once this deal was exposed, the former regent was reported to have plotted Taktra's murder, but the conspiracy failed and Reting Rinpoche was arrested. After Reting's detention his followers, the monks of Sera Je, rose up in revolt. When the outraged monks were unable to rescue Reting through force, they discharged their wrath in the streets of Lhasa. They broke into houses, seized weapons, and fired in the streets, and the city was placed under a state of emergency. The revolt was quickly put down and Reting died in his prison cell—most likely from poisoning—before his trial was concluded.

3

On the Throne in Drikung
The Brilliance of a World in Decline

A T MID-CENTURY, political events of otherwise global significance had little impact on Tibet. While World War II raged on
elsewhere, the country enjoyed a period of economic revival. When
India gained independence on August 15, 1947, hardly anyone in Lhasa
took notice. Hugh Richardson, the last British representative in Tibet,
became the first Indian representative.

But Tibetans did feel the upheavals taking place in China. In January
1949, the government of Chiang Kai-shek succumbed to the Communist
assault and Chiang Kai-shek's government fled to Taiwan. On October 1,
1949, only two days after the National People's Congress had declared
Tibet to be Chinese territory, Chairman Mao Zedong (1893–1976) was
proclaimed leader of the People's Republic of China (PRC). Tibetans
were now considered "national minorities" within the PRC.

The threat to Tibet's sovereignty came at a time of political weakness.
The Dalai Lama was only a boy of fourteen, and the country had no military strength. The only Tibetan response to the new Communist government in China was the expulsion of all Chinese dignitaries remaining
in Tibet and the removal from office of Tibetans accused of collaborating with them. Faced with a potentially catastrophic upheaval, many
Tibetans—including most of the aristocracy—simply shut their eyes.

Meanwhile, the Tsarong family faced a different kind of change
when, one morning in the early summer of 1950, an official delegation
from Drikung Thil Monastery arrived and presented the elder Tsarong
with a report that Tseten Gyurme had been formally recognized as the

incarnation of His Holiness Drikung Chetsang Rinpoche, and officially confirmed as such by the regent Taktra Rinpoche. The delegation requested the elder Tsarong to entrust his grandson to the care of the monks. Dasang Damdul Tsarong respected religious tradition and supported monasteries generously, but he himself was more of a pragmatist than a deeply religious man. He told the delegation that the decision would be made by the child's parents.

After the monks had left his chambers, Tsarong called for his son and daughter-in-law, and told them about the delegation's request. The parents were shocked and reluctant to surrender their son to the monks. Life in a monastery was harsh, even for the incarnation of a high lama; they also wondered whether the child's recognition was only a pretext to forge a connection to their wealthy and influential family. In addition, the mother protested that the child was not even four years old. The elder Tsarong was also reluctant, but did not wish to dismiss the request out of hand. The evidence presented in the documents was astonishing in many respects, and even a Tibetan who was not deeply religious still believed that obstructing a rightful recognition would bring misfortune to the family and child. He advised the young parents not to decide in haste, but rather to think the matter through carefully, although there was not much time to do so. The delegation had claimed that this was the auspicious moment for recognition and that any delay would be inauspicious.

Yangchen Dolkar sought the advice of her parents, who were very religious and familiar with the tulku system, as the Shabdrung tulku of the Taklung Kagyu always reincarnated into the Ragashar family. Phuntsog Rabgye Ragashar urged his daughter to relinquish her little Tseten Gyurme to the Drikungpa, because an incarnate lama who is kept from fulfilling his religious position would die very young. Tseten Gyurme's parents did not want to take such a risk, and in the end they had to acknowledge the significance of the remarkable events surrounding their son's birth. In addition to the child's birth on the auspicious morning of Drukpa Tseshi and the vision of Tara, Yangchen had had recurring dreams of a monastery and stupa while she was pregnant, and once the previous Chetsang Rinpoche, Shiwe Lodrö, had visited the Tsarong home and given a necklace to Dasang Damdul's wife Pema Dolkar, telling her that if she wore it her fields would be fruitful and

LEFT: *Chetsang Rinpoche with his father on a swing.*
RIGHT: *Chetsang Rinpoche at his recognition in the
garden of Tsarong House, Lhasa, 1950.*

she would see him again soon. What had appeared at the time to be an ordinary expression of gratitude for hospitality now seemed to hint at prophecy. With heavy hearts the parents consented to their son being raised and educated in the monastery to take on the responsibilities of the Drikung Kyabgön.

On the day of his formal recognition, Tseten Gyurme's head was shaved, with only a small lock of hair left on the crown of his head, and he was dressed in monk's robes. The mandatory traditional yellow boots could not be found in his size, so the ones he wore were far too large. He was a little unhappy about this, but the Drikung monks were delighted, perhaps thinking it was an omen that he would follow in the great foot- steps of his predecessors. The ceremony took place in the family temple,

Recognition of Chetsang Rinpoche, with the Drikung monk officials Chagdzö Legden, Joma Thrinle, and Drönyer Konchog Samten (from left).

the Chögyalkhang ("room of the Dharma kings"), which contained almost-life-size, gilded and gem-encrusted statues of the three Dharma kings of Tibet: Songtsen Gampo (reign 617–649), Trisong Detsen (reign 755–797), and Tri Ralpachen (reign 815–838). There were also precious woodblock print books of sacred texts behind glass doors, elaborate offering cakes, cloisonné lions, rare porcelain vases, a golden reliquary, 108 water bowls, a golden butter lamp, a mandala made of pearls, and finely executed religious scroll paintings (*thangkas*) that covered the walls.

When the small child mounted the Dharma throne, even the elder Tsarong, national hero and distinguished statesman, bowed down humbly to his little grandson. Tseten Gyurme sat on his throne as if it were his rightful and accustomed place, and when Tsarong presented the customary mandala offering, the symbolic gift of the entire universe, Tseten Gyurme responded with a loving gesture of blessing as seemingly natural as one performed thousands of times.

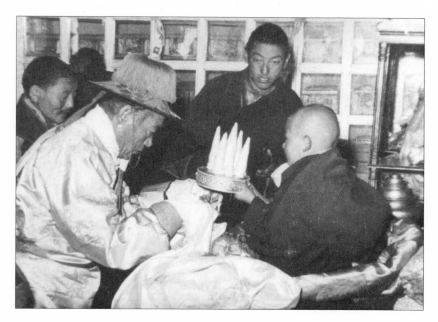

Dasang Damdul Tsarong makes a mandala offering to his grandson Chetsang Rinpoche in the shrine room of Tsarong House in Lhasa.

The dignitaries of Drikung Labrang also made mandala offerings to the precious reincarnation and recited prayers for his long life. Only the family and a few of their closest friends filed past the throne to present their long white *khatags*, silk scarves, which the young Rinpoche then placed around their necks.[1]

Tseten Gyurme became Chetsang Rinpoche, but because he was still so young he was allowed to remain with his family a little longer, and his life did not change completely overnight. He was dressed in the dark red monastic robes and cared for by two monks, but was still allowed to play uninhibitedly. The remaining time with him seemed painfully short to his grandparents, parents, and siblings, but Rinpoche himself appeared undisturbed by the imminent changes.

On August 15, 1950, one of the most powerful earthquakes ever registered shook Tibet. The epicenter was on the Indian border, but it was felt all the way to Lhasa. Many people believed it was a sign that Tibet was heading for catastrophe. For the Tsarongs it presaged Rinpoche's departure in October for his formal enthronement at Drikung. The

Chetsang Rinpoche with hotogthu *hat put on a horse by his personal attendant Solpön Chösjor.*

journey began after an elaborate traditional ceremony in the Tsarong house shrine in which delegates from the Drikung Labrang offered the Drikung Kyabgön symbolic representations of the Buddha's body, speech, and mind. As fragrant clouds of incense smoke rose from huge censers in the courtyard, Chetsang Rinpoche's relatives and his family's friends, tenants, and servants all lined up according to their rank to see him off. Everyone was dressed in their best clothing, the family in their finest brocade robes and elaborate jewelry. Chetsang Rinpoche's eldest brother, Tsewang Jigme, wearing a yellow silk robe, embroidered boots, and a brocade hat, mounted a brown horse to accompany the festive delegation escorting Chetsang Rinpoche to Drikung Thil Monastery.

Rinpoche's personal attendant, Solpön Chösjor,[2] who had also been his previous incarnation's assistant, carried him out into the courtyard and set him on a sumptuously caparisoned horse. Rinpoche was still too small to sit securely in the saddle by himself, so his two attendants— the only ones allowed to touch him—had to help him. He wore a yellow silk robe and a special shallow cymbal-shaped golden hat with a top ornament fashioned like a cut jewel. This style of headdress could only

Procession to the enthronement through the streets of Lhasa.

be worn by the most high-ranking incarnate lamas who held the honorary Manchurian title of *hotogthu;*[3] Chetsang Rinpoche had received this title in his previous incarnation from the Thirteenth Dalai Lama. The designation also entitled him to an escort of ten government officials, with five monastic and five lay officials accompanying his impressive procession.

The group was led by a monk bearing a depiction of the "Wheel of Existence" to symbolize the fact that a bodhisattva had voluntarily reincarnated to help all sentient beings escape from the sufferings of *samsara.*[4] Then came a monk sounding a trumpet, and standard bearers with magnificent red hats and the banners of the three Drikung Kagyu protector deities—Achi, Gonpo, and Chökyong. They were followed by three assistants from the labrang, and then Chetsang Rinpoche himself with a monk holding a golden parasol over him; following Rinpoche were a representative of the Tibetan government, the treasurer of the labrang, members of the family, and a long line of monastic and lay dignitaries. Heinrich Harrer and Peter Aufschnaiter were captivated by the splendid pomp, recording it in photographs which show a grave and serene Rinpoche, his gaze directed into the distance. While joy, pride, and enthusiasm shone in the faces of the people around him, he remained calm and inscrutable. He was the still point at the center, unmoved as he passed through the excited crowds lining the streets to pay him homage.

The Drikung region lies northeast of Lhasa and covers a territory larger than Sikkim. The monastery of Drikung Thil was built in the Shorong Valley in 1179 by Kyobpa Jigten Sumgön (1143–1217), the founder of the Drikung Kagyu lineage, who used to teach on the large terrace in front of its main building. Behind this, many small buildings, mostly meditation huts, lie scattered over the mountain. According to legend, this place was indicated to Jigten Sumgön by a *dri,* a female yak, and the animal's horns are still kept in Drikung Thil. Some say that Drikung was named after that dri, but the region formerly belonged to Dri Seru Gungtön, a minister of King Songtsen Gampo, and it is more likely to have been named for him.[5]

Yangrigar, the second important monastery, is not far off, in the direction of Lhasa. Furthest away, lying to the northwest, toward Namtso Lake, is the monastery of Drikung Tse. Lying between Drikung Thil and Drikung Tse, the stronghold of Drikung Dzongsar Tashizug—or simply Drikung Dzong—was both a monastery and the administrative center of Drikung, whose authority was organized along the lines of the thirteen offices of the Tibetan government. In the upper area lived the household servants, shrine master, cook, teachers, secretary, and commissary of stores. The lower area accommodated the secular administration of Drikung, consisting of the manager, the bursar, the secretary for external affairs, the under-secretary, the head purchasing agent, the steward of firewood, and the head stableman.

These four monasteries were Chetsang Rinpoche's residences. He lived in Tse in the spring, Yangrigar in the summer, Thil in autumn, and Dzong through the winter. There were many other Drikung monasteries in the region, as well as Drikung monasteries in other areas—primarily in Kham in eastern Tibet, in the region of the sacred mountain Gangri Tise (Kailash), and in Ladakh.

A voyage from Lhasa to Drikung normally took two days, but there was nothing normal about this journey. Every stage had been orches-

*Chetsang Rinpoche in Drikung accompanied by his
personal assistant and his mother, behind him.*

trated, with carefully prepared welcoming ceremonies in important villages, where even the number of men to stand guard and of riders and
pack animals to be provided had been specified in advance. Monasteries that lay along the route had meticulously organized receptions for
Chetsang Rinpoche. The procession crossed the Kyichu River in yakskin
boats to find hundreds of people waiting to receive the blessing of the
Kyabgön Rinpoche. After the river crossing, Rinpoche proceeded more
comfortably, carried in a sedan chair by eight men.

The road was paved only to the district capital of Medrogungkar.
Beyond that was Katsel, the first Drikung monastery on the route. According to legend, in ancient times King Songtsen Gampo subdued the

Drikung Tse Monastery in 1948.

land of Tibet, which was the body of a giant demoness named Sinmo, by building four temples on geomantically significant sites, thus symbolically nailing her down. Katsel was built to fix her right shoulder in place. Neither large nor impressive, Katsel has a varied and eventful history that is typical of many Tibetan monasteries. It was founded by the Nyingma, transferred to the Drikungpa in the thirteenth century, taken over by the Gelugpa in the seventeenth century, and then returned to the Drikungpa in the nineteenth century.

According to custom, the actual enthronement of the Kyabgön Rinpoche was held at Drikung Tse, which had originally been built by the Tibetan king Mutik Tsenpo (764–817) as a manor house. It was first consecrated as a monastery in 1560 by Chögyal Rinchen Phuntsog (1547–1602), the twenty-first Drikung throne holder, when it also became his main residence. The most sacred statue there was an image of the Buddha said to have been made during the Buddha's lifetime and consecrated by him personally, and to have been brought to Tibet by the Indian master Jowo Atisha (982–1054).

At Drikung Tse, the young Chetsang Rinpoche met his spiritual brother, Chungtsang Rinpoche. Until the seventeenth century, the Drikung Kagyu throne holders had been a hereditary lineage in the Kyura clan of its founder, Jigten Sumgön. The tulku system of incarnation lineages was only instituted when the family failed to produce a male successor, and the two last hereditary throne holders were the brothers Konchog Rinchen (1590–1654) and Rigzin Chödrak (1595–1659), who were very close to each other. Konchog Rinchen had been "Chetsang" ("older brother") and Chödrak "Chungtsang" ("younger brother"), and their successive reincarnations have been the Drikung throne holders ever since. The Tsarong child, as the reincarnation of Chetsang, was the "older brother," even though he was biologically four years younger than his "younger brother," Chungtsang Tenzin Chökyi Nangwa. Chungtsang Rinpoche scowled at him when they met because it was his habit to look gloomy and morose. He belonged to the Lhagyari family, one of the oldest noble houses in Tibet, and he was already clearly well-versed in questions of etiquette and ceremony, carrying his status with self-assurance. But he could not resist the little Chetsang Rinpoche's warm-hearted friendliness and they were to get along very well.

After the enthronement ceremony, the guests were shown through the monastery, and any lingering doubts Chetsang Rinpoche's mother, Yangchen Dolkar, still entertained evaporated when she recognized details from her recurring dreams of the unknown monastery and the unusual stupa. Yangchen Dolkar was greatly relieved when she realized she had made the right decision for her son.

Following the formal enthronement in Drikung Tse the procession traveled to the main monastery, Drikung Thil, where more than two thousand people, including representatives from the Tibetan government, from all the Buddhist lineages, and from different cities and regions, as well as the local aristocrats and village headmen, awaited them. The treasures in the monastery of Tse paled in comparison to those in Drikung Thil, which testified to the ancient brilliance and wealth of the lineage. In the Serkhang ("Golden Temple") was the most revered treasure of all, a life-size, gold-plated statue of Kyobpa Jigten Sumgön that was a "speaking statue," one known to have communicated prophecies to those who were spiritually pure.[6] Containing many precious relics, including a tooth of the Buddha and two fingers of the great Tibetan yogi Milarepa, it was flanked on one side by a statue of Gyalwang Kunga Rinchen (1475–1527), the sixteenth throne holder, and on the other by a statue of Panchen Sönam Gyatso (1527–1570), the nineteenth. All three were seated on golden lion thrones under finely worked parasols depicting the five deities of the Chakrasamvara mandala. There were gem-encrusted stupas containing the relics of several previous throne holders, and another statue of Jigten Sumgön. A small carved landscape held the sixteen *arhat*s, Buddhist "saints," all carved from white sandalwood. Beneath these were the four worldly protectors and the main deity, Yeshe Gonpo, with his retinue, made from ground gemstones mixed with medicinal substances.[7] A cave in the landscape of the sixteen arhats held a statue of Shakyamuni Buddha carved of wood from the great Bodhi Tree under which he had attained enlightenment. This statue was said to be redolent with the fragrance of moral and ethical purity, emitting a continuous stream of blessings. The twelve deeds of the Buddha were depicted in white and red sandalwood, and a model of the temple at Bodh Gaya, where Buddha attained enlightenment, was encrusted with gemstones. The room was filled with countless images of buddhas, bodhisattvas, lineage lamas, and hundreds of stupas in various sizes. Some huge statues had been pulled by horses from Phagmodrupa's monastery of Densa Thil to Drikung Thil when the Phagmodrupa lineage died out and the throne at Densa Thil was left empty. Covering the western wall were tall bookshelves containing more than two hundred precious manuscripts and woodblock prints, including the collected works of Jigten Sumgön, printed with gold and silver ink on indigo-colored paper and with a shining black finish to enhance the calligraphy;[8] texts of the sutras and tantras; the collected works of the lineage masters; and the writings of all the throne holders of the Drikungpa. The wooden text covers were richly and elaborately carved, decorated with gold and silver, and ornamented with white and red pearls, turquoises, and corals. This incredible repository of sacred objects was merely the first of fourteen shrine rooms in Drikung Thil, all of them as magnificent.

Another day of ritual and ceremony began when Chetsang Rinpoche and Chungtsang Rinpoche took their places on their thrones, which no one else dared touch, for fear that the serpent deities said to reside in them would inflict illness. In front of the statue of Jigten Sumgön, Tritsab Gyabra cut Chetsang Rinpoche's lock of hair and gave him his

Enthronement of Chetsang Rinpoche in Drikung Thil Monastery.

first set of names; another set would be bestowed by the Dalai Lama. The little Rinpoche did not seem to be wearied by the long ceremonies as he sat attentively on his throne, following everything with both alertness and serenity. He swiftly understood what actions and gestures to perform during the rituals, amazing the lamas with how quickly he learned to anticipate the sequences.

The Shemo dances are performed only at the enthronement of a Drikung lineage head. Dressed in garments that were among the oldest known Tibetan costumes, women and men danced with measured steps as they chanted a narrative of the religious history of the Drikung tradition and its reign over the sacred mountains—Tsari, Gangri, and Lapchi—and sang the praises of the mountains, rivers, lakes, fields, and animals in the Drikung region. As was customary, after the dances Rinpoche visited Jigten Sumgön's famous red-earth throne in a field near the monastery.

The following day he toured the entire monastery complex, including many meditation huts in the eastern and western retreat centers, where selected monks spent years in seclusion, sometimes with the doors sealed shut, concentrating one-pointedly on meditative attainment. Chetsang Rinpoche and his parents also inspected the treasury of Achi, which was opened only upon a lineage holder's assumption of office. When Rinpoche's father managed to open the intractable locks, which had refused to yield to the efforts of the monks, the flickering torchlight revealed countless ancient weapons, spears, knives and guns—the ceiling was supported by hundreds of old muskets rather than by wooden beams. There were also curiosities said to date back to the semimythical King Gesar of Ling, such as peacock feathers from the skirt of King Gesar's wife and oversized earrings said to have belonged to his general. The visitors marveled at the jewel of a dragon, the claw of a garuda, the skin of a mythical lion, the sword of a legendary hero, and chests containing brocade garments said to have come from Tilopa, the Indian ancestor of the Kagyu tradition. They saw only a small portion of the remarkable treasures, most of which remained hidden in darkness. When the creaking doors were sealed shut behind them, neither the visitors nor the monks imagined that in the years to come the chamber would be violently invaded by political vandals who would desecrate it, destroying all these treasures of mythical ages and relics from the noble history of the Land of Snows.

While Rinpoche was absorbed in exploring the wonders of his new life at the monastery—even more naturally thrilling to him than the marvels of the Tsarong mansion in Lhasa—his father worried about political developments. When they had left for Drikung there had been disturbing reports from the border region that the People's Liberation Army was advancing on the city of Chamdo. Every evening after they arrived at Drikung, Tsarong listened to the latest news on a radio he had brought with him.

In the spring of 1950 the Chinese Communist government had begun to disseminate their propaganda using well-known religious personalities, primarily the Panchen Lama (1938–1989) and Geda Tulku, the incarnate lama of Beri Monastery near Gandze. In a radio address on May 6, 1950, Geshe Sherab Gyatso (1884–1968), an influential scholar of Drepung Monastery, told Tibetans not to believe the "slanders of the British and American imperialists"—that if necessary, China would make use of force to "free" Tibet, and that the People's Liberation Army (PLA) was unquestionably powerful enough to do so. He concluded with a recitation of the usual formulaic promises of equal treatment for all nationalities and of religious freedom under the protection of the People's Republic of China (PRC). By the end of the month a unit of the PLA had taken the strategically important city of Dengo but had not advanced further. Tibetans wondered whether this was just a test of the Tibetan army's defenses or part of an attempt to bully Lhasa into submitting to China's demands.

The People's Republic of China's "liberation" of Tibet faced potential international complications when the conflict between North Korea, allied with the Soviet Union, and South Korea, supported by the United States, escalated into the Korean War. China was in danger of being drawn into a war with the United States, thus giving the United States a pretext for intervening in Tibet. However, North Korea's initially surprising successes captured the complete attention of the United States, and Tibet seemed not to concern them, even when PRC troops entered the Korean War. General Douglas MacArthur succeeded in driving back the North Korean units and insisted that nuclear weapons be used to expand combat operations into China, but the American government wished to avoid escalation, relieving the general of his command and settling for a ceasefire and a Korea divided in two.

Meanwhile, the new Chinese government attempted to win the Khampas of eastern Tibet over to their cause. They succeeded in part, although some Khampa leaders actively organized a fierce resistance. Lhasa refused to receive any Chinese emissaries and the Kashag was unwilling to grant any concessions, despite having good reason to fear an invasion. The Kashag's decisions reflect the naiveté of Tibet's foreign policy, a result of Tibet's self-imposed isolation. Hoping that the escalation of the Korean War—or the possibility of an armed conflict with the United States—would distract China from its plans for Tibet, the Kashag simply ignored Chinese proposals.

By October of 1950 the PRC was determined to "unite Tibet with the motherland." Without further preliminaries 40,000 troops of the PLA crossed the Drichu river (which the Chinese call the Yangtse) and on October 11 the army stood before Chamdo. Ngawang Jigme Ngabö, the representative of the Tibetan government in Kham, urgently requested instructions from the Kashag in Lhasa, receiving no answer to his first three messages, even though the country was clearly in great peril. Finally Lhasa sent word that the ministers were at their annual picnic and could not be disturbed. Between Lhasa's political ineffectiveness and the lack of a well-organized and well-equipped military, the Tibetans were without a chance of halting the assault of the PLA, and surrendered. After capitulating, the prisoners were forced to endure socialist indoctrination, and were then sent home with provisions and money as the Communists attempted to show their moral as well as military superiority.

When Dundul Namgyal Tsarong heard that Ngabö had surrendered, he wanted to leave immediately for Lhasa with his family. Insulated from events outside their monastery, the Drikung monastics couldn't understand Tsarong's haste; not understanding the nature of the PRC's intentions, they had no sense of the imminent danger. The Tsarong family returned to Lhasa without Chetsang Rinpoche, who remained in the monastery.

As a member of the national assembly, the elder Tsarong was kept fully informed as events unfolded, and a family council decided to send the family members to Kalimpong in India, not far from the border with Sikkim and a relatively comfortable journey by Tibetan standards. Many other noble families were also beginning to transfer their fortunes to country estates or to India, and the capital's aristocratic houses began to look desolate. The Tsarong women and children set off in two parties a few days apart, in the middle of a bitterly cold winter. The journey was made a little easier by a group of servants sent out in advance with provisions to set up camp each night. They traveled down-river on the Kyichu in boats to Chushul, where they continued their journey with horses and mules. Sikkim could usually be reached in seventeen days, but with the parties' many small children it took three arduous weeks. When they finally crossed the Nathu La, an escort of the maharaja of Sikkim received them—the Ragashars were related to the Sikkimese royal family, and Dundul Namgyal's half-sister Tsering Yangzom Taring was married to a son of the maharaja's elder brother.

Meanwhile in Lhasa the two state oracles of Gadong and Nechung were consulted to advise the government about the imminent danger. The message was unclear but was interpreted to mean that the fifteen-year-old Dalai Lama was to be enthroned immediately and was to take over the reins of government. The young Dalai Lama was not sure he was prepared for such responsibility three years before the traditional age of enthronement, especially given the country's precarious situation, but in the end he agreed. His enthronement on November 17, 1950, in the Potala Palace was attended by representatives from India and Nepal and the chögyal of Sikkim.

His first official act was to move Tibet's leading statesmen and himself to relative safety in Dromo, on the Sikkimese border. Rumors of an eight-hundred-man PLA force advancing on Lhasa hastened the departure. At dawn on December 19, the Dalai Lama fled to the south in civilian clothing, accompanied by his two tutors and the members of the Kashag. Remaining in Lhasa, Lukhang Tsewang Rabten and Lobsang Tashi were appointed deputy prime ministers, while Ngabö was instructed to continue negotiations with the Chinese. Dasang Damdul Tsarong and his son secured the Dalai Lama's escape route along the southern bank of the Kyichu River. Four decades earlier, Tsarong had similarly secured the flight of the Thirteenth Dalai Lama; however, at this time his protection was more of a symbolic gesture, with the PLA too far away to present a direct threat.

With the Dalai Lama's departure from Lhasa, the Drikung administrators finally grasped the urgency of the situation and decided to send Chetsang Rinpoche to join his parents in Kalimpong. For young Chetsang Rinpoche the difficult journey through icy landscapes of enchanting beauty was a fabulous adventure. Memories of this voyage would remain vivid throughout his life.

Two men led a dozen pack animals with provisions, tents, clothing, and bedding. Rinpoche himself traveled on the back of a mule he had received as a present from his grandmother, with a second group including his personal attendant, his bodyguard, and additional assistants and delegates from the monasteries. Despite the bone-chilling cold, Rinpoche was delighted by the many wild animals he had never seen before: strange birds, Tibetan antelopes, wild donkeys (*kyang*), and huge mountain sheep (*argali*) with mighty, twisted horns. The group climbed several high passes and traversed dangerous terrain, including a stretch along the bizarre, turquoise-blue lake of Yamdrok Tso, whose frigid shores had to be crossed during daylight, quickly and without a halt, as making camp in those temperatures could be life-threatening. Another deadly stretch lay between Kala and Thula; it had to be crossed before dawn to avoid the strong winds that developed during the day, powerful enough to sweep humans and animals into the abyss.

The final trial along the road was a leech-infested area that had to be crossed with shoes securely tied and long trousers bound at the ankles. By evening the mules and horses were bleeding everywhere—on their legs, bellies, and even on their mouths and eyes. Rinpoche wept bitterly at the horrific sight, but they had all survived. The only casualty on the journey had been a huge pack mule too old to bear the strains of the treacherous road.

In Kalimpong, Rani Chönyi Wangmo invited the extended Tsarong family to live in her house, "Hilltops," an exquisite home with many rooms and an expansive garden. For the Tsarong children this was again a carefree time, and Rinpoche played with an irrepressible energy, despite having arrived from Tibet with a case of whooping cough. The climate seemed to do him good, and he was cured after a few weeks.

Rinpoche was a whirlwind of activity, always a step or two ahead of his attendants and caretakers. He was an enthusiastic soccer player, along with his older brother Jigme and his cousins, the sons of his aunt Tsering Yangzom Dorje. The mischievous boys also snuck cigarettes, hiding in the tall grass behind the house to light them and once even causing a small fire. Another time the young Rinpoche pushed his elder brother into the goldfish pond of a large villa the family was visiting. While the children played and the family lived safely in Kalimpong— unaware of the fateful events back home in Tibet—Dundul Namgyal often traveled to Dromo to visit his father, who had remained there with the Dalai Lama and the cabinet. In this way he was able to follow events closely as they unfolded.

On April 29, 1951, the Tibetan Peace Delegation, headed by Ngabö, had a preliminary meeting with representatives of the Chinese government in an army headquarters in Beijing, followed by meetings to discuss the terms of the PRC's "Seventeen-Point Plan for the Peaceful Liberation of Tibet," what has come to be known as the Seventeen-Point Agreement. It soon became clear that the Chinese would not allow the Dalai Lama to remain in power; when this point was addressed, the chief negotiator remarked that Tibet had the choice of being liberated either

Chetsang Rinpoche (front right) playing soccer with his cousin and brother in Kalimpong.

peacefully or by force. There had never been any possibility of real negotiations but the PRC engaged in the discussions because if the Tibetan government could be forced to acquiesce, it would be easier to convince the Tibetan people to accept the Chinese Communist Party's programs.

Another point the Chinese were pressing was the status of the Panchen Lama. This highest-ranking rinpoche after the Dalai Lama was a friend and ally of the Chinese, and the Tibetan authorities had consequently refused to recognize him. The Chinese representatives now threatened to declare the negotiations unsuccessful unless the Panchen Lama was recognized, so the Dalai Lama and the Kashag gave their consent and recognized Lobsang Thrinle Lhündrup Chökyi Gyaltsen, who was thirteen at the time, as the Tenth Panchen Lama.

The Dalai Lama waited anxiously for news from Ngabö and was shocked when he heard a radio announcement that representatives of the People's Republic of China and the local Tibetan government had signed a Seventeen-Point Agreement; Ngabö had no authority to sign documents on behalf of the government and the Tibetan government would never have agreed to such a deal. On May 23, 1951, under extreme pressure from the Chinese representatives, Ngabö had, in fact, signed the Seventeen-Point Agreement in Beijing, putting an end to Tibetan independence and freedom. The Chinese pretended that Ngabö was authorized to act in the name of the Tibetan government and they even counterfeited the official state seal of the Dalai Lama. The very first point nullified Tibet's independence: "The Tibetan people shall unite and drive out imperialist aggressive forces from Tibet; the Tibetan people shall return to the family of the motherland—the People's Republic of China." Tibet was assured "national regional autonomy," but only "under the unified leadership of the Central People's Government." In addition, the Chinese government committed itself to not altering the prevailing political system in Tibet and to respecting the status, function and power of the Dalai Lama. The Tibetans could not understand what "imperialist powers" were to be driven from their land, nor could they accept the idea of China as the "motherland."

At that point the Dalai Lama could either flee or attempt to cooperate with the PRC according to the Seventeen-Point Agreement. Taktser Rinpoche, the Dalai Lama's elder brother who had already been living in India for some time, urged him to leave Tibet. Other influential government officials tried to persuade him to accept the agreement and return to Lhasa. Following ancient custom, an oracle was consulted on the fateful matter. The oracle's response was that the Dalai Lama should return to Lhasa, and on July 23 the Dalai Lama and his entourage set off on their way back to Lhasa.

The Drikung estate manager feared that the Tsarong family would keep Chetsang Rinpoche along with their other children outside of Tibet despite the country's peace under the Seventeen-Point Agreement, so he undertook the long and difficult journey to Kalimpong to personally bring Rinpoche back to the monastery. Chetsang Rinpoche's brothers and sisters who were to remain abroad and attend boarding school in Darjeeling would miss him, but Rinpoche himself was not unhappy at the idea of returning. Even as a child he was able to accept life's changes with joyful equanimity.

Once back in Tibet, Chetsang Rinpoche traveled to Lhasa for the hair-cutting and name-giving ceremony performed by the Dalai Lama. In

Buddhism, the hair-cutting ceremony symbolizes following the path of the Buddha, who cut his hair when he decided to renounce the worldly life of a prince to seek spiritual truth. After a reception given by the Tsangpa Khangtsen of Drepung Monastery, a magnificent procession escorted Rinpoche from the Tsarong home to the Norbulingka Palace, the summer residence of the Dalai Lama. There, the serious young Dalai Lama performed the rite with deep devotion and love, unruffled by his concern about the country's political future. After cutting the hair, the Dalai Lama gave Chetsang Rinpoche another set of names to add to the first, Konchog Tenzin Kunzang Thrinle Lhundrup.

4

Tutors and Storytellers
Early Years in the Monastery

Wile the ordinary population of the Drikung region paid scant attention to shifts in Tibet's governmental structures, the monastery managers knew that they would have to come to terms with those in power if they wished to retain their privileges. Khenpo Tseten Sangpo was the Drikung representative in a delegation that traveled to China with the Dalai Lama. He was dedicated to helping the poverty-stricken families in the Drikung area, and was deeply respected and loved by the population. He embraced the sociopolitical ideals espoused by the Communists and supported what the Chinese termed the "peaceful liberation" of the country, despite the fact that most Tibetans failed to understand what they were to be "liberated" from.

Like so many others, Tseten Sangpo was transfixed by Chairman Mao Zedong's charismatic personality. He even claimed that Mao Zedong was an emanation of the powerful Buddhist deity Vajrapani, although perhaps this view was calculated to persuade the uneducated population to accept the drastic changes to their country's social and political fabric. Without information to interpret Chinese rhetoric within the context of the realities of the international situation, many Tibetans hoped that the Chinese would in fact usher in positive changes. However, even the most radical of the pro-Chinese faction did not anticipate that the People's Republic of China's transformation of Tibet was intended to exterminate the country's religious tradition, along with all its other traditional social and cultural institutions.

It was in this land, still insulated from the outside world but on the

Drikung Thil Monastery, the founding monastery of the
Drikung Kagyu lineage (1179), in 1948.

brink of upheaval, that five-year-old Chetsang Rinpoche began his monastic education. Instruction began before sunrise. One of his attendants,
Solpön Konchog Tsewang, taught him to read, an essential foundation
for the memorization and study of the Buddhist scriptures. His spiritual mentors, called *yongzin*,[1] were Regent Gyabra and Ayang Thubten
(1899–1966). Gyabra was the abbot of Yangrigar as well as the *tritsab*
(literally, throne substitute) of the Drikung Kagyu lineage; he had been
the heart disciple of the previous incarnations of the Kyabgön Chetsang
and Chungtsang Rinpoches. Regent Gyabra and Ayang Thubten gave
Chetsang Rinpoche his first oral transmissions.

Tibetan Buddhist texts and their meaning are transmitted orally from
teacher to disciple in an unbroken chain within a lineage. The oral transmission, in which the teacher reads the scripture aloud to the disciple,
is believed to confer special blessings which will enable the disciple to

access the most profound meanings of the text, going beyond what can be understood from the written words alone. This guarantees both the authenticity of the teacher and of what is taught. For example, Tantric texts and their complex meditative practices are mostly kept secret. A disciple becomes authorized to study a tantra and practice its special visualizations, recitations, and meditations through an initiation or empowerment (*wang*), a complete oral transmission (*lung*), and instructions (*tri*) on the meaning of the text. In the course of this process, the lama gives profound pith instructions, whose degree of elaboration and complexity are in accordance with the disciple's powers of comprehension and which are aimed at guiding him to the recognition of the nature of mind.[2]

The first transmissions that Chetsang Rinpoche received were for the basic daily prayers and a few teachings on texts by the lineage founder, Jigten Sumgön. At that time in Drikung there was a tradition that empowerments and transmissions to the Kyabgön Rinpoches could only be given by certain lamas. Therefore, venerable masters from various Drikung monasteries in eastern Tibet, such as Bongtrul Rinpoche from Lho Lungkar Gön and Nyidzong Tripa from Nyidzong Gön, were invited.

As both Kyabgön Rinpoches were young children, the interim regent Tritsab Gyabra had to attend to all issues and concerns until they were old enough to assume their offices. Tritsab Gyabra was a tall, portly lama who radiated confidence and power. He was competent, efficient, and even-tempered—qualities that were necessary to guide the lineage through a difficult time, as well as to resolve the innumerable ordinary problems of everyday life, and negotiate the ubiquitous intrigues in the Drikung hierarchy. The regent's encumbrance with duties and responsibilities left Ayang Thubten as Chetsang Rinpoche's main teacher.

Ayang Thubten was an upright elderly tulku from Ayang Monastery in eastern Tibet. He was serious and introspective, living completely in the spiritual dimension. It was said that when he was born his umbilical cord was wound around him like a meditation belt. He had deep insight into the teachings of the Buddha and maintained a continuous meditative state, although he seemed perpetually worried and sometimes experienced strange attacks that made him scream uncontrollably in his room. Twice he jumped out of a window, but fortunately was not seriously injured, only once breaking his leg. No one knew for certain what preyed on his mind, but it may have been the heavy responsibility of caring for the two young Kyabgöns as well as the many Drikung monasteries, which, although full of spiritual treasures, were always short of worldly resources.

Ayang Rinpoche taught Chetsang Rinpoche Tibetan grammar. A correct and deep understanding of the language is essential for grasping subtle Buddhist theory. There are essentially three parallel Tibetan languages: a vernacular form used in everyday conversation, an honorific variety used in formal contexts, and a third used for writing and discussing religious texts. This last one is an exceptionally profound and comprehensive language that provides the framework for complex and subtle philosophical discourse. It arose as early translators of Buddhist texts succeeded in producing a standardized technical language that could capture all of the precision and nuances of the original Sanskrit using Tibetan grammatical structures to express multiple layers of meaning. Ayang also taught Rinpoche the basics of Tibetan astrology, which focuses on the rhythms and cycles of time and is a science of calculation rather than merely a divinatory art.

Writing was taught by the only layman among Chetsang Rinpoche's teachers, Rangdo Ali, a retired secretary of the Tibetan government and an excellent calligrapher. These hours were a welcome change for Rinpoche since, unlike his monastic tutors who were very strict and showed him no deference, Rangdo Ali was humble and respectful. If Rinpoche made a mistake in copying the letters, words, and sentences made with elegant strokes, Ali corrected him with polite deference. Whether fostered by his teacher's gentle encouragement or simply the result of a natural affinity, Chetsang Rinpoche developed a lifelong interest in writing in general, as well as an appreciation of consummate calligraphy and of ancient and rare manuscripts.

When Rinpoche grew a little older, the practice of the Dharma Protector (*Dharmapala*) was added to his daily schedule. While his attendant struck the cymbals and the great drum, Rinpoche chanted the long practice every afternoon. Like any other child eager for new experiences and adventures, he found it a boring waste of time to repeat the same thing for three hours every day. He would have preferred to be outside playing.

Although most of his time was taken up with his lessons and the memorization of texts, the young Rinpoche was allowed some time to play. Playmates were rare, however, since ordinary monks were kept strictly apart from the two Kyabgöns, who lived separated from each other as well as from the simple monks. Because Chetsang Rinpoche's rooms sat on top of the eastern part of the monastery and Chungtsang Rinpoche's rooms were above the western part, they were respectfully addressed as Kundun Shar ("Eastern Holiness") and Kundun Nub ("Western Holiness").[3] The boys were like unreachable deities abiding in the lofty heights of their mandala palaces, far above all that was ordinary and prosaic. Still, both of them yearned for the dust of the ordinary courtyards, the scrubby bushes beyond the monastery walls, the river's rushing waters, the animals grazing in the meadows, and most of all, playmates.

At first, the four-year difference in age, combined with Chetsang Rinpoche's and Chungtsang Rinpoche's contrasting personalities, was too large a gap to bridge. The open, adventurous, and cheerful Chetsang Rinpoche and the more mature, serious, and reserved Chungtsang Rinpoche could find little in common. It would only be later, when Chetsang Rinpoche had grown older and the two had begun to develop similar interests, that they would become close. In the beginning, Chetsang Rinpoche had only Nangse Tenzin Rinpoche, a tulku his own age, and Norbu Rinpoche, only a little older, as occasional playmates.

Chetsang Rinpoche's guardians were always preoccupied with serious matters, but at least his cook, Ashang Paljor, provided pleasant distraction along with the nightly bowl of soup he brought for him to drink before bed.[4] The old man, who had also been Shiwe Lodrö's cook, would sit on the edge of Rinpoche's bed and tell him strange tales about a speaking corpse that the hero of the story carried on his back—bizarre bedtime stories to Western ears, but Rinpoche fell asleep every time. Ashang Paljor's stories are known in Tibet as *Ro Dung* and have been transmitted in many different versions.[5] In them an Indian meditation master gives his naïve young disciple the strange task of bringing him the corpse of Rogen Ngodrub Gyatso from the cemetery, but if he speaks with the dead body it will fly back to the cemetery. When he succeeds at his task, a great goldmine will appear that will be of limitless benefit to sentient beings. This is the frame for a series of stories with

Buddhist morals embedded, as told by the corpse in an effort to get the young disciple to speak to him. After each one the disciple cannot resist commenting on the tale, and the corpse boxes his ears three times before flying away like a falcon. Thus the disciple has to begin his task all over again, and a new story starts. The corpse entrances him each time with another strange fable of daredevil adventurers, cruel witches, clever thieves, enchanted animals, and tyrannical kings—full of magic but also full of deeper meaning. Only after starting over with his assignment many times does he finally grasp the significance of the teachings that underlie the stories, realizing the value of his efforts for his own spiritual growth. His Indian teacher joyfully tells him that he has finally succeeded in climbing the glorious mountain and transforming it into gold, and that he has become the gold that will be of great benefit to all sentient beings. Told as popular fairy-tales in homes and nomads' tents throughout Tibet to children who, like the hero of the narrative, seldom understood the legends' full meanings, these narratives contained a subtext of Buddhist ethics and ideals that infused their young minds with healthy social and religious values.

When the troops of the People's Liberation Army marched through the Drikung region, Chetsang Rinpoche observed them intently. He was fascinated and not alarmed, although there were many soldiers. The first contingents were badly equipped and suffered from the harsh winter and the extremely high altitude. In addition they lacked food, as their supply lines functioned only sporadically, and they had to make do with minimal daily rations for months at a time. They had strict orders not to accept anything from the Tibetans, because at that time the Communist government wished to convince the Tibetans that the troops were only going to benefit the population. The soldiers didn't respond to provocation but instead remained calm and courteous. The Chinese cadres won over the Drikung administrators and other leading monastery employees, putting them on their payroll. Invitations were exchanged now and then. The Chinese cautiously explained party ideology to the lamas, but perhaps they left some aspects unclear or perhaps the lamas didn't devote much attention to such worldly concerns. At any rate, the deceptive peace continued for a few years.

Nevertheless, the PLA troops were soldiers, and in later years

Chetsang Rinpoche watched how their prisoners were tied together and forced to carry the troops' provisions. The prisoners struggled along under their heavy loads, often falling, and those who died from exhaustion were shoved into shallow roadside graves. These sights were horrifying and disillusioning. The soldiers once camped overnight in a park opposite the monastery. After they left, anxious villagers reported that people had been buried and requested Rinpoche to recite prayers for them. He was taken to four or five mounds of fresh earth where he said the prayers, wondering whether they had died of exhaustion or been executed.

In September, 1951, the first three thousand Chinese soldiers reached Lhasa, quickly followed by another three thousand. The army camped outside the city, but the sudden influx of so many people resulted in a shortage of provisions that grew into a famine for the troops of the PLA, and tensions grew between the soldiers and the Tibetans. When their firewood ran out, the soldiers burned yak horns and bones, causing a terrible stench in Lhasa.

The Chinese Communists first concentrated their political efforts on Lhasa and Shigatse, where their protégé, the Panchen Lama, resided. Only specially trained propaganda units visited the villages, where they presented appealing programs of song and dance and provided medical treatment for the sick. The highest-ranking cadres held lavish banquets for the nobility, while the masses enjoyed propaganda films about the Communist victories against the Chinese Nationalist Party (Kuomintang) and the Japanese. The PLA opened a free hospital for the poor that was far superior to the city's public hospital. The Chinese even followed the Tibetan custom of distributing money during Mönlam, adding a propaganda booklet and a photo of Mao.

Thus the Chinese first sought to secure the goodwill of all levels of society, and then they slowly introduced new regulations to transform the organization of Tibetan society. They skillfully established a parallel administrative structure and a secular education system. Education had previously only been available in the monasteries, although a few wealthy families hired tutors or sent their children abroad. Prominent Tibetans, including Dasang Damdul Tsarong, were asked to serve on educational committees responsible for building new schools. They could hardly refuse to participate in such a noble social project, although the new

Chinese schools were actually used as an effective means of indoctrinating the younger generation with Communist propaganda. By 1952 there were several new schools for Tibetan children, as well as "patriotic associations," cultural groups, an office for political consultation, and an editorial board for a newspaper.

After anti-Chinese demonstrations at the Mönlam festival of 1952, the Chinese forced the Dalai Lama to dismiss two prime ministers, Lukhang and Lobsang Tashi, who were driving forces of the resistance. This was a decisive blow to Tibetan autonomy, and from then on the Chinese military leaders gradually gained control, while members of the Kashag became mere puppets.

Every year, usually in late summer, Chetsang Rinpoche visited his parents in Lhasa. The presence of so many Chinese in the streets astonished him, as did the despondent atmosphere that his parents and grandparents could not conceal from him. He saw how intently they listened to the news on the radio, but it was improper for children to ask questions, and the adults kept their worries to themselves. Grandfather Tsarong made every effort to make sure the children felt as happy and secure as possible in his house. One year Chetsang Rinpoche brought Chungtsang Rinpoche, and they both stayed almost four months. The two Holinesses brought their tutors and attendants and received their regular lessons, but they were also able to play with Chetsang Rinpoche's siblings and cousins in the expansive grounds of the Tsarong home.

Grandfather Tsarong remained a member of the national assembly, but since the assembly no longer met, he had plenty of time for his beloved gardening. Every morning, as soon as the sun had risen, he went down to start working in his vegetable garden. Planting fruit trees was his greatest joy, and the specimens he had imported from India bore fruit in abundance. Tsarong gave each of his grandchildren his or her own fruit tree to care for, and when Chetsang Rinpoche was seven years old his grandfather suggested planting a peach tree. Tsarong presented a sapling as tall as his grandson, and instructed him how to plant it. The procedure took hours, but Rinpoche planted his tree all by himself, and when the work was finished, grandfather and grandson gazed at the little tree contentedly. Whenever he came to visit after that, Chetsang Rinpoche first ran to check on how his tree was growing. To everyone's surprise, it bore five or six large peaches in its first year.

In 1959 Rinpoche would see his peach tree for the last time. PLA troops had been stationed in the family's house for a while when he snuck onto the property. The once-blooming garden was neglected and desolate; the beds had been trampled underfoot, with only a few sad little flowers to be seen among the parched grasses. Knowing that he would not return, Rinpoche said farewell to his tree, still growing splendidly.

Although the young Rinpoche was more interested in animals than plants, his grandfather's enthusiasm for botany resulted in an interest in gardening that has lasted to this day. He cultivates many different plants in front of his residence in Dehra Dun, India, collecting the seeds of interesting trees, shrubs, and flowers during his travels, and planting them in his garden in India.

To extend their control over the country as swiftly as possible, the PRC began to construct roads, quickly building the infrastructure needed to bring heavy vehicles and artillery to Lhasa. Rinpoche's father also brought a vehicle to Lhasa, a Land Rover he purchased in India that was disassembled and the pieces carried by porters over the passes of the Himalayas. He reassembled it himself in Lhasa, and used it to drive his son back to the monastery, although the road only went as far as Medrogungkar, where they were met by a delegation from Drikung with horses. Rinpoche enjoyed those rides, sitting on his father's lap with his hands on the steering wheel as though he were driving the huge vehicle himself, while his more timid companions in the back seat said prayers.

Despite the strict daily routine, life in Drikung was full of variety because Chetsang Rinpoche moved to a new monastery every few months. Yangrigar lay in a valley, surrounded by many fields, and Rinpoche enjoyed free time on the river bank, where the monastery's horses grazed. He liked to catch one and ride bareback, racing over the hills. He loved to ride and would try to ride nearly anything, sometimes even climbing onto the back of a bull or a billy goat.

Rinpoche loved animals, wild and domesticated. Some beautiful pheasants, with bright orange feet, white collars, and iridescent feathers lived around Yangrigar, and a variety of large partridges began to sing at about 3 A.M. every morning. Many animals lived on the mountain slopes behind Drikung Dzong. One night a snow leopard jumped through a ventilation hole in a store room next to the kitchen and drank from the

Yangrigar Monastery in 1948.

cauldron of water kept there. Chetsang Rinpoche could see into the ventilation hole directly from his room, and he watched the elegant animal jump out and disappear into the underbrush after it had slaked its thirst. Another time he came face-to-face with a leopard while on his way to the outhouse; he stood perfectly still, and for one endless moment gazed, unafraid and fascinated, into the leopard's bright, shining eyes, until it crept silently away over the cliffs. Occasionally he would hear the cry of a villager's goat that had fallen prey to a leopard. He would rush outside immediately with his field glasses to watch the snow leopard drag its victim into the bushes.

Every summer a delegation from the monastery performed a rain ritual at the sacred lake of Medro Sijin, considered a sacred *naga* lake because a small island shaped like a snake rises from the water.[6] There was an abundance of fish in the lake, clearly visible as they swam in the

crystalline waters above the hundreds of ritual offering urns, accumulated over centuries, shimmering on the lake bottom. Tibetans neither
caught nor ate fish, and the unchecked population died in masses when
strong winds whipped the surface of the lake and the waves swept them
ashore. The skies would then grow black with birds coming to feast on
the fish.

As Chetsang Rinpoche matured, he and Chungtsang Rinpoche grew
closer and began to have many adventures together. Beneath Chungtsang Rinpoche's mask of reserve was a brash and daring character who
took pleasure in shaking people up. Like Chetsang Rinpoche, he loved
animals, riding, and picnics. He also loved swords, rifles, pistols, and
knives, and would sometimes sneak into the shrine rooms of the protector deities just to see the terrifying weapons hanging on the walls. They
fascinated him, but he never actually tried to use them.

Chetsang Rinpoche instigated most of their adventures. One autumn
he persuaded Chungtsang Rinpoche to go on an expedition to pick
the peaches growing on the mountain behind Drikung Dzong. While
Chungtsang Rinpoche moved cautiously on the dangerously steep slopes,
Chetsang Rinpoche quickly scampered up one of the trees. Enticed by
the best fruits, hanging high up in the crown of the tree, he climbed out
on a branch that broke under his weight. Smaller branches slowed his
fall, but when he crashed down onto the steep slope he began to slide
toward the edge of the nearby cliff. Chungtsang Rinpoche clung helplessly to a tree trunk, sure his young friend was doomed to slide over
the precipice, but Chetsang Rinpoche crashed into a small thorn bush
growing at the cliff's edge, saving him from certain death.

Other mischief was less dangerous. The two Rinpoches found a way
to slip under their high thrones in a rarely used Yangrigar shrine room.
They took a couple of butter lamps from an altar table to light their hiding
place, and sometimes brought dried meat and enjoyed a picnic in their
"cave." Chetsang Rinpoche also brought a handful of cigarettes that he
had taken from a cigarette box his parents kept for guests, and one time
the boys heard the heavy wooden doors to the shrine room being pushed
open just as they had lit up their cigarette. They quickly extinguished the
lamps and cigarette, and did not move. They heard the shuffling steps
and the rattling of metal bowls as the temple caretaker performed the
daily ritual of filling the offering bowls. He soon left, but the monk had

Chungtsang Rinpoche (left) with Chetsang Rinpoche in Drikung.

noticed a strange smell that he could not identify, and reported this to the monastery administrator. A few days later, as they were again smoking a cigarette in their secret kingdom, the administrator burst in with the monk and became very upset. "The smell in this shrine room is disgusting! A bad omen!" The Rinpoches had trouble containing their laughter, but they remained undiscovered.

Later, when Chetsang Rinpoche was about eleven years old, the two Rinpoches received a series of empowerments in this same shrine room. During an empowerment one drinks a little *chang* (barley beer) from a skull cup, and after each empowerment the remaining chang was collected in a large pitcher to be disposed of. One day the two Drikung Holinesses took the pitcher to a hiding place in a storage closet in Chungtsang Rinpoche's room and finished off the mild, but decidedly alcoholic, drink. In Rinpoche's family, chang drinkers got red faces, and he was no exception; he felt hot and his face turned bright red. He was supposed to attend a puja but this was now impossible, since it was immediately obvious that he had been drinking chang. Fortunately

Joyful Chetsang Rinpoche with his bicycle at Yangrigar Monastery.

Chungtsang Rinpoche was able to get Rinpoche's attendant to make his excuses for not attending the puja, and once again the boys' mischief went undiscovered.

In the Tibetan calendar each year is associated with one of twelve animals in a regularly rotation. In Drikung there was a tradition of giving a series of important teachings and empowerments in the years of the Monkey, Snake, and Pig. The year 1953 was a Snake Year, and Lho Bongtrul Tenzin Dodul was invited to Drikung from Kham to give the Kyabgön Rinpoches transmissions and initiations. Drubwang Gejung Rinpoche, who was deaf in his right ear, accompanied him.[7] In Drikung Thil, Gejung Rinpoche announced: "I took my Vinaya and Bodhicitta vows from Shiwe Lodrö, and received many initiations from him that are hard to obtain. If the son of the Tsarong family is the indisputable incarnation of Shiwe Lodrö, he will heal me if he blows in my right ear." Kyabgön Chetsang Rinpoche looked at him calmly, took the man's head in both hands, and blew in his ear; from then on, Gejung Rinpoche could hear in both ears. He wept for joy that his revered old teacher had come again, and with him the blessing power of the lineage.

Monks who had spent long periods of time in retreat were required to demonstrate the progress in their yoga practice, called *tsa lung trul-khor,* before a small committee headed by the throne holder. In Drikung Thil these demonstrations took place in a courtyard specially designed for the trulkhor examinations and covered by tenting. Only yogis and rinpoches were permitted to attend the demonstrations; no ordinary monks were allowed in.[8] Rinpoche could hardly wait to see what was going to happen. The yogis sat on small rugs, clad only in short trousers, and began their demanding exercises. One of these movements, called *langbeb,* literally "rising and descending," is an amazing leap in which the yogi springs into the air from the seated lotus posture, folds his legs back into lotus posture in midair, and then lands, still seated, back on the ground. The best yogis appeared to defy the laws of gravity, seeming to fly upwards and pause at the highest point to cross their legs without haste, and then land gently on their rugs. Pachung Rinpoche (1901–1988), the famous yogi of Drikung, sat in the front and could leap highest and most elegantly of all.

In 1954 the Dalai Lama was invited on a propaganda tour through China, along with government officials, members of the aristocracy, and lamas in a huge caravan. Since the delegation was to pass through the Drikung region, the monastery was called upon to accommodate them. A camp with hundreds of tents was set up for the Dalai Lama and his retinue near Mamtsakha, which was far from Drikung Thil Monastery. In fact, Chetsang Rinpoche and his delegation could manage the journey to meet them only by riding yaks over the steep passes. Chinese soldiers made their own camp nearby, and Rinpoche could see them hunting rabbits. It was the first time Rinpoche had seen men hunt, and he watched, both curious and disturbed, to see how they skinned the animals and roasted them over the fire.

Together with their entourage, the two Kyabgön Rinpoches waited to pay their respects to the Dalai Lama, as did many other high rinpoches and a huge crowd of ordinary people. A great cloud of dust appeared on the horizon, and a strange clattering could be heard in the distance. When Phuntsog Tashi, the Dalai Lama's security officer, came into view riding a motorcycle, the nomads—having never seen such a machine before—were utterly astounded and thought he was riding a goat, holding onto its horns. Their reaction amused Rinpoche, whose father had ridden on a motorcycle for as long as he could remember. After a delay during which twenty strong local men had to dig the Dalai Lama's car out of the mud and carry it part of the way, he finally arrived, with his entourage riding on horses and mules. The Kyabgön Rinpoches offered the Dalai Lama their ceremonial white scarves, escorted him into his tent, and were served tea and sweet rice with him while they watched the nomads' dances.

Rinpoche still remembers the unusually beautiful mules in the Dalai Lama's caravan. They were large and strong animals in matched pairs: two black ones with striking white spots on their bellies and flanks, like leopard skin, were followed by two gray ones, then two chestnut ones, and so on. In the comfortable stables of the Norbulingka Palace, the feed troughs were elevated so the animals could eat without stretching their necks down, but in the Drikung camp their feed was placed on the ground, and the bewildered animals sank down on their forelegs to eat. The nomads laughed uproariously at the sight.

Difficulties that had been seen as bad omens on the Dalai Lama's journey to China grew worse on his trip home in 1955. A bridge collapsed in Kongpo while the group was crossing it and the caravan became separated. The Dalai Lama had made it to the other side of the river, but the greater part of his retinue was forced to make a lengthy detour. Still, the Dalai Lama returned from China feeling confident. His conversations with Chairman Mao Zedong and high-ranking party, government, and military leaders had filled him with optimism about Tibet's future. Unfortunately, the menacing omens were more accurate than his optimistic hopes. The PRC leaders failed to keep their promises, and by the end of the year, Communist extremism and excesses had begun to spread throughout Tibet.

5

Inside the Mandala

I N T I B E T ' S S A C R E D G E O G R A P H Y, places where realized masters have spent time in solitary retreat became sealed in a twofold fashion: sealed by spiritual mastery and by tantric practice. Later, yogis on journeys recognized the secret seal of mastery where ordinary eyes could see only fields, mountains, and rivers. They settled in these places to receive their blessings and engage in profound meditation, and by doing so reopened the sacred locations. In this way places have been added to the spiritual cartography, and become Buddhist pilgrimage sites, particularly attracting Vajrayana practitioners.[1]

Not far from Drikung Thil Monastery, surrounded by rocky heights, lies the little valley of Terdrom, still known for its hot springs and many caves. During the eighth century, the Indian tantric master and "father" of Tibetan Buddhism, Padmasambhava (Guru Rinpoche), spent time in this area together with his disciples, of whom the foremost was his consort, Yeshe Tsogyal (757–817). They engaged in tantric practice and concealed spiritual treasures in nearly inaccessible places. These Dharma treasures (*terma*) were mostly profound texts, but also included some ritual objects, relics, and natural objects. They were left so a *terton,* a treasure-finder, would discover them when their contents would be of the greatest benefit to human beings.[2]

Thus, Terdrom has been regarded as a sacred place for centuries, and it is the center of the Drikung mandala. Terdrom means "treasure chest," and the lovely valley is itself a treasure, containing the mythical birthplace of Achi Chökyi Dolma, the protector deity of the Drikung lineage. Nyergyepa Dorje Gyalpo (1284–1350), the tenth Drikung throne holder, perceived the sacred imprint left in the valley of Terdrom by the

Terdrom Nunnery in the valley of Terdrom.

tantric practices of Guru Rinpoche and Yeshe Tsogyal, and he revealed
the place's extraordinary energies.

In Terdrom every bend in the stream, every rock outcrop, every
pass, and every cave has a significance that transcends its material appearance. It is not a symbolic meaning but an actual manifestation that
can be perceived by those whose view has been purified by meditative
practice. Each year in autumn the Kyabgön Rinpoches made a pilgrimage to the valley. The monks of Yangrigar Monastery escorted them to
Kyedrak Thang, Achi's birthplace, where they hung prayer flags and performed purification rituals. The next day they continued on to the plain
of Zenthang, where they were met by a delegation from Drikung Thil
and local officials.

A *chagchen,* an initiate in the geomantic secrets of sacred places,
guided them through the spiritual landscape. He showed them prints
in stone that had been left by Achi's horse, by the mythical Garuda
bird, and by various Drikung throne holders. He explained that certain

boulders were actually long-life pills of the dakinis.[3] As he spoke, the landscape he led them through was transformed into a visionary pure realm. The chagchen conjured up a sacred geography invisible to the profane eye. Rinpoche listened intently to the stories, surrendering completely to the narrative of the spiritual and profane history of his glorious Drikung lineage.

To reach Terdrom they had to cross first a pass and then a river. Directly beneath the hot springs a shell-limestone cliff formed a natural dam and the water was forced through a tunnel fifteen meters long. The gorge cut by the river was deep and precipitous, and on one side a huge boulder had broken off and left a gaping fissure. In earlier times, the chagchen explained, the entire area beyond the natural dam had been a dangerous lake full of malicious water spirits so poisonous that birds flying over it fell dead from the skies. All attempts to drain the waters failed until people prayed to Achi for help. Achi cut the cliff in two with her magical mirror, but only some of the water flowed out. Guru Rinpoche, who happened to be sitting in a cave high above the branching river, noticed that Achi's magical action had only been partially successful and hurled his *vajra* at the cliff wall, opening a tunnel that allowed the water to flow out. The chagchen pointed out the shape of the vajra, which remained as a rock outcrop at the entrance of the tunnel. Guru Rinpoche gave as a dwelling place to the elemental spirits that he had subdued and bound to the Buddhadharma a red cliff that rises to the north of the tunnel. Then he caused the hot springs, said to heal all bodily illnesses, to emerge for yogis and yoginis.

As the pilgrimage continued the chagchen's explanations as well as the receptions and ceremonies become increasingly elaborate and lengthy. Whenever they had climbed a pass or reached a nomad camp or other small settlement, the local representatives stood ready in their best clothes, holding white scarves for a welcoming ceremony. They spent the first night in tents in Tayak Thang, near a famous nunnery that was the residence of the Drikung Khandro, an advanced female practitioner considered to be an emanation of Yeshe Tsogyal.

The next day they climbed to Tsachuka Pass, where the nuns waited in a long line, holding incense sticks and white scarves. They invited Chetsang Rinpoche into the temple of their cloister, where they performed a long-life puja for him that lasted all day.

Chetsang Rinpoche taking a bath in the sacred hot spring of Terdrom.

According to ancient pre-Buddhist beliefs, the serpent spirits (San-skrit *nagas,* Tibetan *lu*) that live in the earth, streams, and lakes guard the energies of the earth. They maintain the earth's ecological balance by countering human depredation of the environment. In their negative aspect they cause diseases, specifically those believed, in Tibetan medi-cal theory, to originate from an imbalance of the water element. Nagas protect the purity of water, and waters under their special protection, such as Terdrom's hot springs, are considered precious sources of health and well-being.

The mouth of the main spring was surrounded by a stone wall higher than a man's head. This privileged bathing spot, where the water flowed out of the cliff with great force and was especially pure, was reserved exclusively for the Kyabgön Rinpoches; ordinary people accessed the waters further downstream. The chagdzö broke the seal on the lock of the wooden slat door, affixed the year before, so the two Rinpoches could take their annual healing bath. The autumn weather would have been already quite cold, but the water at the mouth of the spring was extremely hot. At first Rinpoche was afraid of being scalded and his skin turned bright red, but once he had gotten used to it, he and Chungstang Rinpoche enjoyed splashing and playing in the sacred water.[4]

The pilgrims spent at least a week at the hot springs before continuing on their way, on foot or riding yaks, over the mountain ridge behind the nunnery. The group paused on a knoll crowned by a stupa, and the chagchen pointed out a high plateau and the mountain behind it, which together appeared to form an elephant's head with its trunk. This animal, seeming to emerge from the landscape to watch over the Terdrom Valley as its secret guardian, symbolized steadfastness and strength and bore the lotus throne of Akshobhya—the Dhyani Buddha who also epitomizes stability. Chetsang Rinpoche felt a special kinship with this image since one of his birth names, Gyurme, also means "the Unshakeable One."

Beyond a spring that flowed from one of Guru Rinpoche's caves was a small monastery where there was a black vase, covered with gold, that produced a miraculous steam of water. It was said to have been an offering from a naga. The path grew more difficult behind the monastery, climbing steeply to Norbu La, "the Jewel Pass," where Rinpoche hung prayer flags on the stone cairns, built slowly as every passing traveler added a stone. The path continued around a sharp ridge where Guru Rinpoche had once hidden a treasure, and hours later they reached a cave in a small hollow, where numerous springs flowed from the cliff walls. Here they collected a special earth, *sakala*, which was considered medicinal and full of blessings. Further on they passed through a place identified as a cemetery, below a group of peaks that represented the dakinis of the five buddha families. Lay practitioners practiced *chöd* in the shadows of the cliffs, playing their large hand drums and bone trumpets.[5]

Finally the pilgrims reached the heart of the Drikung Mandala. On the steep cliff wall high above their heads they saw the dark entrance to an enormous complex of caves known as the Kiri Yangdzong Cave. An impressive entrance fifty meters high led into the cliff. Also known as Khandro Drora ("Dancing-ground of the Dakinis"), it is a very sacred place and is considered one of the Eight Great Caves of Tibet.[6]

During Guru Rinpoche's stay in Tibet there was a period in which the ancient Bön religion regained strength and influence in the population, and he and his consort were forced to leave their retreat place in Yamalung. They fled to the Drikung area, where they found refuge in the Kiri Yangdzong Cave. Yeshe Tsogyal is said to have received her three

initiations into the *Khandro Nyingtig* (Heart-Essence of the Dakinis)
here.[7] After Guru Rinpoche had left, she traveled to Nepal and returned
to Terdom with her consort, Atsara Sale, to spend seven months in retreat. She later revisited the valley of Terdrom many times to practice
there. Yeshe Tsogyal is said to have spent a total of seven years meditating in her chamber inside the great cave, and near the end of her life she
performed her final Dzogchen retreat here.[8] She concealed a part of the
Khandro Nyingtig in Terdrom, and the seventeenth Drikung throne
holder, Rinchen Phuntsog (1509–1557), discovered the treasure text
Damcho Gongpa Yangzab in Kiri Yangdzong Cave, thus becoming a
renowned terton.

The ascent to the cave was strenuous and perilous; the more timid
among the monks, and the more portly, preferred to stay behind. A
winding path led up steeply, and soon the voices of those remaining
in the valley could no longer be heard. The huge entrance chamber,
known as the *Tsokhang Chenmo* (Great Assembly Hall), opened under
the highest ridge. Once inside the vast opening, Rinpoche and his companions had to climb long, shaky ladders made of untreated bamboo
canes bound together with straps of yak leather. This was a terrifying
ascent, and Chetsang Rinpoche's attendants were more afraid on his account than on their own. They warned him not to look down, and one
particularly strong monk held his legs firmly while he pulled himself up
the widely spaced rungs. He did glance down once, and saw those who
had remained behind only as flickering red specks at an unimaginable
depth. He climbed the last rungs quickly, until he felt firm ground under
his feet again. The ground was solid, but by no means safe, since the rock
was damp and uneven. Above him, the ice-covered cliff wall disappeared
into darkness where a passage just below the ceiling of the cave led to
Yeshe Tsogyal's secret retreat chamber.

Pilgrimage to this cave was a powerful initiation into the secrets of
the tantric path. Some of the darker passages and chambers deep inside
the cave could only be entered with torches; others fell away sharply and
the pilgrims had to cling to yak-hair ropes to avoid falling into the abyss.
Somewhere in the darkness a waterfall roared into the depths. Chetsang
Rinpoche was astonished at the ease with which the old chagchen made
his way, moving through the shafts and tunnels with calm familiarity. He
said that the entirety of the secret teachings was displayed in the cave,

and all six realms of existence, the worlds of the gods, demigods, human beings, animals, hungry ghosts and hell-beings, could be found there. On another level of visionary consciousness, the yogi saw the maze of tunnels, with their many turnings and branchings, halls and domes, as the energy channels of the subtle body, just as he visualized them in meditation.

In one place there was a narrow twisting passage that was difficult to squeeze through. It was said that one who was full of sin would become trapped. Chetsang Rinpoche was still a small boy, but the opening was so narrow that he was afraid nonetheless. He made his way through safely, and the chagchen pointed out more marvels: cavities in the wall said to be impressions of Guru Rinpoche's head, crystals with spontaneously arisen images of Buddhist deities and Dharma symbols, and a pedestal-like outcropping from the cave wall that was regarded as the throne of Guru Rinpoche and was flanked by shelves for the miraculously arisen ritual implements.[9]

The last place the pilgrims visited in the cave was a small round chamber that had been Guru Rinpoche's meditation room. A striking stone pillar that stood just outside it was associated with the central channel of Vajrayogini, a tantric deity. The group had now arrived at the most secret center of the mandala where the Dharma treasures had been found, the very heart of the spiritual energy field. The smooth stone was a type of quartz crystal and it broke the light of the torches into colorful rainbows. This crystal was regarded as the essence of all minerals and was used in rejuvenation practices.

Many found the descent even more frightening than the ascent. The way down followed a steep gravelly slope beside the cliffs. There was no firm path through the loose gravel, giving the feeling of sliding inescapably into the abyss. The descent was made even more dangerous by the many large stones and boulders concealed by the harmless-looking gravel surface. Only one small group could descend at a time so the stones they dislodged would not hit anyone on the slope below them.

Replete with impressions of his journey into the interior of the mountain, Chetsang Rinpoche conducted a *tsog* ritual of food and drink offerings for Guru Rinpoche, and then set off for Drongur, where they camped for the night near the small ancient retreat hut of Rinchen

Phuntsog, the terton who had founded the hermitage here. The day's experiences seemed to have plunged Rinpoche into a magical super-reality in which past and mythical realities blended seamlessly into ordinary reality.

The pilgrimage continued over a pass into a deep valley, and two days later they reached Tsa Ug Ritö, the renowned retreat cave of Kyobpa Jigten Sumgön. In 1191 lineage founder Jigten Sumgön had come here to do retreat, but it had seemed too small and dark to the faithful attendant accompanying him. And so, Jigten Sumgön expanded the cave by magical means and struck a window into the south cave wall with his vajra. Since then the cave has also been called Tsa Ug Lhokar, "Cave with the Opening to the South."

Other caves in the area also became retreat places for yogis and yoginis, and Rinpoche was attracted to these retreatants in ragged clothing, who had dedicated themselves completely to a life of Dharma and subsisted on the simple offerings brought to them by kindly patrons. They prostrated to the young Kyabgön, and regarded him with a gaze that was more open and calm than that of the monks living in monasteries. He did not yet fully understand why they spent their time in retreat, but he instinctively sensed the special merit and power of their aspirations. The retreatants' years in these isolated and remote places connected them to the sacred landscape Chetsang Rinpoche had traversed in the past weeks; their practice both sustained the spiritual power of the land and allowed its blessing energy to flow into them. As they perfected the complex practices of tantra, they transformed their profane bodies, speech, and minds as well as the environment around them—becoming the deity's body, speech, and mind at the center of a sacred mandala. These heirs of the tradition founded by Jigten Sumgön, who sent thousands of yogis into retreat in the sacred mountains of Tibet, struck a resonant chord in young Chetsang Rinpoche awakening vague memories, like fragments of an almost-forgotten dream.

The travelers stayed a few days in the area, ostensibly so that Rinpoche could rest from the strenuous journey, but he preferred to visit hermitages and ask the yogis how they lived and what they had experienced in their many years of retreat. He sensed that they held the key to strengthening and reconnecting the fragments of memory he felt stirring deep inside himself.

As his journey approached its end, Chetsang Rinpoche performed ceremonies with a delegation of khenpos,[10] lamas, and monks from Drikung Thil for two full days in Ngoyig Thang before proceeding to the monastery on an astrologically auspicious day. When Rinpoche entered the monastery's Golden Temple and made three prostrations to the main statue of Jigten Sumgön, it felt as though something had changed, either in the monastery or in himself. He offered the long silk scarf not to the golden statue, but to Jigten Sumgön himself, to the lineage lamas, to the yogis in their hermitages, to the Buddha, and to his teachings. The pilgrimage was officially complete after the final procession to Yangrigar Monastery was concluded with further ceremonies, and Rinpoche entered his winter quarters in Drikung Dzong.

Back in Lhasa, once the Chinese cadres in the city had established their schools, they announced that Tibet—with Chinese assistance—was now fully capable of educating its children, pressuring the remaining aristocratic families with children being schooled in India to force them to return. Afraid of what the People's Liberation Army might do otherwise, even the Tsarongs brought their children back to Lhasa during the winter of 1953.

At first Chetsang Rinpoche's siblings regarded the new Chinese schools as a pleasant change. Class differences were suppressed, and soon all of the pupils wore identical uniforms. The children enjoyed learning the Communist propaganda songs, which they sang enthusiastically in class and on the streets without really understanding the songs' purpose, and they enjoyed liberties forbidden to them under the previous social order. In this way the Party molded Tibetan youths into enthusiastic advocates of their propaganda. For example, Chetsang Rinpoche's sister Namgyal Lhamo joined a political drama group, which even performed before the Dalai Lama.

During the Dalai Lama's visit to Beijing a preliminary committee had been initiated to establish the Tibet Autonomous Region (TAR). Unfortunately, "regional autonomy" was a misnomer intended to disguise the complete subjugation of Tibetan authority to PRC rule. When the Preparatory Committee for the Autonomous Region of Tibet (PCART) was formed in March 1955, Namgyal Lhamo belonged to a troupe of young Tibetans sent to the rural areas to perform political theater. The

plays they enacted extolled Chairman Mao and the People's Liberation Army, praised the end of the "feudal" regime and exploitation, and
promised that Communist reforms would ensure the country's bright
future. With their radiantly happy faces the members of the troupe
were attractive, persuasive, and unquestioning proponents of Mao's
ideological programs. Most of them, including Namgyal Lhamo, were
so enchanted with their newly gained freedom from traditional social
strictures and conventions that they did not notice how they were being
manipulated to do the work of the new rulers. They were completely
unaware of the brutal assaults in Kham and Amdo, where, far from central Tibet, families were forcibly separated and children sent to China
to be indoctrinated or to vanish forever. Women were sterilized without their knowledge or consent, and during the infamous *thamzing*
("struggle") sessions, children were forced to denounce their parents, to
beat them, and sometimes even to kill them. Monks vowed to celibacy
were forced to have sexual intercourse with women, nuns were raped,
and high-ranking lamas were imprisoned or condemned to hard labor
on road construction crews. Monasteries were left deserted, plundered,
and destroyed.

When Namgyal Lhamo and her sister Norzin Yangkyi started to attend the newly founded Middle School, they slowly began to realize that
the new social freedoms granted the youth were only bait to entice them
into a harsh system of oppression. Teachers were no longer subtle and
accommodating, and the previously appealing propaganda slogans were
now ruthlessly put into practice as brutal retaliation against the nobility.
Children of aristocrats were harassed and confrontations between social
classes were openly encouraged. Many disillusioned Tibetan pupils became hostile toward their Chinese teachers, and sometimes engaged in
bloody encounters as the tensions that had originated in eastern Tibet
spread across the country.

As early as 1954, when the Dalai Lama had passed through Kham
on his way to Beijing, the local rulers had made it quite clear that they
would not peacefully tolerate the barbarous Communist reforms. These
eastern Tibetans' obstinacy, independence, tribal loyalty, and fighting
spirit were well known to central Tibetans, who sometimes disparaged
them as untrustworthy, brutal renegades. In the Dalai Lama's speech at
the inauguration of the Preparatory Committee for the Autonomous

Region of Tibet he quite wisely observed that reforms in eastern Tibet would have to be implemented with great caution.

In April 1956 the PCART was inaugurated with great pomp, with the Dalai Lama and the Panchen Lama as Tibetan figureheads. The PCART was to integrate Tibet into the PRC's administrative structure by replacing the Chinese "Tibetan Military Commission" that had forcibly controlled Lhasa politics since 1951. Installing the Dalai Lama and the Panchen Lama in the PCART was a means to gain acceptance among the population, while the ultimate goal was to discreetly transfer the Dalai Lama's governmental authority to the Communist Party of China. Making the Dalai Lama chairman was successful in disrupting resistance to the Committee; many who wanted to rebel against it hesitated to oppose the Dalai Lama. There were fourteen ministries in the PCART, and members of aristocratic families were recruited to serve by means of subtle compulsion. Dasang Damdul Tsarong—experienced in the construction of bridges, hydroelectric plants, and canals—was put in charge of the department of construction. Owners of large estates were compelled to place their homes at the committee's disposal, and within two weeks the entire ground floor of the Tsarong mansion was filled with Chinese employees of the department.

Meanwhile, under pressure from the Chinese the Drikung regent Tritsab Gyabra moved to Lhasa and was appointed General Secretary of the newly created department of religious affairs and member of the Tibet Committee of the Chinese People's Political Consultative Conference (CPPCC). The Consultative Conference was developed to create the outward appearance of a democratic commission that integrated other parties and national minorities, but any claim to democracy was a sham. All delegates were selected by the Communist Party of China, and were promptly removed and put on trial if they failed to please.

Additional troops of the People's Liberation Army were brought into the country as Chinese cadres spread to the most remote parts of Tibet to compile a comprehensive and detailed census of the population and complete inventories of the possessions of the aristocrats and the monasteries.

Although often heavy-handed, the Party tactics in U-Tsang, in central Tibet, were generally diplomatic and strategic; an entirely different approach was used in Kham and Amdo in the east. A *de facto* Chinese

sovereignty had existed in some parts of eastern Tibet since the Qing
Dynasty (1644–1911), and the Tibetan government in Lhasa had never
seriously attempted to impose their sovereignty over Kham and Amdo.
When the PLA defeated the Kuomintang, it moved into eastern Tibet
without much opposition, and since then the PRC had regarded Kham
and Amdo as directly subordinate to the Chinese central government
rather than as parts of Tibet, and thus outside the jurisdiction of the
Seventeen-Point Agreement. As regional military administrations tried
to immediately integrate both provinces into the "motherland," they
found themselves facing an armed and militant population of Tibetans ready to fight for what they considered their traditional right to
self-rule.

In 1955 and 1956, when the Communists implemented massive land
reforms and so-called "democratic" modernizations, the Khampas saw
these measures as attacks on their traditional values, and their resentment boiled over. Sporadic skirmishes took place between armed Khampas and Chinese in 1955, and they had developed into open revolt by the
time the PCART was installed in Lhasa. The conflict came to be known
as the "Kanding Rebellion," after the city of Kanding, which the Tibetans
call Dartsedo. In Lithang, Gyalthang, and Changtreng, Chinese cadres
were attacked by the local population, and when the People's Liberation
Army marched against the rebels, thousands fled to the great monastery of Changtreng Sampheling. The monastery was besieged and then
bombed from the air; hundreds of Tibetans were killed and the famous
monastery of Trijang Rinpoche, the junior tutor of the Dalai Lama, was
left in smoking ruins. This opened a campaign to annihilate the monasteries, symbols of Tibetan identity, and also fortresses that had provided
refuge against various invading armies in Tibet's history.

Armed conflict was confined to eastern Tibet for the time being, but
refugees streamed out of the disputed regions and fled to Lhasa, where
resources were already strained by the presence of Chinese troops. At
first the genteel people of Lhasa didn't believe the rough and rebellious
Khampas' reports of the atrocities in Kham, and many Khampas moved
on to India, where they drew the attention of the international media to
the rebellion in Kham.[11]

In autumn 1955 Rinpoche's parents were pressured to be part of
a group of governmental and monastic officials and merchants on an

eight-month propaganda tour of China. After the dangerous and uncomfortable trip to Beijing, their program included innumerable repetitive visits to factories and collectivized farms accompanied by long-winded lectures about the merits of Communist reforms. Several of the visitors seeing industrial factories for the first time were impressed, but Rinpoche's father, who was familiar with factories in India and well informed about modern industry in other nations, was not. They were not allowed to see any problems or failures, although they did get a glimpse of trouble in Shanghai: in what had once been a busy harbor with a thriving international shipping industry, the docks were abandoned, with only one foreign ship to be seen.

When they returned to Lhasa, just in time for the inauguration of the PCART at the end of April 1956, they found that conditions there had worsened. Everything seemed to be under the control of the occupying forces, and Yangchen Dolkar Tsarong found Chinese guards stationed at the gate to her parents' home; her father, supposedly a general in the new hierarchy, was essentially a prisoner in his own house.

Meanwhile in Drikung, the traditional annual prayer ceremonies were held in each of the monasteries, and they typically required the presence of the throne holder. Chetsang Rinpoche grew easily into his role in the regular cycle of ceremonies and relocations that punctuated the year. Teachings and ceremonies for the lay population were held outside the monastery of Yangrigar from the eighth to the fifteenth day of the fourth month, and at the conclusion of the summer retreat of the Yangrigar monastic community in the sixth Tibetan month there was a great four-day picnic with dances from *Lhamo*, Tibet's form of opera, until it was time to return to Drikung Thil. The Tibetan New Year's festival, *Lhosar*, always lasted several days in Drikung Dzong, and from there the Kyabgöns proceeded to Drikung Tse on the first day of the second Tibetan month.

While Rinpoche was still undergoing his basic education, he received a series of special oral instructions and initiations from Yongzin Tritsab Gyabra, among them the *Kagyu Ngag Dzö* ("The Kagyu Treasury of Oral Instructions") and the *Yangzab Wangchen*, an empowerment for a meditation practice on Guru Rinpoche. Bhalok Thubten Chödrak Rinpoche gave Chetsang Rinpoche teachings on all the Dharma Protectors of the

Drikung Kagyu lineage, and Lho Bongtrul Rinpoche bestowed teachings on various practices,[12] including the *Damcho Gongpa Yangzab,* the treasure text that Rinchen Phuntsog discovered in the Kiri Yangdzong Cave.

The year 1956 was a Monkey Year, of special significance to Tibetans since the mythical ancestor of the Tibetan people is said to have been a monkey. Monkey Years are dedicated to Padmasambhava, or Guru Rinpoche, and throughout the country trance oracles were consulted in the Monkey Month (the seventh month) of a Monkey Year. This was also when the Drikung *Phowa Chenmo,* the most important festival of religious instruction and pilgrimage in the Drikung lineage, was held. It is said to have been in the Monkey Year of 1308 that one of the early throne holders, Dorje Gyalpo, geomantically reopened the valley of Terdrom to pilgrimages. He decreed that ritual dances connected to Padmasambhava's primary deity, Dorje Phurba,[13] be held in the Monkey Month, when Padmasambhava's birthday is celebrated, and he also introduced the tradition of giving special teachings in connection with these ceremonial dances.

Two centuries later, the great Rinchen Phuntsog integrated teachings of the Nyingma School into the Drikung tradition and shifted the site of the Monkey Year Teachings to his secluded hermitage in Drongur. To the traditional set of Monkey Year Teachings he added the treasure texts that he had revealed in Drongur. In the seventeenth century, the first Chetsang and Chungtsang Rinpoches gave the cycle of Monkey Year Teachings the form it has kept up to the present. The Drongur Monkey Year Teachings became a major public event, retaining the instructions that Rinchen Phuntsog had introduced and now also including a long-life initiation according to the tradition of the yogini Siddharajni. The climax and conclusion was the transmission of *phowa* on the final full moon day of the teachings, and hence the festival became known as the Drikung Phowa Chenmo, "The Great Conferral of the Transference of Consciousness at Drikung."[14] This series of teachings and initiations became so famous that pilgrims from the remotest parts of the country journeyed for months to participate in the Drikung Phowa at Drongur.

In 1956 the Drikung Phowa Chenmo was held in the Monkey Month from the seventh day to the full moon on the fifteenth day. It was to be the last one held at Drikung for several decades. The ten-year-old

Crowd attending the Drikung Phowa Chenmo in Drongur in 1956.

Chetsang Rinpoche was to grant the long-life empowerment, and to prepare for it he undertook a two-week retreat at Drikung Dzong. Then he and Chungstang spent several days traveling to Drongur, with receptions and rituals at the sacred places in the Terdrom valley. In Drongur the Drikung Rinpoches and the head administrator of the labrang had simple quarters in Drongur Monastery, near Rinchen Phuntsog's old meditation hut, while the monks from Yangrigar and Drikung Thil pitched their two great assembly tents on the seventh day of the month—the tent from Thil was named "Blue Sky," and that of Yangrigar "White Snow Mountain." In the Monkey Year of 1932 a quarrel between Yangrigar and Thil had threatened to split the lineage, and to prevent further disputes they were ordered to sit in separate tents, starting a tradition which continued after the quarrel subsided.

The great tent of empowerment (*wangur*), introduced by the Fifth Chetsang Rinpoche Thukje Nyima (1828–1885) was pitched over the courtyard of Drongur to hold the thrones of the Kyabgön Rinpoches and the seats of the incarnate lamas, the *khenpo*s and the monastic officials, elevated according to their rank. The entrance to the valley was ritually sealed, and a sacred domain came into being. Several hundred tents belonging to lay associations, nomad families, and individual pilgrims dotted the valley. Thousands of people attended the festival despite the political tension in Lhasa and the fighting in Kham and Amdo; Chetsang Rinpoche's parents, his brother Jigme, and an aunt from Bhutan all sat at his feet in the tent.

On the tenth day of the month, the Kyabgön Rinpoches were garbed in the ceremonial robes of Oddiyana and Zahor,[15] woven capes like the one given to Jigten Sumgön by an emperor of China were laid across their shoulders, and parasols of peacock feathers were held over their heads. After Chungtsang Rinpoche conferred the initiation of the peaceful Guru Rinpoche, Chetsang Rinpoche, although he was still very young, gave his first empowerment, the long-life initiation.

The initiations on the following days were bestowed by Chungtsang Rinpoche, Tritsab Gyabra, Nyidzong Tripa, and the young Togden Rinpoche, head of the Drikung lineage in Ladakh. In the afternoons, the high-ranking lamas and khenpos gave instructions on Jigten Sumgön's Heart Instructions and *Gongchig* (The Single Intention)[16] as well as special teachings for monks who were advanced in their meditation practice. On the fifteenth day, the fourteen-year-old Chungtsang Rinpoche gave the phowa transmission; among Drikung lamas, only those with a long incarnation lineage were permitted to confer the teaching of phowa. A peaceful stillness descended on the participants as, deep in contemplation, they followed the instructions of the Kyabgön Rinpoche, who was no longer an ordinary mortal, but rather a transformed, exalted being. They listened to every word with devoted attention, and some showed signs of the unbroken spiritual power of the transmission, either momentarily fainting or trembling and twitching in ecstasy. Afterward, everyone made their way home, back to the profane world that was undergoing violent and catastrophic change.

6

Tibet at the Abyss
Rebellion and Oppression

WHEN THE DALAI LAMA was invited in 1956 by the Indian government and Prince Döndrup Namgyal of Sikkim to the ceremonies in India marking the 2,500th anniversary of Shakyamuni Buddha's birth, the PRC feared that he might seek asylum abroad, and thus elude their grasp. They proposed that he send a representative instead, but they had not anticipated the outrage this suggestion would draw from the Tibetan public, and had to back down. On November 20 the Dalai Lama and the members of the Kashag left the capital.

The news of the imminent journey of the Dalai Lama was alarming to many wealthy families, and they felt that pilgrimage to the religious celebrations might present their last chance to get themselves, their families, and their fortunes safely out of the country. Dundul Namgyal Tsarong decided to take advantage of the opportunity to take his children to safety; the family reached Dromo in three days traveling by car on the new road, and after two more days of riding horses and mules they crossed into Sikkim.

While in India the young and inexperienced Dalai Lama sought the advice and counsel of other world leaders, particularly Indian Prime Minister Jawaharlal Nehru, but the Chinese representatives sent to the celebrations limited the Dalai Lama's opportunities for candid meetings, and Premier Zhou Enlai, who was also visiting India then, pressured Nehru with the threat of strained relations with China. Nehru invited the Dalai Lama to stay in his country until conditions had been stabilized in Tibet, but he recommended that he return and work out an

Chetsang Rinpoche (front right) with his siblings: (from left) Norzin Yangkyi, Paljor, Jigme, and Namgyal Lhamo. Their last picture together, taken in 1956 before his siblings left Tibet.

agreement with the PRC. At the end of January 1957 Premier Zhou Enlai met with the Dalai Lama in the Chinese embassy in Delhi; he gave him a message from Mao stating that the reforms in Tibet would be deferred for the next five years and, if necessary, an additional five-year deferment could be granted, but that if a revolt persisted, it would have to be put down by force. In Kalimpong, the Dalai Lama's brothers, Gyalo Döndrup and Thubten Norbu, as well as former government officials Lukhang and Shakabpa, all living in exile, urged him to seek asylum in India, but he remained indecisive. In the end he decided, on the advice of the Nechung and Gadong oracles, to return to Lhasa at the beginning of March.

In August 1957, the Chinese did make a few of their promised changes in Lhasa, including a reorganization of the PCART so that 90 percent of the committee was Tibetan and abolishing several ministries, including the department of construction. With most of the family staying outside Tibet, the Tsarong mansion was left almost empty after the former department employees vacated the ground floor.

For a while it looked as though China's new policies would lead to a stabilization of the situation in Tibet, but a different set of standards was being applied in eastern Tibet, and the reforms were not being halted or delayed, but merely watered down. This was not enough to stem the tide of refugees fleeing Kham or to pacify the militant Khampas who preferred to fight. By autumn of 1957 their rebellion had spread. Tibetan rebels attacked Chinese cadres supervising road construction, and even a garrison of the People's Liberation Army.

In April 1957 Dundul Namgyal Tsarong had returned to Lhasa with his wife after his mother had become seriously ill; she died that July. Chetsang Rinpoche was at Yangrigar at the time, and for fear that he would grieve deeply, the monks kept the news of Pema Dolkar's death from him for an entire week. When they finally told him Rinpoche did not weep, but scolded his attendants for not having informed him. He allowed himself a short moment of sorrow and reflection, and then it was over.

Chetsang Rinpoche's mother planned to join the children in Darjeeling in October and take them on pilgrimage to Buddhist sites in India during their winter vacation from school. Hoping to also get Rinpoche out of the country, his parents requested that he be allowed to join them on the pilgrimage, but their request was denied. The abbot explained that it was time for Rinpoche to undertake a three-month retreat, and his religious training should not be disrupted for a family pilgrimage. In addition, Rinpoche was in his thirteenth year according to Tibetan calculations, and thus in a so-called "obstacle year" in which journeys were to be avoided.

After his wife's death Dasang Damdul Tsarong fell into a deep depression, and in December his son Dundul Namgyal convinced him to request a leave of absence from the government. Dundul Namgyal planned to go into exile and urged many other relatives and friends to flee as well. He was frustrated by those, including his sister and brother-in-law, whom he saw as shutting their eyes to the reality of the changes around them, those who preferred to stay and wait for things to improve. His father was granted a permit to spend several months on pilgrimage in India, and while Dundul Namgyal was only supposed to accompany him to the border, they both left the country. The following spring the government ordered the return of all officials who had left Tibet and remained in India, but very few of them obeyed. Dundul Namgyal Tsarong stayed with his father, who still had a few months before his official leave expired. But when it did expire in September, the elder Tsarong returned to Lhasa despite Dundul Namgyal's efforts to persuade him to stay. He said that he belonged in Tibet, in service to the Dalai Lama and to his country. The rest of the family remained in exile.

Dasang Damdul Tsarong, the former commander general who had weathered all kinds of military and political storms and was not easily frightened, was truly alarmed by what he heard in Kalimpong and saw on his return journey. With the Thirteenth Dalai Lama he had tried to implement reforms that might have prevented the current crisis, but they had been blocked by conservative factions of monastics and aristocrats. Now he could clearly recognize the truth of the farsighted but tragically ignored prophecy the Thirteenth Dalai Lama had written shortly before his death in 1933:

> Efficient and well-equipped troops must be stationed even on the minor frontiers bordering hostile forces. Such an army must be well trained in warfare as a sure deterrent against any adversaries. . . . Furthermore, this present era is rampant with the five forms of degeneration, in particular, the red ideology. . . . In the future, this system will certainly be forced either from within or without on this land that cherishes the joint spiritual and temporal system. If, in such an event, we fail to defend our land, the holy lamas, including "the triumphant father and son" [the Dalai Lama and Panchen Lama] will be eliminated without a trace of their names remaining; the properties of the incarnate lamas and of the monasteries, along with the endowments for religious services, will all be seized. Moreover, our political system, originated by the three

ancient kings, will be reduced to an empty name; my officials, deprived of their patrimony and property, will be subjugated like slaves by the enemy; and my people, subjected to fear and miseries, will be unable to endure day or night. Such an era will certainly come![1]

The situation in Kham remained grim, and the exodus of eastern Tibetans continued unabated. By the beginning of 1958 more than 15,000 Khampa families had relocated to Lhasa and its environs, and many others moved to Lhokha in southern Tibet, where Gonpo Tashi Andrugtsang, a wealthy Khampa merchant from Lithang, formed an alliance among several Khampa clan chieftains. They founded the *Chushi Gangdrung* ("Four Rivers, Six Ranges") guerilla movement, giving it the ancient name of their homeland.[2] Chushi Gangdrung soon had more than 15,000 volunteer freedom fighters, all passionately determined but lacking sufficient weapons and ammunition. The American Central Intelligence Agency supplied some arms, but not enough and not soon enough.

In spite of their inadequate equipment, Gonpo Tashi's guerillas enjoyed some astonishing successes. To the west of Lhasa, in the region of Nyemo, a series of significant victories left more than 700 casualties in the People's Liberation Army. But although Chushi Gangdrung successfully plundered PLA warehouses in Damshung, near Namtso Lake, and won a few skirmishes, the Tibetans were overwhelmed in the open terrain, where Chinese planes easily spotted them.

Near Drikung Thil the resistance fighters set up a tent camp, which Chetsang Rinpoche observed through his field glasses. They sent three monks to the monastery to scout out the best escape routes, since PLA troops were already close on their heels. As the three monk-scouts were returning to their camp from the monastery the PLA attacked the camp, and when the rebels ran out of ammunition they were forced to flee. By September of 1958 Gonpo Tashi and his men had been forced back toward Kham, and the resistance was falling apart as many of the starving and exhausted fighters were defecting to join bandit groups.

The violence continued to creep closer to Drikung's peaceful sanctuaries. Since many Khampa refugees were passing through Drikung, the Chinese forces hunted for rebels who had taken cover there, and

*Chetsang Rinpoche
in Drikung Yangrigar
Monastery in 1956.*

one night five Chinese officers and an interpreter demanded entrance
into Yangrigar Monastery at midnight. The monastery had taken in no
strangers but the commanding officer was not satisfied, and to intimidate the monks he ordered his men to shoot off a flare gun and set up
an encampment of about 100 soldiers just outside the monastery walls.
They moved on the next day, but it was understood that they could return at any time.

Meanwhile, Rinpoche began his philosophical studies at the Nyima
Changra, the monastic institute of Buddhist philosophy. The building had once been the summer palace of the Fifth Chetsang Rinpoche
Thukje Nyima, and when his subsequent incarnation, Shiwe Lodrö,
converted it into a philosophical academy, he named it "Nyima" for
the Fifth Chetsang Rinpoche, and "Changra" for the beautiful willows
(*changra*) in the park around it. Shiwe Lodrö persuaded a renowned
scholar, Nyarong Tulku Jamyang Wangyal of Kham, to come and teach
there, and the institute grew in fame and Drikung enjoyed an intellectual

upswing. The institute's basic texts, the *Thirteen Great Treatises*,[3] were re-edited and new printing blocks for them were commissioned. The Drikung community attributed the Nyima Changra's rise to prominence to the blessings of the Rinpoches, Thukje Nyima and Shiwe Lodrö.

Rinpoche's studies with tutors in his private chambers came to an end and he began to receive instruction in the Nyima Changra a group of ten to fifteen tulkus and selected monks. Now, although he was four years younger, he studied with Chungtsang Rinpoche in a group that included students from all parts of Tibet. Their teacher, Böpa Tulku Dongag Tenpa (1907–1959), introduced them to the philosophy of Madhyamaka.[4] They began with basic texts such as the *Thirty-Seven Practices of a Bodhisattva* and *The Way of the Bodhisattva*,[5] but their studies would soon come to an abrupt and brutal end.

In autumn of 1958 some leading Drikung lamas went to Lhasa to judge the situation themselves. Some of them, including Drönyer Konchog Samten and Chetsang Rinpoche's personal attendant Solpön Chösjor, felt that it no longer made any sense to stay in Tibet, and they were considering sending Kyabgön Chetsang Rinpoche to India until the political situation had stabilized. Chagdzö Tsephel, the manager of the Drikung Labrang, seemed to agree with them. They informed the elder Tsarong of their intention, and he immediately drew up a plan for Chetsang Rinpoche's escape and sent for his grandson to come to Lhasa. He wanted to get moving right away, before the monastic administrators could change their minds. While Rinpoche was on his way to Lhasa, the chagdzö sought an audience with Tsarong; in general he would follow the great lord's advice, he said, cautiously weighing his words, but no preparations had been made for an immediate departure. He would send someone to Drikung who would take care of everything. Tsarong was not sure whether this was a tactic to politely stall the departure or just the slow-moving caution of a monastic official who failed to recognize the urgency of the situation.

When Chetsang Rinpoche arrived in Lhasa he stayed in the house of an aunt, away from the discussions at the Tsarong house. He was happy at the thought of being reunited with his family in India. The drönyer and the solpön had also sent an assistant to Drikung to pack up the most important valuables and what was easy to transport from Rinpoche's chambers, especially his distinctive amulet belt of reliquaries, without which he should not travel. But the assistant did not return. Instead, a week later an entire delegation of dignitaries came to the Tsarong mansion. The manager of the monastic administration of Drikung Thil, the former drönyer of the labrang, senior monks from Yangrigar Monastery, village headmen, chieftains and high-ranking officials of the Drikung district—all were determined not to let their lineage holder depart under any circumstances. They argued that the Dalai Lama was still in Tibet, and that no one from the great labrangs of other monasteries had fled, and they insisted they be allowed to take Rinpoche back to Drikung.

Tsarong was beside himself and summoned the chagdzö, who put on an innocent face and claimed to be taken by surprise by the Drikung dignitaries' arrival. Tsarong did not believe him and the dispute between the former commander general and the Drikung manager dragged on for half a day. Tsarong pointed out that the child was doubly at risk, given the Communists' agenda to completely eliminate the two traditional repositories of power and authority in Tibet, the monastic hierarchy and the aristocracy. Chetsang Rinpoche's grandfather was both furious and deeply disappointed. Buddhism is said to be a path to overcoming ignorance, the worst of mental poisons,[6] but these representatives of Tibet's religion appeared blind and inflexible in the center of a disaster that was closing in on them, in the face of an impending catastrophe. The monastery manager did not yield, and he even threatened to press charges against Tsarong, who finally gave in with rancor and bitterness. In a final burst of rage he demanded that the chagdzö take Rinpoche and leave his house immediately: they would soon see what their decision would cost them.

Tsarong concealed his dejection when he told his grandson to return with the delegation to the monastery. Rinpoche was very disappointed, but he remained valiant in the face of this final separation from his family. Chetsang Rinpoche would not see his family again for eighteen years.

On February 8, 1959, the Tibetans celebrated the New Year, a Pig Year. The Dalai Lama's final examinations in Buddhist philosophy at Drepung Monastery were scheduled to take place during the Mönlam festivities, but there was concern that he would be invited to attend the National People's Congress in Beijing, which would result in a deferral of his examinations. Lhasans were also uneasy because PLA presence was

Chetsang Rinpoche in a field near Lhasa in 1958. This is the last picture his father took of him before his parents left Tibet.

strengthened to prevent any repeat of the pro-independence demonstrations that had taken place during Mönlam in previous years. The Chinese forces were especially concerned that the freedom fighters would use the Mönlam crowds to stage an uprising. In a desperate attempt to mediate between the Chinese and the resistance fighters, the powerless Tibetan government convened the National Assembly and appointed Dasang Damdul Tsarong to be the chief negotiator with the Chinese, but the revolt broke out before the first round of discussions could take place.

On the last day of the old year, the Dalai Lama had been invited to attend the performance of a dance troupe in the newly built auditorium of the PLA headquarters. The Dalai Lama had accepted the invitation to avoid giving the impression of being discourteous, but was able to get around setting a specific date until March 7, when he finally agreed to come three days later, on March 10. His hosts demanded that he appear without the usual ceremonial entourage of ministers and dignitaries, and without personal bodyguards; they promised to ensure his safety.

Officials in close contact with the Dalai Lama were shocked when they heard about this strange invitation, issued at such short notice; the demand that he attend without bodyguards was especially disturbing. A few days earlier the Nechung oracle had warned that the Dalai Lama should not go out, and a rumor that the Dalai Lama was to be kidnapped and detained by the Chinese spread like wildfire.

On the morning of March 10, a few thousand Tibetans gathered before the Norbulingka Palace and demanded to see the Dalai Lama, and in the heated atmosphere some Tibetans believed to be collaborators were attacked. A small group remained to barricade the streets leading to the palace while the mob moved into the center of Lhasa chanting anti-Chinese slogans. Two days later, fifty Tibetan officials calling themselves "The People's Assembly" gathered in Shol, the village just below the Potala Palace, in support of the uprising. The largest demonstration that Lhasa had ever seen was held in Shol the next day, on March 13. Thousands of Tibetans flooded into an open area to cheer the speakers, who demanded the restoration of Tibet's independence. When weapons were distributed from government arsenals the situation intensified and the PLA opened fire, hoping to intimidate the crowd. The Nechung oracle advised the Dalai Lama that it was no longer safe to stay in the palace, and that night the Dalai Lama fled, disguised as a layman. A select group of Khampa fighters aided his escape from the palace, past outraged demonstrators and the Chinese army, and it seems the Dharma Protectors guarded them carefully.

Lhasa's residents were distressed to discover that the Dalai Lama was gone and suspected he had been kidnapped. The People's Liberation Army opened a massive attack on the city, and after three days of intense fighting the PRC flag flew from the roof of the Potala. Zhou Enlai declared that the uprising nullified the Seventeen-Point Agreement and that China was no longer bound by any agreements. The gloves had come off.

The Dalai Lama reached India on March 30, to be followed by thousands of fellow Tibetans in the coming weeks and months, among them tulkus, lamas, and freedom fighters, all of whom had given up hope of opposing China's overwhelming power.

The disappearance of the Dalai Lama, the Kashag, and other spiritual and secular dignitaries left a vacuum of national leadership to be filled by the Chinese leaders without fear of opposition. Officially, the Preparatory Committee for the Autonomous Region of Tibet was to govern, but all real power was now effectively held by the newly created Military Control Commission of the People's Liberation Army, which instituted violently repressive measures throughout the country.

The Panchen Lama was the only major traditional spiritual and secular authority remaining in Tibet, and the occupiers groomed him to become a substitute for the Dalai Lama. They installed him as chairman of the PCART, but the population largely distrusted him and regarded him as a puppet of China.

Up to now the Chinese had mainly engaged in dialogue with Tibet's aristocratic rulers, but now they tried to win over the common people by elevating them to positions of authority. Converted Tibetans were to serve as shining examples of revolutionary zeal for their countrymen, while those who resisted, including large numbers of monks and the old aristocracy, were persecuted—they were harassed, imprisoned, and sent to labor camps.

7

In the Grip of the Chinese
Humiliation and Indoctrination

A MIGHTY OLD STUPA stood on the bank of a river near Drikung
Tse Monastery, and Chetsang Rinpoche sat with Nangse Rinpoche
next to it, watching the monks wash their robes in the river, the cloth drifting in the current, making red trails like long streaks of blood mixed with
water. They heard a rider approaching long before they could see him;
mounted messengers had small bells on their horses' bridles to keep them
from falling asleep on their long routes. The rider stopped his horse only
long enough to shout to the chagdzö that Lhasa had been bombarded and
taken by the Chinese and that the Dalai Lama had disappeared. Then he
was gone, to spread the news further on down the road.

The monks were bewildered. They had seen the People's Liberation
Army only sporadically, as troops occasionally passed through Drikung,
making little impact outside of the Lhasa area and the places where they
had battled resistance fighters.

A monastery council was convened and the dough-ball divination
in the main shrine indicated that it would be better to remain in Tibet.
The monastic officials decided to move to their administrative seat in
Drikung Dzong and sent for Chungtsang Chökyi Nangwa, who was in
Lhasa for a major ceremony. Prayers were recited around the clock in the
temple of the three protector deities of Drikung Dzong, and a few monks
began retreat in order to perform the powerful practice of the wrathful
protector deity Yamantaka.

After a few days a mounted group of Khampa warriors arrived at
Drikung Dzong. Their leader, Drakpa Namgyal Ponritsang, was one of

Drikung Dzong, administrative center and monastery, in 1948.

about two dozen clan chieftains in Kham. For generations his family had produced the chieftains of the clan, the village headmen, and the leaders of the Drikung monasteries, of which there were many, in his area of northwestern Kham. Drakpa Namgyal knew the Chinese and had traded with them, as had many in the eastern part of Tibet. He was aware of their intentions, and their strength. The Khampas could not win the war, but he did not wish to surrender to the People's Liberation Army, and he led a band of loyal warriors on several successful raids until they were forced to disperse by massive PLA troop deployment and air strikes.

The people of Kham revered the lineage holders of their monasteries even more than they did the Dalai Lama, and Drakpa Namgyal now thought only of the well-being of the Drikung Holinesses; he was determined to shield Chetsang Rinpoche and Chungtsang Rinpoche from the grasp of the Chinese.

Drakpa Namgyal's band—exhausted, hungry, and wounded, but still unbroken—had reached Drikung. He and two companions entered the monastery, and they first went to pay their respects to Chetsang Rinpoche in his private chambers. After they had prostrated themselves on the floor before the young Drikung Holiness, Drakpa Namgyal explained to Rinpoche that the Chinese had taken over the country. The situation was grave and very dangerous, so they had come to escort him and Chung-tsang Rinpoche to India. Chetsang Rinpoche listened to his speech calmly, and then told Drakpa Namgyal to speak with the chagdzö.

Of course, the chagdzö had no intention of letting the Holinesses leave. He had already refused the same request to the elder Tsarong, and he would not be intimidated by Khampa warlords brandishing weapons. He informed them of the oracle's recommendation that the Rinpoches remain in Tibet, and, tired but unsatisfied, the Khampas left.

According to some of the survivors' stories, reported later in India, the next day they spoke with the chagdzö again, this time accompanied by Drakpa Namgyal's brothers, Drakpa Chögyal and Pema Lodrö. They had no time to lose because Chinese troops were pursuing them, but the chagdzö was unmoved. He told them that his nephew had a good relationship with the Chinese, so he felt relatively secure even in the face of this new threat. The Khampas became angry, brandished their weapons, and shouted that the nephew deserved to die if he was collaborating with the Chinese. The nephew had prudently already fled, and the frustrated Drakpa Namgyal pointed his rifle at the manager's breast, threatening to kill him on the spot unless he let the Holinesses leave.

Up on the monastery roof, Rinpoche watched the arrival of the Chinese troops through his field glasses. Uniformed men on horseback were followed by an army of infantry. Gradually, he made out one soldier up front who was examining Drikung Dzong with his field glasses. The sound of angry voices rose up to him from the rooms below and Rinpoche sent his personal attendant down to find out what was happening. The confrontation in the office of the chagdzö had now reached its dramatic climax, with the Khampas pressing the chagdzö against the wall with their weapons. Rinpoche's attendant implored them to release the manager and to leave the premises at once. They agreed, but wished to see Chetsang Rinpoche once more before leaving.

Rinpoche gave each of them an *Achi Tsönsung,* a consecrated protective needle, wrapped in mantras and five-colored ribbons. On the way out, one man turned in the doorway and placed his rifle at Rinpoche's feet in an extravagant gesture of remorse. He said the weapon had killed many wild animals and even more of the enemy; it was an instrument of sin, and he requested that Rinpoche take it, destroy it, and pray for the men killed by it. Chetsang Rinpoche took the rifle and, following the Khampas down to the great portal where the broad stairs led down into the valley, he laid it on the highest step. The weapon seemed old and strangely harmless to him, now that it was detached from someone willing and able to use it. He lifted the heaviest stone he could manage over his head and smashed it down onto the rifle with all his strength. The Khampas turned when they heard the crash. Relieved, they folded their hands in reverence, sprang onto their horses and galloped away. Rinpoche hastened back up to the roof to watch the large band of Khampa fighters with their noble horses disappear into the Shorong Valley.

Years later he learned that Drakpa Namgyal had succeeded in fleeing with several of his men, although many, including his brother Drakpa Chögyal, died in their last battle with the PLA on the Indian border. Just the evening before, Chögyal had shown the others that his protective needle was broken.

From the roof, Rinpoche watched the Chinese cavalry approaching the monastery on their large, powerful horses. A Tibetan who tried to flee was captured, bound, and led off; his small Tibetan horse would have been no match for the faster Chinese steeds. The troops crossed the bridge and made camp on the pastures directly below the monastery. Across the river, three soldiers dismounted and positioned three high-caliber artillery guns.

The monks were all frightened, wondering whether the People's Liberation Army was going to attack Drikung Dzong. The chagdzö ordered that white scarves be tied to staffs placed next to the main entrance, but the Chinese soldiers seemed not to take note of these. They set up their field kitchen, lit fires, and cooked their midday meal. The chagdzö and the monks decided to speak with the Chinese as a delegation, approaching the camp with white scarves in their hands and according to rank, as tradition required: first the chagdzö, followed by the treasurer, the chief secretary, the undersecretary, the commissary of supplies, and finally, the head of the monastery lumber yard. The PLA officers demanded the surrender of all weapons in the monastery, including every knife with a blade of a hand's length, and threatened the delegation with severe penalties if even one weapon was to be found later. A single old rifle was handed over, along with many swords, daggers, and knives that had hung on the walls of the Dharma Protectors' Temple.

Additional troops arrived through the course of the day and tents lay scattered over the open fields. The soldiers seemed to have been on the march for a long time; some dropped down onto their packs and did not move, while others leaned against the walls of villagers' houses and fell asleep. They weren't given much time to rest, as the troop commander soon roused them to chase the Khampa fighters. The local people indicated that the Khampas had ridden off into the Lungshö Valley, but the truth was that they had gone in the opposite direction. Fortunately for the Khampas, the PLA commander believed that the locals would help him, and his soldiers marched off in the wrong direction.

The following day a siren wailed in the distance, signaling that combat aircraft were approaching, and everybody had to leave the building immediately. Chetsang Rinpoche hung all of his precious amulets around his neck and ran to the hill behind the monastery to hide behind a large peach tree, surrounded by frightened monks. A plane approached and circled a few times above the monastery complex before turning aside and flying off toward Lhasa. Before it disappeared they saw flames on the horizon and heard the deep thunder of explosions. Later they were told that the warplane had bombed a group of fleeing Khampas.

After a tense but quiet week, a company of soldiers appeared again and settled permanently in Dzongshol, the village below the monastery. The PLA requisitioned the largest house in the area and turned it into their local headquarters. Tibet was under martial law and the Chinese soldiers herded all of the leading monastic officials and the chagdzö into a single room, placed them under house arrest, and began a systematic search of the monastery complex. Rinpoche's field glasses and seven or eight old seals of gold and silver were confiscated. The offices were all ransacked in a search for suspicious documents and then sealed off. The commander treated the young Drikung Holinesses with marked respect, however, and twice he invited them to dine with him. The two Rinpoches were too intimidated to start a conversation, despite the officer's efforts to put them at ease. After the meal he offered his astonished young guests cigarettes, which they declined, but the officer laughed and insisted until they accepted.

One day Chagdzö Tsephel and leading monastic officials were to be transferred to the prison in the district capital, Medrogungkar. When the villagers saw them heaved onto horseback, they surrounded the Chinese soldiers, begging them to let the monks stay. The soldiers were annoyed but not yet willing to resort to harsher methods, and the monks were taken back to the monastery.

Every day officers came to conduct interrogations. The timid Chungtsang Rinpoche usually ran away and hid so the soldiers sought out Chetsang Rinpoche more often. Once, the troop commander burst into Rinpoche's room with another PLA officer and an interpreter. He sat down, looked calmly around the room and took some snuff before having the monastery's chief secretary and his assistant summoned. The commander's manner suddenly changed when they came in, and he shouted violently at both of them, accusing them of being agitators and shaking a bundle of papers he claimed were subversive letters. The commander shouted in Chinese, the interpreter in Tibetan, "Did you write these letters or not?" When they did not respond, he sprang up, shouted, and stamped his feet so hard the noise reverberated throughout the entire monastery. Chetsang Rinpoche had never witnessed such a frightening spectacle as this display of fury, with the officer's trembling thighs and his red, distorted face and cruel expression, like the mask of a demon. Rinpoche escaped from the room and cowered in a corner behind a terrace wall. After a while, when he heard a few curt orders and many footsteps going downstairs, he cautiously crept out of his hiding place and saw the secretaries being bound and locked up in some rooms the military had taken over. Some days later they were sent to a labor camp near Medrogungkar.

After a month of the monastery's occupation, a group of civilian Chinese cadres and Tibetan supporters arrived to begin a "program of patriotic reeducation." All of the monks were subjected to repetitive speeches informing them that religion existed only to delude and exploit the populace, to secure the power of the privileged classes, and to oppress ordinary people. The monks were assembled at Nyima Changra, where the Chinese had set up their regional administration, while the tulkus, khenpos, and high-ranking lamas convened at Drikung Dzong. They were all forced to listen to tedious propaganda speeches, which often lasted for hours, and to study Communist pamphlets.

Each monk was asked to articulate what he had absorbed, and if the instructors did not like what they heard, the victim had to endure a tongue-lashing about his reactionary thinking, obstinacy, and backwardness, and about the necessity of cultivating a revolutionary spirit. When it was Chetsang Rinpoche's turn to respond, he was petrified, as everything the instructors had been saying seemed like incoherent ranting to him. He begged Rigyal Rinpoche to help him, although the latter, too, understood very little of what the instructor said. When a young Tibetan woman with a fanatical expression on her face turned to Chetsang Rinpoche, Rigyal said, "He is too young, he understands nothing." The Tibetan woman looked at the frightened boy and seemed to attempt a contemptuous face without success. She appeared confused for a moment, but then turned to the next monk to be questioned. Rinpoche was relieved, until he was informed that he would be questioned the next day. He didn't know what to do; there were so many topics, and he could not make sense of any of them. He decided to memorize one of the texts, and did so easily, although he desperately hoped no one would ask him what it meant. When his turn came, he hastily recited the text he had prepared, and the instructors seemed to be amused and placated by his performance. At least they laughed dryly, and from then on, no one asked Chetsang Rinpoche any more questions, although he still had to attend all of the assemblies.

The reeducation program lasted a few months. Even though no one in Drikung Dzong was forced to disrobe and take up a relationship with a woman—something that was often imposed in other monasteries—many of the monks were unable to bear the psychological terror. They expected to be put in labor camps or prisons, or even to be killed. Some committed suicide, throwing themselves into the river, while others managed to sneak away; fewer appeared for indoctrination with each passing day. Soon only half of what had been sixty inmates remained. Chetsang Rinpoche's playmate Nangse Rinpoche tried to flee with his tutor and another monk, taking cover during the day and traveling by night, but a military patrol spotted them and opened fire. Nangse Rinpoche fell and broke his legs. Recaptured, he was treated in an army hospital.

One afternoon, soldiers appeared in the assembly hall and made a list of the remaining inmates. When they left they assured the monks that they would not return, and said their farewells courteously, but no one trusted them. The senior monks—convinced that they would be sent to prison—prepared to leave, packing their few possessions and donning laymen's clothing.

When the villagers heard about the visit by the military and the ominous list, they came to the dzong in hordes, wailing and lamenting and pleading with the occupiers not to carry off the monks and rinpoches. The Chinese soldiers were astonished and troubled by this spontaneous outburst of civic courage and promised to leave the remaining monks in peace. But the villagers did not trust them, checking later that night to see whether all of the monks were still there. Everything seemed quiet, so they returned to their homes.

During that night Chetsang Rinpoche woke from a deep sleep to find Norbu Rinpoche shaking him and shouting: "Wake up! Fast! The soldiers have come back. We have to go down right away or they will shoot us! Everyone is downstairs already, only you are still here!" In the blackness of night Rinpoche hastily slipped into his robes, but in his agitation he could not find his belt and had to hold his lower robe up with one hand. He groped the wall with the other to find the door and stumbled downstairs, where he saw Chungtsang Chökyi Nangwa together with the other rinpoches and monks standing in the middle of the assembly hall, crowded together like a herd of timid sheep. All were wearing laymen's clothing, and some had bundles tied together. Soldiers surrounded them. As soon as Chetsang Rinpoche and Norbu arrived, the soldiers raised their rifles and barked an order to march. Paralyzed with fear, no one moved and the soldiers began to shout insults and strike the men with their rifles. Finally Chetsang Rinpoche pushed his way to the front and began to walk in the direction the soldiers had indicated. Chungtsang Rinpoche followed him, and then the others. Chetsang Rinpoche thought they were going to be executed and wondered if it would hurt when the bullet ripped through his body. He was trembling, but he continued down the three flights of stairs to the ground floor of the monastery.

Outside, a severe storm was raging, as if the elements were as agitated as the humans that night. It thundered in rapid succession and lightning bolts revealed terrified men kneeling on the ground with arms raised to defend themselves from scowling soldiers. In another flash of lightning Chetsang Rinpoche saw Chagdzö Tsephel and his deputy, with lacerations on their heads and arms, cowering in front of a wall, their hands tied behind their backs. Rinpoche could make out eight other men standing in front of the wall, all bound in a row with their hands tied. They were the Drikung officials. Rinpoche struggled to hold up his robes in the violent storm, and he didn't know whether his body was shaking from the cold or fear. In a flash of light, a Tibetan interpreter for the Chinese army saw the boy and tried to comfort him, whispering that nothing would happen to him, but Rinpoche didn't know whether he could believe him or not.

Then the Tibetan translated the commander's curt words: "These ten shameless creatures will be imprisoned. The others will work for the benefit of the people in a labor camp. If they confess their faults in the right and proper fashion, they will enjoy better conditions and will be able to return home soon. Otherwise they will face the same fate as these incorrigibles here." Finally, the Tibetan interpreter announced, "The two Drikung tulkus and Norbu Tulku have successfully completed the re-education program. They may return to their rooms."

The three ran back into the building, and Chetsang Rinpoche dashed up all five floors to the roof, where he tried to make out what was happening down below. In the lightning flashes he saw the field filled with soldiers ready to fire on their captives, some of whom seemed to be rolling around helplessly on the ground. At the shrill sound of a whistle the troops assembled and ordered the monks to line up in a row. Flanked by soldiers they were marched down the broad steps and away into the dark valley. The concerned villagers who had tried to prevent this would wake to find only three under-age rinpoches left in the otherwise empty stronghold.

The three boys were helpless; until now, attendants had taken care of everything, and they didn't even know how to cook their food. While they were discussing what to do, two Gelug monks appeared—sent to look after them, but also, obviously, to monitor them. The elder of the two turned out to be very good-natured and kindly, and when they were alone he whispered to Chetsang Rinpoche that he could be trusted, as he was related to Drikung Gochok Rinpoche. Chetsang Rinpoche found that reassuring, but he did not have as much confidence in the younger of the two monks.

Their provisions consisted of nothing more than barley flour and *sema,* a type of pea normally used as feed for horses and mules, occasionally supplemented by small pieces of dried meat and potatoes provided by villagers. The boys had little to do in Drikung Dzong, and no one knew what to expect next. The Rinpoches passed some time exploring the huge monastery complex—much of which had been previously off-limits to them—and Chetsang Rinpoche was curious to know what the newly sealed rooms might contain. Tibetan doors stand on high sills that can be removed with some skill and effort, so the boys were able to wriggle under the doors without damaging the seals. But they found only empty rooms; everything of value had already been removed, except for a small amount of gold leaf and mercury, used for gilding statues, left in one sooty chamber.

In Kham, where people's feelings for the monasteries ran far deeper, the villagers removed and safely hid many valuable objects from the Drikung monasteries, including ritual objects and musical instruments. After the Cultural Revolution had ended, and sanctions somewhat relaxed, these objects of vital importance to Tibetan religious life were brought out of their hiding places and returned to the monasteries. But this was not so in Drikung, where the villagers sold the artifacts to Nepalese dealers for a pittance, returning nothing to the monasteries.

Norbu returned to his nomad family. Chungtsang Rinpoche sank into a listless, gloomy state, but spirited Chetsang Rinpoche's energy remained unbroken. The empty dzong soon lost all mystery and he wanted to venture further afield. He had always been under the strict supervision of attendants and guards who had not allowed him to engage with ordinary people and their everyday experiences, and now only the two Gelug monks trailed after him. At first he was shy when he ventured down to the village and so many people stared at him. The army quarters, with a few remaining soldiers, was still in the village, straining the atmosphere. Many Tibetans wanted to receive Rinpoche's blessing, but they were too intimidated to approach him. But Rinpoche soon became accustomed to their behavior and enjoyed his outings into a previously unknown freedom.

Every day, Chetsang Rinpoche went down to the village, led the mules to pasture and rode them, and fetched water from a shallow tributary of the Lungshö River. Winter was coming and a layer of ice covered the stream, so he had to break a hole in the ice to draw water. He would then load two mules with the containers and lead them uphill again. Fetching

water was supposed a job for ordinary monks—out of the question for a
Rinpoche, and unthinkable for a throne holder—but he thoroughly enjoyed this simple activity. He felt as if he had been deprived of the most
delightful tasks all those years.

Chungtsang Rinpoche never left the building, though he sometimes
watched his friend from the roof terrace, lost in his own thoughts.
Chetsang Rinpoche roamed alone, exploring the surrounding area thoroughly. Three neighboring families who lived apart from the others se-
cretively invited him into a kitchen, offered him the place of honor, and
served him tea. When he left they gave him a piece of dried meat so large
he could hardly carry it.

Every now and then a tall army officer came up to the monastery, carrying an air rifle for shooting birds. Rinpoche knew almost no Chinese,
and the few fragments he understood were bad words, as far as he could
tell. He made a game of answering, straight-faced and calm-voiced,
with Tibetan words that were at least as bad, while the officer looked at
him with both scorn and confusion. Rinpoche welcomed every change
in routine, and so enjoyed even this grumpy, ill-tempered man. Once,
wanting to show off his agility, he climbed onto the high wooden frame
of a gate, but it broke apart, and he tumbled down onto the stone stairs
below. Luckily, he wasn't badly hurt, but the officer scolded him with
gestures suggesting that if he had struck his head, it would have been
the end of him.

One day a messenger from Tristab Gyabra appeared with a summons
to bring Rinpoche to Lhasa. Thanks to his good contacts, the Drikung
regent had obtained permission to take in the boy as his adoptive son.
Rinpoche could hardly believe his luck, but he was sorry, too, because
Chungtsang Rinpoche had to stay behind. He did not have much to
pack; Tritsab Rinpoche even advised him to leave his amulet belt with its
beautiful reliquaries with his nephew Geleg for the time being. Rinpoche
would not learn until much later of the reign of terror that began in
Drikung after he had gone; a few days after his departure, Chungtsang
Rinpoche was taken into custody and transferred to the army's main
headquarters in the Nyima Changra.

8

School Years under the Red Banner

S HORTLY AFTER THE FLIGHT of the Dalai Lama, the People's
Republic began to implement training programs to raise class consciousness throughout the country. Even in remote rural areas people
were charged with having counter-revolutionary attitudes. Nomads who
had never laid eyes on a rebel and knew nothing of what had happened
in eastern Tibet and in the major cities were accused of having given aid
and comfort to rebels because they had offered food to pilgrims who
had subsequently fled to India. At the same time, the destruction of the
monasteries that had been going on for years in Kham was now spreading throughout the country. Tibetan functionaries often looted the monasteries together with collaborators. Priceless religious antiquities were
sold on the international art market for hard currency, less-valuable statues were melted down, and most of the rest was senselessly destroyed.
Instead of winning over the ordinary Tibetans, as was intended, these
policies resulted in deepening the antagonism between the Chinese occupiers and the Tibetans into an unbridgeable rift. A massive exodus
of Tibetans began in 1959, driven by the zealous programs intended to
uproot and destroy everything in the traditional order.

Monks all over the country were forced to spend their time in mass
meetings and public "struggle sessions" rather than in religious studies
and practice. For months at a time the same propaganda slogans blared
over loudspeakers heard everywhere in the monasteries. A number of
monks from Drikung monasteries in Ladakh had been pursuing their
religious education in Drikung Thil and Yangrigar when the PLA took
these over. Although the monks were Indian citizens, they weren't allowed to leave the country; rather, they were accused of being agents of

imperialist powers, and interrogated as though they were exposed spies. Finally, after a few months, they were expelled from the monastery and deported. In Yangrigar ten Ladakhi monks, Togden Rinpoche among them, were thrown in prison before being eventually taken to Lhasa on horseback and then deported.

The remaining monks and the local population were summoned to the regional headquarters of the People's Liberation Army at Nyima Changra, where the political reeducation and struggle sessions intensified. First the high-ranking monks and tulkus had to describe in detail everything their subordinates had to do for them, thus providing examples of how the ordinary monks had only been "exploited" in the clerical hierarchy. Then the People's Tribunals, the dreaded struggle sessions, began, in which laypeople made accusations against individual lamas, tulkus, and aristocrats. But rather than giving spontaneous performances, the selected accusers had been forced to rehearse their statements and actions. Naturally, there was always someone who bore a grudge of some sort against one or another of those to be accused, and Communist Party ideology simply provided the excuse for petty revenge and the settling of old scores. Others were bullied and intimidated into participating. Chungtsang Rinpoche was brought before a People's Tribunal, where he was forced to bow his head and kneel down to confess his alleged faults. The crowd closed in around him, with Mönlam, one of his attendants, in the front row. Mönlam was forced to attack him viciously, place a pointed dunce cap on his head, and write insulting words on it. The crowd vilified Chungtsang Rinpoche as a capitalist and exploiter, spat on him, threw stones at him, and kicked and beat him. Some women took off their underskirts and pulled them over Chungtsang Rinpoche's head. Those whose zeal was not up to par were taken aside by a Chinese officer and berated for being incorrigible and condemned to further indoctrination themselves—or sent to a labor camp.

Tritsab Gyabra could read the signs of the times and he knew how to come to terms with those in power. He had left the monastery in 1956, after the Monkey Year Teachings, and married the beautiful young Acha Chönyi, who some said was an emanation of the Drikung protectress Achi Chökyi Dolma; sadly, she died shortly thereafter. Tritsab Rinpoche went on a pilgrimage to India, and considered remaining there, but eventually decided to return to Tibet. On his journey he met the renowned Nyingma master Dilgo Khyentse Rinpoche (1910–1991) in Gangtok, and requested that the master come to Drikung to give the Holinesses the initiation of the *Dam Ngag Dzö* (*Treasury of Oral Instructions*) containing the essential teachings of the Eight Practice Lineages.[7] Khyentse Rinpoche consented, but the revolt in Lhasa broke out soon afterwards and he fled with his family to Bhutan. Religious life had come to a dead end in Tibet, and the party officials rewarded Tritsab Gyabra's change to lay status with a high position in the department of religious affairs.

Chetsang Rinpoche returned to his native city in layman's clothing, without an escort or attendants. The city and its inhabitants looked different; the houses bore scars of machine gun fire, and people's faces appeared tense with suffering and fear. Rinpoche was informed that his family home had been confiscated and that his grandfather had died in prison. Neither he nor Tritsab Rinpoche asked any questions, for fear of drawing unwanted attention to themselves, since denunciation and harassment were ever-present dangers that could be triggered by the wrong word or the wrong question. Many years earlier, Dasang Damdul Tsarong had shown a small box of diamond splinters to Heinrich Harrer and said that he would swallow them when all other avenues were closed, but the details of his actual death aren't known. Rinpoche did not brood over his tragic situation; his concern was to survive without losing his optimism and joy in life, even in the face of catastrophe. He always had a special ability to minimize the attention he devoted to his own suffering, recognizing it as it crossed his mind and then departed like a passing guest.

Tritsab and Chetsang Rinpoche lodged in a government guesthouse that had formerly been the residence of the aristocratic Phala family. A short time later, Tritsab Gyabra was sent to accompany the PLA on an expedition against the still-rebellious Khampas, since Gyabra both knew the routes through the wild region and was highly respected by the rural population. Some Tibetans later accused him of having been a collaborator, but he only cooperated because he knew that if he refused he would be put on a work gang building roads or thrown into a lightless dungeon.

After Tritsab left, Rinpoche lived in the guesthouse with Geleg,

Tritsab's nephew, for a few months. This description of their lodging was, at best, a euphemism. The building was dilapidated, with broken windows and a façade peppered with bullet-holes. In his dreary room the bed sheets were smeared with dried blood, and Rinpoche preferred to sleep on the floor with blankets. The kitchen was also squalid, but it was slightly more bearable than his room, so he and Geleg spent most of their time there, although they had hardly anything to eat. As Tritsab Gyabra and his family were not natives of Lhasa, they did not qualify for ration cards, so it was almost impossible for Geleg to get food.

Chairman Mao wanted to transform China into a great industrial nation overnight, and in 1959 he announced the "Great Leap Forward," and forced millions of people, mostly farmers, into industrial communes. Miniature blast-furnaces were set up in almost every village, but the steel they produced was worthless and many workers became ill from the unhealthy labor conditions. The mandatory conscription into the industrial labor force left too few farmers, especially since the quotas for agricultural production were quadrupled in order to export meat and grain to the Soviet Union in exchange for aid in constructing an atomic bomb. Radio Beijing announced harvest surpluses while the country experienced the greatest famine caused by human action in history. Estimates vary, but in 1961 and 1962, some twenty to forty million people died.

In Tibet, the communal management of land and animals and the state-controlled distribution of products, coupled with the food crisis in China, caused the food supply system in Lhasa to collapse, whereas the traditional system had functioned without problems for centuries. In the formerly prosperous capital city, which had never seen food shortages before, it became almost impossible to obtain even a little tsampa without the precious ration coupons.

Each day Chetsang Rinpoche had to walk with the neighbors' children a long way north to the plain of Kyangthang to glean the potatoes left after the army fields had been harvested. Sometimes they were able to collect a cabbage that fell from a truck hauling produce from nearby fields. As he was gathering firewood in the eucalyptus grove behind Chakpori Hill one day, he discovered some monks from the residence of the Panchen Lama, who still enjoyed a favored status in the new social order. They tossed old dried ritual offering cakes (*tormas*) to the birds, and sometimes let the hungry children have some, too. The tormas did not taste very good and were only edible after being softened in tea, but they were food.

When Tritsab Gyabra returned, they moved into another temporary accommodation in the vicinity of the Lubuk quarter in Lhasa, where Tritsab's new girlfriend had a house. It was a simple, old dwelling, but far better than the miserable guesthouse, although food still remained scarce. Due to his position, Tritsab had to entertain many visitors, and tsampa was always in short supply. Although Tritsab Gyabra was in charge of religious affairs, no one ever spoke of the Dharma or the spiritual life of the monasteries, and Rinpoche's impression was that the real function of this government agency was to drive religious matters out of people's heads.

When Tritsab had to travel with the army again, Rinpoche moved in with the Gatro Khangsar family in Lhasa. They were Nubpa Rinpoche's parents, and he enjoyed his stay there. Nubpa Rinpoche had three brothers, all of whom loved to play soccer. Every day they set off, together with Chetsang Rinpoche's cousin Jigme, for the great courtyard of the abandoned Meru Monastery, where Rinpoche received his initiation into the mysteries of soccer. The anarchic game he had played with his brothers and cousins in his early childhood now took on structure and rules. He was zealously dedicated to the game, and when the others grew tired and went home, Jigme stayed to play goalie while Chetsang Rinpoche tirelessly kicked the ball against the wall.

Nubpa Rinpoche attended a lower school in the neighborhood, where only the basics of the Tibetan alphabet were taught. He took Chetsang Rinpoche to school with him a few times, but Rinpoche already knew everything they were teaching there. Then all the high-ranking lamas and tulkus were summoned to Gyume Dratsang, the former Lower Tantric College, to endure a political reeducation program similar to that in Drikung. They were given various pamphlets and articles and were instructed to write their opinions and observations on them. Of course, they were expected to produce the correct Communist Party view and harassed if they didn't. Younger participants such as Chetsang Rinpoche, who understood little of the occupiers' policies and had even less interest in them, preferred to stare out the window, watching the people passing by, envying the boys and girls walking to school. Chetsang Rinpoche, with his friends Reting Rinpoche and Taktra Rinpoche—the reincarnations of the two deceased regents who had fallen out with each other—and Tsemonling Rinpoche, would much rather have gone to school than attend the mind-numbing reeducation program, and the boys asked Tritsab Gyabra whether the latter could help them through his connections.

Gyabra didn't dare approach the Chinese authorities directly, but he recommended the boys write a petition for admission to a school. Reting, who had the best writing skills, wrote what his friends dictated, a skillfully sycophantic text that ended with the words, "We, the signatories, are too young to comprehend the true significance of the reeducation program. We therefore beg to submit this petition for admission to a school, so that we may be better equipped to be of use and service to ourselves, the government and the people."

The gambit worked, and they were allowed to attend school, although the friends were split up among three schools in the city; Rinpoche was assigned to the Second Primary School in Lhasa. He had to take an entrance examination, and he naturally could not answer any of the questions on mathematics and the natural sciences. In a monastic education mathematics was only taught in the context of astrology, which was a complex science of calculation, but one that had little in common with scientific mathematics. In 1961 he was admitted to the Primary School's second grade. At almost fifteen he was the oldest pupil in the class and he immediately decided to learn the most, going beyond the planned curriculum. He took to heart the advice of an old Muslim teacher who instructed his pupils to never waste their time, but to constantly use it for their studies, even when they went to the toilet. Rinpoche pored over his lessons by candlelight late into the night. The subjects opened up completely new worlds to him: the natural sciences, history, geography, biology, art, and music. Everything was taught in Tibetan and the teachers were strict, but they were not allowed to beat their pupils. Rinpoche was one of the best pupils by the end of the third grade; he skipped the fourth grade, and mastered the material of the fifth and sixth grades in half a year's time each, thus completing the six grades of the Primary School after three years. He passed his examinations for admission to the Middle School in 1964.

At this time there was a political assembly in the Great Hall of the Tibet Autonomous Region in Lhasa which all rinpoches and members of the aristocracy were expected to attend. The People's Liberation Army had recently trapped a notorious bandit, Jagpa Samphel, and his two sons. Samphel had made a cunning bargain with the Chinese administration and he had come to Lhasa to tell his life story, which was to serve as an eloquent example of Communism's benevolence and transformative power. The story Samphel related to the assembly included many digressions, but its remarkable details remained in Chetsang Rinpoche's memory. The reformed bandit came from Nagchu and had begun stealing as a small boy. At thirteen he led his first ambush as a highwayman, and subsequently built up a thriving trade in stolen goods. He joined forces with a resistance group in 1959 and engaged in many skirmishes with the PLA, killing hundreds of Chinese soldiers. In the last battle his band took cover on a mountain as the army encircled them. After everyone except he and his two sons had been killed, the Chinese called out to him that he was surrounded, but if he surrendered he would be given his freedom, some land, and animals. Samphel did not believe them. Still, his situation was desperate. Without any water on the mountain they had to kill blue sheep and drink their blood. He was wounded and couldn't move his right arm, so he had to shoot with his left, taking aim with his left eye, which he was not used to. To make sure his right eye didn't misdirect his aim, he bound it shut with his bootlaces. When he was down to his last two bullets in two rifles, he turned himself and his sons in, curious to see if the soldiers would try to cheat him. If they did, he intended the commanding officer to be his final target. However, they kept their word, and he was given his freedom, animals, and land.

When he had finished his overblown speech, a man—a Tibetan and a Communist Party functionary who was not on the list of speakers—stood up. He went up to the stage, introduced himself to the assembly, and assailed Jagpa Samphel with harsh words, accusing him of making propaganda, spreading lies about the PLA, and trying to present himself as some kind of national hero. Two guards dragged the uninvited speaker from the stage and a cadre wearing a regulation blue suit and a Mao cap announced the next presentation on the program. Rinpoche was astounded at the lengths the Chinese occupiers would go to in their efforts to convince the Tibetans of the benefits of their policies. He was even more surprised at their naiveté in believing that such presentations were convincing to anyone but themselves.

In February 1961, Chetsang Rinpoche returned to Drikung, with Tritsab Gyabra, for the first time since he had left Chungtsang Rinpoche there alone. The monasteries were empty and it was not prudent to go near them. They went to enjoy the New Year celebrations with Tritsab's family in Wururong, a small village near Yangrigar. An opera and dances were performed, but the atmosphere was tense because members of the local administration had also come, and no one knew who could be trusted and who would carry tales to the Communist government officials. People who had once been relaxed, open, and cheerful now whispered among themselves and exchanged shamefaced looks. Afraid of being marked as "incorrigible," or worse, no one dared approach Tritsab Rinpoche and the Drikung Holiness to receive their blessing.

During his second school year, Chetsang Rinpoche took time off to accompany Tritsab Gyabra on a journey to the nomad regions in the north. Because he cooperated with the new government, Tritsab's properties had not been confiscated, and he was still permitted to profit from the earnings produced on his large estates with thousands of animals. Once a year he traveled to his tenant farmers to collect his income. Rinpoche looked forward to exploring unknown stretches of land, and Gyabra was counting on his mathematical abilities to do the bookkeeping. A group of four set off: Tritsab Gyabra, his nephew Geleg, Chetsang Rinpoche, and an assistant. They traveled in nomadic fashion, on horseback with six yaks carrying their food and equipment. They departed each day before dawn, and by noon set up camp, where Gyabra fetched water from a stream, Rinpoche unpacked and tended to the yaks, and Geleg made a fire the traditional way, using dried dung as fuel. They ate their tsampa and a little dried meat before going to sleep.

The group passed by Drikung Thil, and after a few days they reached the area of Baga—with its springs that feed the Kyichu River—where some nomad families were camped. When the nomads invited the prominent visitors to their tents, they first did prostrations and offered them a piece of butter and *thu,* a special cheese, as a gesture of welcome.[8] Tritsab and his companions were offered places to sit on the left side of the oven, the place reserved for guests of honor. First they were given yogurt, which according to tradition had to be served overflowing from its bowl. The nomads had difficulty obtaining barley, so there was not much tsampa, but they compensated with immense amounts of cheese.

The thu was served again at their departure. The nomads made a gift to Tritsab Rinpoche of a brown horse he particularly liked, and Geleg and Chetsang Rinpoche packed up the butter that the nomads gave them as rent. It was pressed into blocks and stuffed into airtight containers made of yak intestine so that it remained edible for a long time. At that time government policy allowed the nomads to keep one third of their butter and milk production, the landowner was paid another third, and the rest was for the nomads' young animals.

The travelers moved on, and the mountainous landscape opened into treeless grass steppes stretching endlessly before them. In the morning they could make out their destination in the distance. Nonetheless, even after a long day's ride, it seemed as though they had not come any closer. It had rained constantly in the previous weeks and great marshy bogs had formed in places, dangerous to those who strayed from the solid raised pathways.

Their destination was the tent camp of Gochok Rinpoche's nomad family, the wealthiest family in the area. The previous Chungtsang Rinpoche, Chökyi Lodrö, had recognized Gochok Konchog Nyedon as a tulku and had him brought to Yangrigar after he had finished his studies in the Gelug monastery of Drepung. In 1917 the previous Chetsang Rinpoche, Shiwe Lodrö, appointed him Khenpo of Yangrigar, where he introduced strict rules and a fasting retreat in summer. The monks of Yangrigar revered Gochok Rinpoche and his family for their continuing generosity toward the monastery and the region's poorest people, and Chetsang Rinpoche was eager to meet this renowned family, which was spoken about with such reverence in Drikung.[9]

Their camp lay in a bare patch surrounded by lush pastures. Black tents arose like islands in a sea of white sheep, extending as far as the eye could see. Chetsang Rinpoche had seen large tents before, in Drongur during the Monkey Year Teachings and at receptions for the Dalai Lama, but he had never seen such an enormous one. The Gochoks were obviously very wealthy. The several thousand sheep that grazed in the area were only selected rams intended for consumption; the ewes were pastured elsewhere. Great yak herds with two thousand yak calves, and more than a thousand white horses were also pastured in a different place. They had so many animals they couldn't actually keep count of them all. There were eighteen tents in the encampment, each one guarded by a ferocious Tibetan mastiff. At night all of the dogs were let loose to protect the camp, and they sniffed around the visitors' tents, chewing on the wooden tent pegs and snapping and pulling at the ropes. They even pulled Geleg's blanket from his bed and tussled over it. Rinpoche hardly slept that night, and as much as he loved animals, he was glad when it was time to move on.

On this trip Chetsang Rinpoche was able to come to know a very different way of life from that which he had experienced growing up in central Tibet: different homes, different food, different clothes, and different customs. Rinpoche was especially fascinated by the richness of the nomads' language, which had names for so many things that had no equivalent in the Tibetan dialect he spoke. It struck him that, unlike city-dwellers, the nomads never used obscene language, never joked or made fun of others. Their reserve lent them an air of nobility that he found lacking in the sophisticated world of deceit and treachery that he knew from Lhasa and life in the monastery.

Incessant rain made the group's return journey more difficult with every passing day. The heavily laden animals struggled in the mire, and Tritsab Gyabra could not take all he had collected with him, as it would have required a caravan of 30 yaks, so he arranged to have it sent to him later. Soaking wet, the travelers rode through swampy areas for days in the rain, without even being able to light a fire to warm food or prepare tea. Geleg kept a piece of dry yak dung like a treasure in the large fold of his *chuba* (traditional layperson's dress), and the idea that the dung was now their most precious object appealed to Rinpoche's sense of humor. Eventually it did stop raining, and Geleg's care to keep the dung dry made it possible for them to light a fire and enjoy a cup of hot tea.

Further on, they had to cross the dangerously swollen Miti Tsangpo River. The young stallion Rinpoche rode became very restless and nervous when they approached the flooding river. It took hours to cross because the river had overflowed its banks, and as the group became separated, Rinpoche lost control of his agitated horse and it plunged ahead into deep water. The guide's shouted instructions were lost in the roaring of the river, while the horse struggled against the powerful current. When they had almost reached the far bank, the animal's entire body suddenly submerged; one step in the wrong direction and it would have completely lost its footing. At that point the river bed had been so deeply cut that the stallion's leap was unable to bring them up onto the bank. They fell back into the water and drifted with the current downriver, where the panicking horse tried a second jump, and failed again. Chetsang Rinpoche made ready to save himself with his own leap to the riverbank and was pulling his boots out of the stirrups when the stallion attempted a final desperate jump. At last the horse succeeded in scrambling onto the bank. Both horse and rider were exhausted and shaken, but the animal had found the only place it was possible to exit the deep water, and all the others had to come the same way. The rest of their return was dreary with incessant rain and mud, but, to everyone's relief, without further incident.

In May 1962 the Panchen Lama strongly criticized PRC policies in Tibet, much to the surprise of both Tibetans and Chinese, although most Tibetans found out about his courageous stand only much later, if at all. In his public appearances the Panchen Lama appeared to support China's policies, and his attempts to work within government channels to defend Tibet's interests remained largely hidden from his countrymen.

The thorough and detailed criticism coming from the Panchen Lama, the PRC's protégé, shocked the Communist Party. Mao and the Party's new leadership had just begun a new policy of encouraging criticism, but they never expected the relentless document that became known as the Seventy Thousand–Character Petition.[10] It is a harrowing record of the mismanagement and destructive policies of the People's Republic of China in Tibet, laid out clearly and fairly by someone never suspected of harboring such views, much less of having the nerve to express them. It was the sharpest and most detailed attack on China's policies in Tibet that had ever been formulated, and included a burning plea for religious freedom. Mao was outraged and termed the petition "a poisoned arrow aimed at the Communist Party of China."

Outwardly, China remained unmoved in the face of this massive attack for some time; apparently the party leadership was entirely focused on trying to limit the damage from the economic disasters caused by the Great Leap Forward. The border dispute between China and India in October 1962 provided a much-needed boost to national morale and patriotic fervor, as the PLA had swiftly inflicted a devastating defeat on India's forces. India then began to take a greater interest in the Tibetan exile community, funneling support to the CIA's covert program for training and assisting Tibetan freedom fighters, and giving the Dalai Lama permission to set up a government-in-exile in Dharamsala.

Meanwhile, Chetsang Rinpoche was finding a suitable channel for his energy, agility, and drive in sports. He was selected for a team of athletes under 18 years of age who would represent Lhasa in a competition against the country's two other great cities, Shigatse and Chamdo. He excelled in many track and field sports—sprint, shot-put, discus, javelin, high jump, and long jump—and eventually collected two dozen awards, even holding third place in all of China, as well as the Tibetan record for throwing discus. He received a certificate with Mao's portrait and Chinese stamps on it, useful credentials that guaranteed the respect and cooperation of those who believed in the superiority of patriotic revolutionary education. It also afforded some protection against the attacks on representatives of religion and the aristocracy that increased in direct proportion to the Panchen Lama's gradual fall from grace. In yet another purge of the Communist Party and government, Mao had ordered the annihilation of all reactionary forces, and the Panchen Lama was now labeled a "capitalist roader" and, for the first time, he was not invited to the Chinese National Day in the summer of 1963. Finally, following the purge of his most important advocates, the Panchen Lama was accused of obstructing the introduction of socialist reforms and gradually removed from his offices.

Chetsang Rinpoche was summoned by the department of religious affairs to participate in a meeting of tulkus and lamas making preparations for the Mönlam of 1964. This was a delicate situation, since representatives of Tibetan religion were now in the cross-hairs, as Gochok Rinpoche had warned him. Gochok had recently returned from Beijing after completing his studies at the Tungyang Mirig Lobdra, the Central Institute for National Minorities. He and Tritsab Gyabra were both in the Tibet Committee of the Chinese People's Political Consultative Conference, and Gochok had obtained accommodations for Rinpoche and Tritsab where he and his wife also lived, in an apartment house for officials of the committee.

One Sunday when Tritsab was away with the Chinese army, Gochok was on the telephone, a public phone on the ground floor, for hours, speaking in Chinese. When he finished, Gochok took Chetsang Rinpoche aside and told him he was leaving Lhasa to visit his family, and he urgently advised him to avoid any event organized by the department of religious affairs. He exhorted, "Do everything possible to have them throw you out of such events. If you are called upon to take part, refuse. Make yourself out to be younger than you really are, and keep on going to school! Mark my words!" He then insisted that Rinpoche not tell anyone about their conversation, and especially not Tritsab.

Chetsang Rinpoche trusted him. Gochok understood Chinese politics and was very well informed about the new, harsher policy toward the representatives of religion. He wanted to prevent Rinpoche from being pulled into the vortex of intimidation, violence, and subjugation, and although Rinpoche knew nothing of the specifics for this warning, he was nonetheless certain that Gochok's advice should not be taken lightly.

Gochok shouldered an old British rifle that had been officially issued to him and, with his wife and their baby, departed. Although Chetsang Rinpoche did not know it, they were attempting to escape, but they were stopped at the border. Gochok's wife came from a very poor family and therefore enjoyed a high status under the Communists, so she was released after a few months. Rinpoche later saw her on the streets of Lhasa with her small child, selling matches. He quickly dodged into an alleyway, realizing that it could be dangerous to be seen speaking with her and thus associating with suspected "traitors."

With Gochok's warning in mind and a gloomy feeling, Rinpoche went to the Mönlam Chenmo meeting, which was compulsory for all tulkus and the leading representatives of religious life in central Tibet. The meeting was chaired by the Gelug Tsokhang Lama, who sat in the middle; next to him sat a Chinese officer, and then a translator. Rinpoche obeyed neither the dress code, which required his monks' robes, nor the prescribed seating order. He took a seat directly next to the door, sitting listlessly and staring at the ceiling. The officer found his behavior outrageous, glared angrily in his direction, and muttered something to the translator. The translator asked Rinpoche why he was wearing such old, ragged clothes, since Tritsab Gyabra received government money to take proper care of him. In point of fact, Rinpoche never wore new clothes at that time; if a piece of clothing was torn, he patched it. He

answered truculently that he held to the principles of a recent government campaign to "raise productivity and reduce expenses," and he did
not want to waste anything. Tritsab Gyabra gave him what he could,
but he had to keep the campaign in mind, too. Silence reigned in the
hall as his answer was translated, and the other tulkus exchanged horrified looks at the insolence of his response. He was ordered to shave his
head and don his monk's robes—"lama clothes," as the Chinese called
them—for the Mönlam Chenmo. Chetsang Rinpoche remained stubborn and replied that since the Communist Party proclaimed religious
freedom, which was also guaranteed by the constitution, it was his decision whether he wanted to take part in the Mönlam or not. The Chinese
officer's face reddened with fury; he mumbled something inaudible and
opened the meeting.

The PRC government's overriding concern appeared to be control.
The Communist Party regarded religion as "poison," as Mao had put
it, but rather than completely eliminating religious life they apparently
intended to preserve its empty forms as folklore and harness it to serve
their political purposes.

As soon as the meeting was over, everyone else hastened to leave while
Chetsang Rinpoche lingered by the door. The Chinese officer came over
to him and tapped Rinpoche on the head with his finger, a bit annoyed
and even more astonished at so much audacity. He mumbled something
like "naughty boy," laughed and left the room. After this incident, the
authorities no longer requested Chetsang Rinpoche's participation in
the events of the department of religious affairs, since he clearly seemed
to have been very successfully reeducated and to have internalized Communist values.

The Panchen Lama's fate had already been sealed before he repeated
the accusations from his petition, this time to a large audience in Lhasa,
during the Mönlam; at the end of his speech he described the Dalai
Lama as his "refuge in this life and in the next." Shortly thereafter, in
September 1964, the Seventh Enlarged Meeting of the PCART brought
him to trial, accusing him of secretly preparing a counter-revolution.
Public exhibits were set up in Lhasa and Shigatse that purported to show
the evidence of his supposed crimes, and he was even accused of having
a secret weapons factory built behind his monastery. School children,
work units, and members of the neighborhood committees were guided

through the exhibits. The public might not have been convinced by the display, but they probably got the underlying message—that favor and privilege could be taken away as easily as they were given.

The Panchen Lama was abused in the vicious struggle, but he refused to confess to having committed any crimes. He was put in prison and not released until 1977.

Rinpoche entered Tibet's only secondary school, the Jerag Lingka Middle School behind the Potala, in 1964. The Middle School was the showplace of Chinese educational policy in Tibet. The carefully selected teachers were mostly Chinese, with a few of the very best Tibetan teachers, including Seshi Tsewang Namgyal, author of a 1958 Tibetan dictionary that is still highly regarded.

The classes mixed boys and girls, although they hardly spoke to each other, but the nationalities, Tibetans and Chinese, were strictly segregated. Friendships between Tibetans and Chinese were practically impossible; they had separate classes, separate dormitories, and separate kitchens, even eating separate foods. Chinese students were served mostly rice and Chinese wheat, while the Tibetans generally ate tsampa. Once a month the students obtained a ration of meat, and they were given some vegetables as compensation for garden work they were required to perform every Saturday. The quantity of food was seldom enough to appease their hunger, especially that of sports enthusiasts such as Chetsang Rinpoche, who needed a high-calorie diet. But they did drink very good tea. When the PLA had searched the Potala Palace for valuables, they had found large stores of tea blocks that to them looked worthless and unfit for consumption, and some of these blocks had been sent to the school, so the students enjoyed the finest quality black tea.

The dormitories were spartan, with fifteen to twenty boys in a small room, and their days were strictly regimented. Every morning a shrill bell rang before dawn and the students had to quickly dress and rush to the playground for morning gymnastics. Afterward, they washed in buckets of ice-cold water. There was a tight schedule of meals and classes, and the students were always closely monitored and disciplined. Each week a large assembly of all five hundred students was held, in which individual students and entire classes were praised or criticized; those accused of misconduct had to stand up before the entire assembly, listen with bowed heads to the recital of their wrongs, and then confess and express contrition.

Rinpoche was pleased to find in his first year that an intensive course in Chinese was being offered for the first time. The students were required to master three thousand characters in a very short time, and after one year they would be able to speak and write Chinese better than the classes ahead of them, which had completed a regular course in Chinese. Their teacher, Mo-han, was astounded that Rinpoche consistently achieved scores of 98 or 99 percent, which Rinpoche attributed to his great interest in learning the language.

In early 1964, the Tibetans were called upon to raise their level of class-consciousness. In China this campaign was aimed at purging the Communist Party apparatus, but in Tibet the traditional Tibetan leadership was targeted and this policy led to the inversion of the former social hierarchy, although the division of the populace into discrete classes remained the same. The children of former serfs and of poor families enjoyed privileges, above all if they joined the Communist Youth League, which was open only to them. While the other students had to pay fifteen yuan per month for food and lodging, they were charged nothing, and after graduation they were given the best positions in the Communist Party and in the local administrations. They had become the new elite.

The inverted system of discrimination could be strange and confusing. Once, Chetsang Rinpoche received a little money from Tritsab Gyabra and hid it under his pillow, but the next morning when he returned from gymnastics, it had vanished. Since he was left without money to pay for his room and board, he was forced to report the incident to the classroom teacher. A meeting of the entire class was called, and the guilty party, a boy who had stayed in bed that morning claiming to be sick, was soon found. He confessed his guilt before the entire class, and most of the students thought that the matter was now settled. But the teacher gave a lecture using Communist dialectics to turn the tables, casting the victim as the perpetrator, and then called upon the students to discuss what conclusions were to be drawn. Many were of the opinion that half of the responsibility was Rinpoche's and half the thief's, some were inclined to say the thief was responsible, and others thought Rinpoche was to blame. The teacher skillfully steered the discussion in such a way that, in the end, Rinpoche was the only truly guilty party, having caused the theft by bringing the money into the school in the first place. The real issue was the supposed "fact" that Rinpoche was influenced by the mentality of the capitalist upper class. Thus, it was not the thief who should confess his fault publicly, but Rinpoche, who had to concede before the teacher and his fellow students that this conclusion was the only correct one.

By now familiar with the game of vilification, Rinpoche stood up dutifully, and with an expression of deepest contrition confessed that everything had happened because of his errors. But then suddenly a girl student spoke up and defended him, saying that theft was wrong and reprehensible under any circumstances. She won amazement and admiration from the students for her courageous stand even after the teacher seemed to have won the rhetorical battle. As Rinpoche's supporters saw a chance of reopening the discussion, the teacher ignored her protest and abruptly called on Chetsang Rinpoche to conclude the meeting. The matter was now settled and there would be no further argument.

Despite the social tensions, Rinpoche's time in the Middle School was a fulfilling one. He had a few very good friends, was respected by most of the teachers for his prudence and industriousness, and enjoyed success in sports. In 1965 he represented the school on a soccer team in a major competition organized as part of a program to celebrate the founding of the Tibet Autonomous Region.

That July, the stores began to fill up with food and merchandise that had not been seen in Lhasa for years, as Lhasa was spruced up to impress the foreign journalists who would be visiting the city for the first time. Elaborate preparations were made for the celebrations, which lasted several days. On August 29, 1965 there was a parade and a reception of important political leaders from Beijing, cheered by dutiful Tibetans in regulation blue worker suits. On September 1, the First People's Congress of the Tibet Autonomous Region convened in the newly built Workers' Cultural Palace directly under the Potala, and Ngabö was appointed as the first governor of Tibet. After years of serving the Communist Party's interests he lacked any political credibility among Tibetans, but his appointment was intended to prove that Tibetans were taking an active part in their country's politics.

*Chetsang Rinpoche (front row seated, far left) with the soccer team of the
Lhasa Middle School representing Tibet Autonomous Region in 1965.*

The most significant event for Rinpoche was the great soccer match in
the new stadium, which had been built with the forced labor of prisoners. First, four teams competed, one from the People's Liberation Army,
one from the transportation workers, one from the government offices of
Lhasa, and one representing the Tibet Autonomous Region. The winning
team was then to play a demonstration match against Tibet's only professional team. Chetsang Rinpoche, several of his schoolmates, and a few
members of the press played on the Tibet Autonomous Region team.

The PLA team was given six months to train, and the best provisions
and training facilities, while Rinpoche and his teammates had only three
months free of school obligations, and used miserable training facilities; nonetheless, they not only made it to the finals, but even defeated
the Chinese Army team, thrilling the Tibetan spectators and winning
them the honor of playing against the professional team. The stands
were overflowing for that extraordinary final match, which Chetsang
Rinpoche won for his team by scoring a spectacular goal in overtime.
Rinpoche remembers it as the best game of his life; afterward, his nick-
name became "Golden Foot."

9

Theater of Cruelty
The Cultural Revolution in Lhasa

O N M AY 29, 1966 a group of students of the Qinghua Middle
School in Beijing founded the first Red Guards. They were fanatical supporters of Chairman Mao and unquestioningly obedient to his
directives. Similar groups arose in schools and universities throughout
the country as the new generation, nurtured on increasingly delusional
indoctrination, came of age. They had been educated to worship and
obey power, not to think, and now they were ready to act and become
powerful themselves. Without any coherent plan, the students were
nonetheless a force to be reckoned with, and most of the men in power
were at a loss as to how to deal with them.

President Liu Shaoqi (1898–1969) made a vain attempt to repress the
chaotic and unpredictable student groups, but Mao immediately grasped
the potential of harnessing the immense energy of the youth for his purposes. He gathered the young radicals around him and censured Liu for
obstructing the students' revolutionary zeal. At the eleventh plenum of
the Eighth Central Committee on August 1, Mao had reassumed control
of power.[1] A few days later, his ground-breaking article, "Bombard the
Headquarters," was published. A campaign against party bosses "tread-
ing the capitalist path" was officially launched when the plenum passed
a Sixteen-Point Directive on the Cultural Revolution on August 8. Lin
Biao now rose to become the second most powerful man in the CCP.

Mao skillfully succeeded in transforming the arena of the struggle
for political power from the quiet and subtle manipulation of party
theory and ideology into a show of popular support, where he had no

competition. In August 1966 one million young people cheered him on enthusiastically at the Square of Heavenly Peace, seemingly not for his ideology, but just to feel, and show, their own strength. All of a sudden, youth had power. Schools, universities, businesses, and factories were closed so students could travel throughout China to exchange revolutionary experiences with other Red Guards. In a country that had been characterized for centuries by filial respect toward parents, and by strict hierarchical obedience, Mao endorsed the upending of values: his young supporters were allowed, even encouraged, to revolt, especially against tradition, parents, and superiors, and violence was expressly permitted. The Cultural Revolution had begun.

Red Guards terrorized the country, leaving a trail of blood in their wake, as they burst into houses and forced ordinary people to confess to "bourgeois" errors, or as they beat, humiliated, and arrested people on the streets. The Red Guards conducted their own style of struggle sessions, even more extreme than those of before, and the general level of physical and psychological abuse increased. Brutal torture, mutilation, or execution by the marauding groups of young people became part of the daily routine of the Red Guards.

The Cultural Revolution began to affect Tibet in February 1966, when the Mönlam festival was prohibited for the first time. In May 1966 the party set up the Cultural Revolution Committee in Lhasa, headed by Wang Qimei, who, as army commander, had conducted the negotiations with Ngabö during the attack on eastern Tibet in 1951. The committee launched the campaign against the "Four Olds" that were to be eliminated: old ideas, old culture, old customs, and old habits. The radical developments set in motion by the Red Guards did not reach Tibet immediately. In July the regional Communist Party still sent out invitations for the traditional summer picnic, a custom they had taken over from the old Tibetan government, and former Tibetan aristocrats who upheld the party line were feted at a lavish banquet. Soon afterward, the members of the aristocracy would be cast as class enemies and counter-revolutionaries.

After the promulgation of the Sixteen-Point Directive in August 1966 the Cultural Revolution's focus in Tibet was shifted from old values to the local party elite. On August 24, a unit of Red Guards was set up in the Middle School and the Teacher Training School in Lhasa. Some suspected that the local party leadership had installed these groups hoping to keep the Chinese Red Guards out of Tibet, and thus avoid being targeted themselves. But a handful of Chinese students from the University of Beijing and Qinghua University infiltrated the Middle School, held secret meetings, and founded the first unit of the aggressive Chinese-style Red Guards in Tibet, recruiting their members from the children of higher-level officials and from poor families. They armed themselves with homemade spears, tied on red armbands, and roamed the streets on their way to public assemblies, which everyone had to attend, including Chetsang Rinpoche and his Tibetan friends.

For a time, the local party leadership succeeded in directing the Cultural Revolution as a campaign against the Four Olds. All religious symbols were removed from public life; the Norbulingka, former summer residence of the Dalai Lama, was renamed "People's Park;" a young Red Guard from Rinpoche's school named Genyen Chöpel ("Propagator of the Dharma [holding] Novice Vows") was rechristened Mao Hui Biao, "Protector of Mao." Women and girls were no longer allowed to wear their hair long, and Red Guards cut it off forcibly.

More serious was the unprecedented wave of demolition of almost all historic buildings and monuments, and of any monasteries that had not previously fallen prey to vandalism. By 1965, 80 percent of all of Tibet's monasteries had already been devastated; what was left would now be destroyed.

The Red Guards demanded that all schools take part in the destruction of the Jokhang in Lhasa and marched everyone to the temple. Rinpoche and his companions hung back toward the end of the line, but they could see there was a dispute between the Chinese Red Guards and some representatives of the department of cultural affairs who had taken up positions in front of the entrance to the Jokhang. The officials were able to prevent the temple's destruction, but they could not keep the mob from plundering it. The Red Guards went into the temple and started ransacking the sacred ritual objects and ranting against "superstition." Many children rushed in to join them, dismantling the shrines and dragging the sacred statues with ropes through the filth of the streets. Rinpoche and his friends slipped off to the nearby house of a classmate to watch what was happening from the roof. The excited children in the streets may have simply enjoyed the opportunity to vent their youthful energy in the destruction, while some shrewd adults took advantage of the general tumult to carry off priceless sacred treasures, which they could sell to Nepalese dealers.

Rinpoche thought that the Jokhang had always been the stage for the *comédie humaine* in the Land of Snows: a penitential path for pilgrims with their leather aprons, marking out their way here with body-lengths—one full prostration after another in the dust; a vanity fair for the wealthy; a podium for opulent spectacles of the clerical elite; a court of justice for stern masters of discipline; an open-air museum for short-lived monster sculptures made of butter; a hang-out for hustlers and pickpockets. A place of dramas and legends. A backdrop for lofty and tragic moments in the history of the Tibetan people. It was considered to be the heart of the country's ancestral demoness, Sinmo, whose body was formed by the topography of the country. King Songtsen Gampo had rammed the Jokhang into her heart like an oversize *phurba,* the ritual dagger with which the powers of evil are exorcised. To Rinpoche it seemed as though the demoness was reawakening. The sacred monasteries that once rendered her innocuous were being destroyed. Her heart was bleeding again, bleeding in the center of Rinpoche's country. It was bleeding in the hearts of the people—a poison of baleful portent.

The Red Guards invaded the homes of the wealthy and confiscated everything that looked like capitalist goods to them. The government set up a large storage hall for all the statues and antiques from monasteries and private homes, but valuable objects entered the international art and antiquities market, and were to end up in major public and private collections in the West. Everyone was forced to turn over their valuables. Things were simply seized from those suspected of having supported the rebels or otherwise worked against Communism, but others were at least offered some compensation, albeit a pittance. The precious objects were carelessly weighed in the storage hall and then tossed onto a heap, and their owners were handed a sum that was merely symbolic, since any personal accumulation of wealth was considered a crime.

A great mountain had grown that included some sizeable statues from the surrounding monasteries. The largest of the statues could not be stored inside and were piled up next to the storage hall. The area was swampy and the effigies began gradually sinking into the ground. Some months later Chetsang Rinpoche could still recognize the heads and shoulders of some of the figures from a distance, like tragic monuments to a dying culture. Later, the swamps would be drained and houses built.

No one dared keep religious objects any more, and Tritsab Gyabra dumped a chest containing vajras, beautiful reliquaries, precious statuettes, and a few Buddhist texts into the Kyichu, entrusting his last Dharma treasures to the river rather than the rampaging vandals. Nevertheless, he was one of the many lamas and tulkus subjected to public humiliation. In front of a mocking crowd he was paraded across the Barkhor, Lhasa's famous circular road around the Jokhang, wearing a white cardboard dunce cap that said "I am a demon."

To avoid being attacked for keeping company with Tritsab Gyabra and other tulkus, Chetsang Rinpoche moved into the shabby dormitory in the Jerag Lingka Middle School, which had essentially shut down—the teachers having gone into hiding, and the students having taken to the streets to carry out the Cultural Revolution. At first the representatives of the old aristocratic and monastic society had come under fire from the Communist Party, but now even the party's faithful servants were being paraded through the streets in disgrace and subjected to the well choreographed "wrath of the masses." Under the pretext of a Maoist reformation of social conditions, the actual goal was to completely annihilate Tibetan identity.

The Barkhor became a theater of cruelty. Rinpoche tried to avoid it, afraid of being dragged into participating in the anarchic proceedings. Tulkus and aristocrats were humiliated by being forced to wear bizarre costumes and wooden signs with the catalog of their supposed evil deeds hung around their necks, or compelled to beat drums and wear hats that symbolized their "crimes." At the school, Rinpoche was accused of being a class enemy—a lama and an aristocrat. He was ordered to confess his crimes and express contrition, but he answered that he had nothing to confess as he was not guilty of any crime, and that if his accusers had something specific to bring up, they should do so. The accusations were merely insubstantial ideological slogans, reiterated over and over, and the classroom tribunal was repeated every few days for some months, but no one dared attack Rinpoche physically. Still, he had to be very careful, as spies and informers were everywhere. One of his teachers, who had performed a traditional New Year's ceremony, was denounced and subjected to a massive struggle session, and people were constantly grilled about who they visited and what was discussed.

Handwritten posters reminding people of the three duties of the Great Proletarian Cultural Revolution ("struggle, criticize, and correct") covered the walls along the major streets, and new directives and slogans were put up every day, creating more confusion than clarity. The Red Guards weren't interested in the political theory or logic behind the Sixteen-Point Directive, it was enough to simply memorize the lofty-sounding slogans and, interpreting them however they pleased, enact them with courage and determination. The confusion surrounding the actual purpose of the Cultural Revolution was so great that Wang Qimei felt compelled to clarify it; he convened an assembly, which Rinpoche and his school friends attended, along with all other students, journalists, actors, and members of the Communist Youth League. During this period it was essential to keep track of the daily policy realignments to avoid running afoul of the ever-shifting winds of power.

Wangdu, the influential head of the Communist Youth League, sat on the podium next to Wang Qimei, and as soon as Wang Qimei ended his speech, Wangdu arose and accused him of being a "capitalist roader." Everyone began yelling at once: Wang Qimei defending himself and pounding on the table with his fist; the actors saying he had helped to shape the peaceful liberation of Tibet, and was a loyal supporter of Chairman Mao; and the journalists and students accusing him of securing privileges for himself and being a complacent reactionary. The conflict escalated into sharp polemics and ended in chaos. Chetsang Rinpoche did not realize that he had been present at a significant moment in the history of Tibet; one that would decisively influence the developments that were to follow. Wang left protected by army security officers, and two factions emerged from the dispute that continued fiercely even after his departure. The majority of the students belonged to the camp opposing Wang Qimei. They would soon organize themselves into a group known as the Gyenlog (rebels), and Rinpoche would find himself involuntarily caught up in this faction.

Up to this point, the Red Guards in Tibet were mostly fanaticized young Tibetans who were fierce advocates of a total overthrow and renewal of society and were dedicated followers of Mao. Resentment and hostility after years of humiliation at the hands of the occupying power mixed with Maoist ideology in their attacks on the Chinese authorities in Lhasa.

The first full contingent of Chinese Red Guards from Beijing arrived in Tibet in November 1966 and accelerated the radicalization of the factions backing Wang Qimei and Wangdu, the debate being conducted primarily through accusations made on posters plastered along the Lhasa streets. Sometimes the posters of one party were pasted over by those of the other before the glue had even dried. The Red Guards sent Chetsang Rinpoche and his friends in the school out to do errands, deliver messages, copy propaganda texts and so on, and once one of Rinpoche's schoolmates, a zealous supporter of the Red Guards, told Rinpoche to take a ladder to put the posters up higher, so they couldn't be pasted over so quickly. It wasn't safe to go out alone in the tense streets of Lhasa, and Rinpoche responded, "Why don't we go together?" His schoolmate reacted angrily, and the two combative boys had to be separated by a couple of other students. Eventually everyone in Lhasa stopped going out and the town shut down. Hardly a soul was to be seen on the abandoned streets, and not even dogs roamed in the eerie silence.

Toward the end of 1966, the personality cult around Chairman Mao intensified. On the formerly Buddhist altars found in every Tibetan home, Mao's portrait, framed by the mantra of Chenrezig, *Om Mani Peme Hung*,[2] and lit with flickering butter lamps, replaced the Buddhist deities. This sort of veneration was not only acceptable, it was required.

Wanting to spread the fervor of the Cultural Revolution throughout the land, Mao directed the Red Guards to travel and make contact with students everywhere. He also invited students to visit him in Beijing, and four students were selected from Rinpoche's school to make this journey. Chetsang Rinpoche and many of his Middle School schoolmates, more than twenty in all, decided they would also travel from Lhasa to Beijing, on foot. Rinpoche was enthusiastic about this plan since it would provide an escape from the increasing terror in Lhasa and the opportunity to engage in a daring adventure and test his well-conditioned body. The young people presented their proposal to local officials and were given food coupons for three months. Samten, a schoolmate who was the only

Red Guard member among them and whose uncle was in the Communist Party, would be their leader. He carried an official letter explaining their intentions and requesting support.

They set off one day in December, so heavily laden with supplies and clothing that they only managed twenty kilometers, but after lightening their packs they were able to put forty kilometers behind them the next day. From Medrogunkar they took the road eastwards that led to Rutok, where they rested for a few days, soaking their aching legs in the nearby hot springs. From here, a narrow path led over three high passes to Lhamo Latso, the oracle lake where Tritsab Gyabra had sought a vision of Rinpoche's birthplace. Some of the students developed huge blisters and required treatment in the villages along the way, but no one wanted to give up. Trucks stopped now and then, and when the drivers asked where they were going and the students replied, "To Beijing!," the response was usually an incredulous laugh.

When the travelers crossed the high snow-covered pass of Kongpo Pa La, the sun was shining in a cloudless sky, but it did not warm them. After descending, they passed the place where, as a small child, Chetsang Rinpoche had once received the Dalai Lama. At that time the campground had seemed like an immense field to him, but now to the young man twenty years old, it looked small and narrow, as if the world had shrunk. He reflected on how our consciousness constructs the dimensions of reality relative to our own body size, and then realized how reality as such unfolds according to the expansiveness or narrowness of one's mind.

His friends flagged down a truck that would take them into Kongpo, where the climate was milder thanks to the moist air that came from the south. They walked on, and after a night in Kenang, their letter of recommendation secured them a ride to Bayi in an army truck. Until recently this had been a tiny village with only a few families, but in 1951 the People's Liberation Army had moved in with ambitious construction and development projects, and renamed the city Bayi ("August 1") for the date of the PLA's founding. The city had developed into a center for industry and commerce and boasted Tibet's largest military hospital, as well as some much-feared labor camps. Samten stretched the truth, telling the truck driver that they were all Red Guards, which gained them recognition and the convenience of sleeping in the army truck station that night. They also enjoyed a good meal, one not limited by the precious ration coupons.

One PLA officer asked if the young people from Lhasa could put on a musical performance to cheer up the clinic's wounded. The students were not prepared but some of the girls could sing and dance, and some of the boys could play the musical instruments available. Rinpoche played the flute, the Tibetan *lingbu*. The great hall was filled with the wounded, who applauded wildly. They demanded encores, but the students had exhausted their repertoire, so the performers started over from the beginning, to the delight of their audience.

The next day, the commander of the army unit invited the group to his spacious house and made a speech. He praised their commitment and their comradeship, and commented on how wonderful it was that young people were acting on Mao's ideas to help the country's development. Chetsang Rinpoche noticed how skillful he was at charming his young guests, winning their trust and admiration with exciting stories about bandits and wild animals in the forests. When he was finished he gave them some advice: "In China everything is red, even the traffic light's signal for 'go' is red now instead of green. The Red Guards are a very good institution, but still, one shouldn't overdo things."

Later they were shown a textile factory in the neighboring city of Nyangtri, where wool blankets for export were produced on brand new machines from Shanghai. It was Tibet's most modern enterprise, and, like all important production sites, it was under the control of the PLA, although the group was not informed of this. Chetsang Rinpoche was unaware of it at the time, but Chungtsang Rinpoche was working somewhere in this region felling trees for a wood processing factory in the Kongpo area. The workers in the woods and in the factory were all labor camp prisoners working under inhumane conditions. It is not known how many died in the labor camps; many simply disappeared with no record. Once, Chungtsang Rinpoche received a serious head wound from a falling branch and was sent to the very same hospital where the students had given their musical performance. His fellow prisoners were convinced that the only reason he had survived the accident was because of his paranormal abilities and protection as a tulku.

Rinpoche and four others who were in top physical condition went ahead to scout a shortcut over the pass at Serkhyim La, which would have taken some days to cross by following the road. The advance guard began their climb at three in the morning, in a dense forest growing on swampy ground, with rotting wood, brooks, fallen trees, and huge cliffs to hinder them. The forest of gigantic trees crowding around them was so dense they could not make out where the sun was rising when dawn came. The ground became firmer the farther they advanced, but it grew bitterly cold and there were bear tracks in the snow, a disturbing sign. Around midday, three of the party fell behind, but Rinpoche and one other continued on to reach the high pass the next day, several hours before the others. Everyone was exhausted, and starting to find the journey tiresome.

They continued almost entirely by truck through the beautiful landscape of the Rongchu Valley, with its rhododendrons and azaleas. The group spent a few days in Pema, an inhospitable region with no vegetation and plenty of red dust, before continuing on into Kham. The city of Chamdo lies in breathtakingly beautiful surroundings, at the roaring confluence of the Dzachu and the Ngomchu (Mekong), and with a backdrop of panoramic mountain ridges, but the city itself looked ugly and faceless. The students arrived in January 1967 and found accommodations in a state hostel. Young people were continually passing through the city, some on their way to Beijing, others returning from there. Rinpoche and his friends wanted to move on, too, but they needed transportation, so they claimed to be Red Guards on a mission to take part in the patriotic struggle, and after three weeks the authorities gave them a truck to use. Some of the girls decided to stay behind in Chamdo, while about twenty of the others traveled on to Chengdu, the capital of the Chinese province of Sichuan.

The group had intended to go on to Beijing, but Samten, who kept the official letter of recommendation, decided that Chengdu was the end of their trip. He had fallen in love with a girl who had stayed behind in Chamdo, and wanted to go back there as soon as possible, but they spent a little time in Chengdu, which was as a filthy place. The sun never shone and the city was filled with the stench of smoke from low-quality fuel. The streets were congested with crowds of people, all of them continually rushing to somewhere or other. Megaphones blared while units of Red Guards could be seen everywhere, throwing "bourgeois junk"—antique furniture, porcelain, paintings, Western musical instruments, and old statues—out of windows and bullying older people on the streets. They had hung a heavy chandelier around one man's neck and kicked him into the gutter. This was the full-blown Cultural Revolution.

The young Tibetans had recently seen a Chinese propaganda film about the revolutionaries' struggle against the Kuomintang in which a few daring soldiers fight a heroic guerilla war behind enemy lines. Now, in the brutal atmosphere of this alien and ugly city, Rinpoche and his friends imagined themselves as the heroic guerillas with a mission to accomplish. They decided not to speak Chinese under any circumstances, and solemnly swore to stand by anyone in the group who might get into trouble. A large rally was taking place on a city square, and Rinpoche and his companions were determined to march straight through the crowd. They made a game of insulting the Chinese with their rich vocabulary of rude Tibetan such as, "Look out, or we'll switch your ribs from the right to the left side!" The Chinese didn't understand what these tall, sturdy, and self-assured Tibetan youths said, but they felt intimidated and made way for them. The crowd parted, and they marched through. Anyone who refused to make way for them was shoved out of the way or frightened off with a drawn knife.

However, they ran into a group of young Chinese who made fun of them, saying Tibet was primitive and backward and that Tibetans knew nothing of the world. An officer asked them in all seriousness if they had heard of Mao Zedong, but they didn't deign to answer. Another Chinese student asked them if they liked Mao Zedong and Samten finally shouted, "Of course! We became Red Guards because we totally revere him!" He then began to rave about Tibet, about the country's great wealth, all the gold and wonderful things to be found there, and the incredibly beautiful girls. He knew how to impress the Chinese students and promised to introduce the arrogant officer to a very pretty girl from Tibet if he would come to their hostel the next day. When the officer arrived with a few comrades the next morning, Samten began to attack him in the style of a fanatical Red Guard cadre. He screamed Mao quotes at him and accused him of having a capitalist mentality and nothing but bourgeois ideals and girls in his head. The young Chinese officer crumpled under Samten's tirade, finally bowing his head and confessing meekly that he had acted wrongly.

For three weeks the Tibetans amused themselves play-acting in the surrealistic world of a city descending into anarchy. Some of them still hoped to travel on to Beijing; the group was to be issued bus tickets back to Lhasa and they thought they might be able to trade tickets with Chinese students going to Beijing who wished to go to Tibet. But the situation in the city had become so desperate that the PLA had to intervene to prevent complete chaos; people were being arrested on every street corner, and Rinpoche and his companions were all loaded onto buses and sent home by order of the central government.

The trip back to Lhasa took two weeks, and Chetsang Rinpoche's feeling of being in a nightmare intensified. Wherever there were people, there were even more soldiers. The bus was often forced to halt and make long detours over very poor roads because the army had blocked the main road through certain cities. Soldiers seemed to be everywhere: soldiers intimidating crowds, soldiers shouting orders, soldiers marching, soldiers arresting people. So many people were being arrested it was hard to imagine enough prisons and camps to hold them all.

10

The Death of Sanity
Red Guards, Rebels, and Reactionaries

WHILE THE STUDENTS had been traveling, the situation in Tibet had also become critical. Radical members of the faction that had previously attacked Wang Qimei were not content with the fact that the high-ranking functionaries were sacrificing the lower-level cadres to appease the young Red Guards. They singled out General Zhang Guohua as the arch-revisionist who was treating Tibet as if it were his own private kingdom. Zhang had led the attack of the PLA on Tibet in 1950 and later was given the post of first secretary of the Chinese Communist Party's Tibet Committee. On December 22, 1966, about sixty groups joined together, most of them Red Guards from China. They called themselves Gyenlog ("The Rebels") and founded the Lhasa Revolutionary Rebel Central Headquarters. Lower-ranking cadres supported the Gyenlog, who seemed to present an opportunity to overthrow their superiors and rise to leading positions themselves. In early 1967 the opposing group named itself *Nyamdre* ("The Great Alliance") and founded the Great Alliance Rebel Headquarters of the Lhasa Proletarian Revolution. The Nyamdre included those regarded as the conservatives among the Red Guards and was supported by the dominant high-ranking party functionaries and the greater portion of the People's Liberation Army. Now, the split between the Communist Party leadership and the lower ranks in Tibet was complete.

The Gyenlog were strongly represented in Lhasa, while Nyamdre supporters were more numerous in rural areas, with the exception of Nyemo. In January of 1967, violence in Lhasa escalated into a pitched battle between the two factions. Supporters of the Gyenlog stormed the offices of the authorities, ransacked them, and kidnapped the directors. Finally, they sought to have Wang Qimei investigated, since his family had been exposed by Red Guards in Beijing as members of the class of landowners and subjected to struggle sessions. The Rebels wanted him expelled from the party because of his class background. The Gyenlog tried to smuggle in supporters from China but failed because the Nyam-dre controlled the border areas and prevented Red Guards from entering Tibet. But chaos had broken out all over China, and at the end of January 1967 Mao gave the army the order to disband all "counter-revolutionary" organizations. The PLA interpreted this directive as a welcome excuse to brutally crush the Gyenlog, and on February 10, thirteen Gyenlog leaders were arrested.

This was the situation Chetsang Rinpoche and his companions re-turned to; when they arrived in Lhasa from the chaos in Chengdu they found that it, too, was in a state of anarchy. As students of the Middle School they were automatically associated with the Gyenlog. Rinpoche did not dare go out into the street during this period. Most of the stu-dents who had homes returned to them, and only Rinpoche and a few of his friends remained in the school building, with Rinpoche cooking for them. There was not much to do, so he read books from the damp and decaying school library. First he browsed through a thick volume containing the complete resolutions of the General Assembly of the Chi-nese Communist Party, but when he discovered a Chinese biography of the Dalai Lama, he read it thoroughly. The author also wrote extensively about Lhasa's aristocratic families, including the Tsarongs and Tarings, which were judged "Western-oriented" because they had Western fur-niture in their houses and—the Tsarongs especially—had many visitors from the West. Even his parents' beautiful brown wallpaper, differing from the traditional wood paneling, was mentioned in the book. His aunt's Phunkhang family was judged more "Chinese-oriented" because they had only Chinese furniture in their house—but this hadn't pre-vented the Red Guards from paying the Phunkhangs a visit and throw-ing their clay statues of the arhats out the window.

While Rinpoche was holed up in the relative security of the school, the assault against the Gyenlog was halted on the orders of Communist Party officials in Beijing, but the PLA still organized a mass demonstration at the beginning of March to celebrate the "defeat" of the Gyenlog. The Red Guards were sent back to China, although with a parade; the local party leadership purged many cadres who had sympathized with the rebel faction; and the ringleaders of the Gyenlog were subjected to vicious struggle sessions.

But in April the Military Affairs Committee issued a directive that the PLA was to restrict itself to political work and the Gyenlog began to regroup. They set up a faction using the name the Provisional Command Post of Rebel General Headquarters.

After Zhang Guohua had been transferred to Sichuan, Zhou Renshan became acting first secretary of the regional party committee, and the first Red Guards began returning from China in May to complete the Great Proletarian Cultural Revolution. The regional party committee recognized both factions, the Nyamdre and the Gyenlog, as "revolutionary mass movements" with basically correct ideological outlooks. Two factions had also arisen within the military as a result of a power struggle between Zeng Yongya, the new acting commander of the Tibet Military Region, and Ren Rong, the top political commissar of the armed forces in Tibet. When Zhang Guohua had unexpectedly sided with the Gyenlog, Zeng Yongya allied himself with them as well, planning to overthrow Wang Qimei and then to "rehabilitate" the members of the Gyenlog. Ren Rong, on the other hand, announced his support for the Nyamdre.

Although both were now authorized, the factions continued to compete for public support. This new competition was waged primarily through the airwaves, rather than on the walls, of Lhasa. The Gyenlog took over the Tsuglagkhang (Jokhang) and set up a propaganda broadcast station in the temple, with loudspeakers placed on the roof and professional announcers continually broadcasting slogans all day, every day. Most of the temple's rooms were locked and sealed, but the broadcasters were able to install their technical equipment in a former audience hall of the Dalai Lama. Chetsang Rinpoche and other students from the Middle School were commandeered to protect the broadcast station, and guards were also recruited from the Teacher Training School and the Military Cadre School. The Jokhang became their new home, and they spent their days and nights in the temple. About fifty guards had moved into a large hall on the third floor, next to the room with the technical equipment, and with everyone all together in one room, without clean clothes or washing facilities, the stench was overpowering. Rinpoche used to creep into a large wardrobe to sleep, trying to get away from the disgusting odor. He had to curl up to fit inside.

The Nyamdre's broadcast station was further to the east, and it also continuously filled the air with high-volume propaganda, screeching, and crackling. The constant cacophony prevented any peace or stillness in people's minds, no matter where they were in the city. The Gyenlog had only one monstrous old amplifier and urgently needed additional equipment to compete more effectively. One day, three very young Chinese students from a school in the eastern part of the city, which was firmly under Nyamdre control, came to the Tsuglagkhang. Rinpoche struck up a conversation with them and they told him that they were the sole supporters of the Gyenlog in their school, and they wanted to supply some secret information. The Nyamdre were getting ready to move their broadcast station, and their apparatus was now in a certain school guarded by only eighteen of their people.

Rinpoche and his companions began discussing plans to seize their opponents' amplifier, and finally agreed upon Rinpoche's suggestion. They would sneak into the enemy camp at three in the morning, when everyone was fast asleep, and post one of their powerful Khampa comrades, armed with a club, spear, or dagger, next to each sleeper. Their task would be to keep their adversaries at bay in case they awoke. Others would protect their escape route, a lookout was to be posted at every corner to warn of danger, and Rinpoche himself would carry off the machine.

They decided to do it that night, and at two in the morning they arrived in the vicinity of their target. All of the details the Chinese boys had given them were accurate. Rinpoche and his team posted their lookouts in the school's great courtyard and waited in the shadows, because a light was still burning in the main building. An older Chinese man opened the door and tossed water from a bowl; it was a Chinese custom to wash one's feet before going to bed, so Rinpoche's group expected the last residents would at that point go to sleep, and the light was then, in fact, extinguished. After a while, they ran swiftly and silently, one after the other, across the great courtyard and, finding the door locked, tried the windows until they discovered one that was open. The Khampas instantly took their positions next to the sleeping Nyamdre and Rinpoche began disconnecting the amplifier, with a tough Khampa named Lodrö, one of his closest friends, standing watch behind him. The amplifier was connected to a multitude of cables and made noise at every movement, and one of the nearby sleepers turned over. Lodrö immediately leaped over to him, prepared to strike him down with a club if he awoke, but he continued to sleep. Once Rinpoche had finally detached all the cables, he and Lodrö lifted the amplifier and carried it through the rows of unsuspecting sleepers and then across the city to the Gyenlog station.

They now had a second amplifier, but no additional loudspeakers. Rinpoche and his friends decided to get some Nyamdre loudspeakers from the roof of a large building that was used as a movie theater and meeting hall. They decided to carry out this particular special operation on their own, without consulting with the whole Gyenlog organization, since it seemed fairly simple. It would be easy to use the iron grating on the rear side of the hall to climb onto the roof; the real danger was in approaching and leaving the hall, as the entire area was in the hands of the Nyamdre, whose headquarters was close by.

They decided to strike that night, as before. A few of their group of twenty-three were chosen to be lookouts, five were selected to bring the loudspeakers down from the roof, and one boy who would go ahead of them holding a Nyamdre flag—if they were challenged he would say that they were Nyamdre on their way to headquarters. The others were to follow him one after the other, each at a distance of about twenty meters, so that they would not be identified as belonging together; Rinpoche was among the last in the rear guard. The occasional Nyamdre guards they passed by on their way did not challenge them, although a few began to shoot rocks from slingshots at the rear guard without pursuing them. The Gyenlogs knew, however, that once they had the speakers they wouldn't be able to return the way they had come. When the first group went up on the roof, those following behind decided to run the few hundred meters further to the Gyenlog headquarters to get reinforcements. At first the leaders were angry at their having gone it alone, but they quickly decided to help. The first group had seized the loudspeakers by the time the reinforcements arrived, and the large group carried them off quickly, before the Nyamdre had time to organize their pursuit.

The Nyamdre soon retaliated with a vengeance. On the evening of July 14, 1967, a convoy of trucks rolled up to the Jokhang in a mighty cloud of dust, and vehicles closed in on the temple from all sides. The Nyamdre had mobilized their supporters in the surrounding villages to storm the Jokhang broadcast station. The attack was not entirely unexpected, as the situation had escalated, with numerous skirmishes in the past few days. The strongest of the Gyenlog were posted on the roof to repel the attackers' ladders, while the others hastily barricaded the doors and passageways inside the Jokhang. There were two entrances to their third floor area, one directly at the staircase, and the defenders threw all pieces of furniture, wood paneling, reading tables, benches and everything else that was to be found in the rooms down the stairs to block it. Rinpoche was busy trying to secure the second entrance when he heard the attackers on the other side battering the door. His companions jammed a large ornamental lintel and planks against the entrance and pressed their own weight against it. A unit of firefighters working with the Nyamdre succeeded in chopping openings in the barricade, and spears were shoved through the slits; one of Rinpoche's friends lost an eye in this attack. The Gyenlog defended their quarters valiantly throughout the night, but when insecticide was sprayed through the holes slashed in the door some of the defenders became dizzy and others doubled over with convulsions; they had to withdraw immediately.

Meanwhile, a large floodlight had been placed on a house across the street to illuminate the defenders on the roof of the Jokhang. A barrage of hundreds of stones forced them to take cover, and the firefighters were able to place their ladders. The besiegers overpowered the Gyenlog on the roof, and while Rinpoche's group was still trying to defend the doorway and protect themselves from the noxious chemicals being sprayed inside, their opponents broke through the roof entrance and started thrashing them from behind. Now there was no escape. Tremendous confusion and little visibility prevailed in the darkness full of dust, filth, and sweat. Some defenders had the wits to destroy the technical equipment before it fell into enemy hands. One of Rinpoche's friends suggested they jump out the window, but such an attempt to escape seemed much more dangerous than staying and waiting to see what would happen. His friend dashed to the window and jumped the three storeys down. Hopelessly outnumbered, the Gyenlog accepted defeat and were driven out, stumbling over broken objects and wounded people lying contorted in pain on the ground. Everyone was covered with filth and blood, and thousands of people were waiting in the streets to beat them. A few Chinese Red Guards from Qinghua University were with the defenders in the Jokhang, and the mob saved its greatest fury for them, beating them mercilessly.

A young Muslim with whom he had played soccer recognized Rinpoche and reproached him, "You're a lama, what are you doing here? Why are you mixed up in something like this?" Rinpoche answered, "I came to protect our equipment." The Muslim slapped his face and shoved him into a group of onlookers. Fortunately, Chetsang Rinpoche was never injured, not even in the fiercest battles, and he had the remarkable gift of feeling very little pain from external wounds.

Rinpoche and his schoolmates were herded into a bus and driven to Nyamdre headquarters. The young men felt strong and fearless, and above all, furious. They briefly considered overpowering the driver and the three Nyamdre guards and taking control of the bus, but there would still be no escape from the crowds of people in the streets. Stones flew when they got off the bus and were led into the Nyamdre building, and one tall Chinese man standing in front of the entrance struck each of them as they passed.

The Nyamdre building was filled with people. The Chinese Red Guards were shoved into a small room and Rinpoche could hear the blows and screams of a terrible beating. The students of the Middle School took care not to be separated, because those who could be singled out were led off and bludgeoned. At dawn the Nyamdre called an assembly in the courtyard. Wang Qimei appeared, and an army officer, obviously a supporter of the Gyenlog, was put up on a small platform, his arms twisted behind him, and his head yanked back. In this position he was forced to endure a *thamzing*, or struggle session, while Rinpoche and the other Gyenlog captives watched from a window and shouted encouragement to him. Soon afterward, they were released. The early morning light revealed swollen faces, dried blood, and bruised bodies. They were so filthy and badly battered they had trouble recognizing each other, but they were still alive. Rinpoche had lost a shoe and was covered with dirt, but otherwise he was fine.

Some time later there was a major gathering in the movie theater where they had stolen the loudspeakers. As thousands of Gyenlog supporters were assembling, including the students from the Middle School, several trucks drove up, and the members of an especially combative Gyenlog unit jumped onto the truck beds. Called the "Lhasa City Development Workers," they were a crew of young street fighters, boys and girls alike, and included many *Lama Gyupa,* former monks from the monastic universities of Sera and Drepung. Rinpoche's friend Lodrö was excited and wanted to join them, so they both sprang onto a truck. A Gyenlog truck had been seized north of Lhasa and their comrades had to be rescued from a large automobile-parts factory in Drapchi.

In front of the factory was a courtyard with a row of houses and shops and a soccer field. When the Gyenlog trucks arrived they could see an army convoy of about twenty trucks approaching in the distance. During this phase of the Cultural Revolution, the PLA was instructed not to participate in conflicts; the unarmed soldiers were only supposed to try to prevent fights and keep the hostility between the factions from escalating. The PLA trucks were still far enough away that, if the Gyenlog acted quickly, they would be able to attack and succeed in their mission to free their friends. The large contingent of several hundred Lama Gyupa with their homemade spears took up position in the rear, while the rest of the Gyenlog ran across the soccer field with their slingshots ready; the girls collected stones along the way to provide the boys with ammunition. A handful of Nyamdre appeared and began slinging stones at them, but Lodrö and Rinpoche, who were in the front ranks of the Gyenlog attackers, told their companions to wait to return fire until they were closer. Vastly outnumbering their opponents, they simply marched on toward the Nyamdre, waiting until they were very close to let loose a barrage of stones. The assaulted Nyamdre fled with the Gyenlog right on their heels, and the Lama Gyupa began to advance from behind them.

Some Chinese Nyamdre in a lookout post on the roof of one of the shops began slinging rocks at the attackers as they entered the courtyard. Since most of the Gyenlog group were Tibetans who spoke no Chinese, it was Rinpoche who called to them, "Give up, you're surrounded!" But they ignored him and continued to hurl stones down on the attackers. The courtyard was paved with gravel, ideal ammunition for the Gyenlog slingshots.When hundreds of stones hit the roof, some Nyamdre fell wounded, and the rest of the intimidated defenders climbed down. Many Gyenlog had already forced their way into the factory and were freeing their comrades and taking the Chinese Red Guards as prisoners. The PLA arrived and bore off the wounded but otherwise let events take their course.

The street battles with slingshots continued over a period of about five months, and the students of the Middle School were summoned to defend the Gyenlog more and more often. They collected stones on the banks of the canal in front of the school building, while stones were being hurled at them from the direction of the Potala. Rinpoche had a spear that he had picked up somewhere, and once he hit the spear of an opponent exactly on the tip, making sparks fly, and at almost the exact same moment, a stone also hit the tip of his spear. Rinpoche reflected on the strange conjunction of forces in that moment, reminded of things he had learned long ago, in an almost forgotten world.

There were numerous armed conflicts between the Gyenlog and the Nyamdre from May to the end of 1967, and chaos ruled everywhere in the country as the Red Guards were allowed to oust party cadres and take over their positions. The situation had become so uncontrollable that in autumn of 1967, Mao Zedong declared that he wished to conclude the Cultural Revolution within the year. But the madness that he had conjured up could not be so easily banned, and he was unable to check this tidal wave. On September 18, Zhou Enlai, Chen Boda, and other party leaders issued a directive that the factional fighting in Tibet was to stop, but in October, the confrontations between the Gyenlog and the Nyamdre grew even more violent.

Those days most young men had nothing but revolution on their minds, and there was no one to help the elderly school stablemen harvest the school's fields, so Rinpoche was asked for help. The stablemen knew him, and they had become friends, since Rinpoche had been commandeered to work in the fields twice before, on account of his class background.

For Rinpoche, this request was a stroke of good luck, because the fighting between the hostile factions had gone beyond spears and slingshots and escalated to automatic weapons. He persuaded two friends to join him and they left the increasingly deadly battlegrounds of the city.

The school's fields lay alongside the Kyichu River in Lamo (Tsangtok), between Lhasa and Medrogungkar. There were no accommodations in Lamo, so they had to sleep in a deep hole they had dug and lined with grass, blankets and jackets. Over it they placed a primitive wooden frame covered with a cloth and then a coarse tarpaulin to keep out water.

The work was not very hard. They had six mules, and if they were tired they simply stopped, as no one was there to supervise them. Lamo was an isolated spot, far from any settlement, and there, by the peaceful rushing of the river, it was easy to forget the slaughter taking place in the city. They cooked over a campfire and slept soundly in the quiet countryside.

The harvest took three months, and by the time they returned to the city, the most ferocious battles had all been fought and Lhasa looked like a war zone. There were many dead and wounded on both sides. The PLA had secretly supplied the Nyamdre with weapons, including machine guns and grenades, by transferring them at the cinema. After the films the soldiers "forgot" their weapons in the dark theater, and the Nyamdre came in and picked them up. PLA members also took off their uniforms to secretly train Red Guards, and to fight themselves, on the side of the Nyamdre.

Beijing had ordered the military to remain neutral in the Cultural Revolution, but there were also two factions within the PLA itself, and this was the main reason the fighting continued in Tibet. The Regiment of the City of Lhasa sided with the Nyamdre, while the Eleventh Brigade, a unit of the border patrol stationed outside Lhasa, supported the Gyenlog. The soldiers of the border patrol were more powerful because they were under the direct command of the central government in Beijing, and they despised their comrades from the Lhasa Regiment. In June 1968, after the Gyenlog returned to occupy their quarters in the Jokhang, the temple was stormed again, this time in fact by the PLA with assault rifles, in a bloodbath that left many dead and seriously wounded, and that would go down in history as the "June 7 massacre."

After returning from the countryside, Chetsang Rinpoche moved back to the Middle School and cooked for his remaining schoolmates. Everyone brought food so that he could make a good meal for the wounded comrades in the clinic. Rinpoche had to take it to them himself, though, which nearly cost him his life. The Nyamdre and a number of soldiers armed with automatic weapons had taken up positions on the walls of the Potala Palace, and they fired on anyone in the vicinity who was incautious enough to move into the open. To reach the clinic, Rinpoche had to pass the rear of the Potala, but he managed to arrive at the hospital thanks to his agility as well as his luck. The rooms were filled to capacity with the wounded. Medicine was in short supply, and many were lying in agony. His school comrades, some of them badly injured, were very happy to see him and to finally eat a good meal. One was a particularly timid student who had never left the school building, always finding excuses to stay inside. He had finally dared to go to the Gyenlog headquarters, where his comrades teased him, "Congratulations, you made it!" On the way back to the school he wasn't so lucky and was hit by a bullet fired from the Potala.

Rinpoche spent time with each of the group in the clinic, telling stories and trying to cheer them up, and he promised to bring food again soon. On the way back he stopped by the headquarters, and then set off for the school with a handful of his comrades. All of a sudden they were being fired on and took cover behind trees, dashing from one to the next. One young boy suddenly stopped and ran back from an especially heavy hail of bullets, and Rinpoche, who was right behind him, was forced to stop as well. He heard a piercing whistle as a bullet passed his ear, missing his head only by a fraction. Though still in shock from the close call, he finally reached the safety of the school walls.

Even this incident didn't keep him from taking food to the hospital. On one of these excursions he met a group of Gyenlog carrying homemade hand grenades and two air rifles. Rinpoche met up with them just as a lone army truck carrying bricks turned onto the deserted street, and they decided to hijack it so that they would not be fired on from the Potala. They planted themselves in front of the approaching vehicle with their rifles pointed and hand grenades at the ready, the truck stopped, and they climbed up onto the load of bricks it was carrying. They hoped that observers would think that they were road workers going to work. They weren't sure whether the driver would obey their instructions and take them to the clinic or turn off and drive to the part of town controlled by the Nyamdre, so one of the riders knocked vehemently on the window twenty meters before the critical turn. The driver was startled and slammed on the brakes so the truck screeched to a halt in the middle of the road. Alarmed by the noise, the snipers on the Potala immediately opened fire with their army-issued assault rifles.

There was a mad scramble to jump down from the load of bricks, which wasn't easy because the bricks were stacked very high and the Gyenlog got in each other's way. Two men in front of Rinpoche blocked his way, and someone was pushing him from behind, as bullets flew past their ears. Rinpoche was shoved down by a blow from behind, and just where he had stood a second before, the bricks were shot full of holes. He took a leap into the roadside ditch and watched as some of the group ran away, fell down, jumped up again, took cover, and otherwise tried to elude the bursts of bullets. Rinpoche did not move from his hiding place until silence returned. The snipers evidently assumed everyone had fled because no one shot at him as he ran to the clinic. The Gyenlog had been lucky this time—none of the men had been hit and the medics waiting for them at the clinic entrance had only scrapes and bruises to treat.

In early 1968, the fighting between the rival factions began to die down in most of China, but in Tibet the conflicts continued. Two new PLA divisions were dispatched into the country to contain the fighting and the army took over the schools; students were now given paramilitary training instead of instruction in school subjects. The students of the Middle School were drilled like army recruits, and PLA troops were posted in every classroom and every dormitory. Senior students and Red Guards were trained in close-combat techniques with fixed bayonets, while Rinpoche and his classmates were mostly drilled in marching and standing at attention.

Once, the entire student body was summoned to witness an execution. It began with a rally to inform the crowd of the crimes of the delinquents, one Tibetan and one Chinese. The Tibetan was a former monk accused of being the ringleader of a network of imperialist spies and the Chinese man was charged with having smuggled watches. They were paraded before the Jokhang, the Tibetan ceaselessly repeating the Dalai Lama's name. The guards brutally pounded the Tibetan's head against a stone wall, and blood streamed over his face and dripped from his fingers. Distressed, Rinpoche and his friends slipped away into the crowd and headed back toward the school. Just before they arrived, they saw a small group of people next to a truck and ran over to see what was happening. They pushed their way to the front and were horrified to discover that the condemned men had been brought there, a mere stone's throw from the school, to be executed; the two men were dragged from the truck to a wall and summarily shot. The crowd immediately began to push and shove forward, and Rinpoche, standing in the front, was only able to keep himself from being toppled onto the dead bodies by making a desperate leap over them. After this experience, he fell into a depression and could not eat for days.

On September 5, 1968, a Revolutionary Committee was set up in Tibet, the last region under Chinese control to receive one. The Revolutionary Committees were to be a three-way alliance between the army, civil cadres, and workers, and the previous party functionaries and military commanders were removed from power. Wang Qimei was neutralized and Zhou Renshan committed suicide. The Revolutionary Committee was supposed to officially end the fighting between the Gyenlog and the Nyamdre, but resentments simmered.

In October 1968 Mao finally succeeded in removing his rival Liu Shaoqi from power and expelling him from the Communist Party, and in spring of 1969 Mao had the PLA disarm and dissolve the Red Guards. The rabid young students had saved Mao from losing his grip on power, but now they had become a liability. They were to be dispersed, sent to the countryside in order to thoroughly purify their old modes of thinking through physical labor. Fields and livestock had been neglected during the years of intense factional fighting, and agricultural production had reached its nadir. The students and Red Guards would now be more useful as agricultural laborers than as cultural revolutionaries. They were sent to remote regions to purge and renew their minds, but the city youths disdained the dirt-covered peasants and their miserable living conditions, and saw their exile as an undeserved punishment. Many were unable to cope with the unfamiliar circumstances, the harsh living conditions, and the brutally hard work.

Rinpoche and a few of his classmates were fortunate enough to be sent to communal labor camps in the district of Thölung, about thirty minutes by bus to the west of Lhasa. Rinpoche's closest friends wanted to keep the group together to protect their "Middle School Lama," afraid that he would be badly treated on account of his class background. They succeeded, and the group of six young men set off to their work brigades and production teams in the Thong Ga Commune of Thölung, consisting of four villages and their subcommunes.

Rinpoche and one of his schoolmates were assigned to the production team of the People's Commune. The other four were divided up between two other communes. The director was a high-ranking party functionary, and each work team was led by a village headman. Rinpoche shared a small room in a modest building with his companion; each had been given a cup and a cooking pot, and nothing more. Except for the local authorities, no one in his new surroundings knew that he was the Drikung Kyabgön Rinpoche. He rose before dawn, cleaned the stables and fed the animals, and then went to work in the fields until late in the evening. He walked twenty minutes to fetch water from a stream, carrying it in a large canister strapped to his back. Now and then he had to attend commune meetings. The villagers were generally fearful of informers, and therefore suspicious of the cadres and all other outsiders, but they felt comfortable and safe with Rinpoche. He was ready to help whenever he could, and right from the beginning he was esteemed by both the peasants and the leadership, who all trusted him and treated him with natural, spontaneous respect.

Rinpoche had been in Thong Ga only a few months when the wife of the village headman was about to give birth. The headman asked Rinpoche to accompany them to Lhasa since his wife was no longer young, and the delivery was not without dangers. When they arrived in Lhasa, the village headman called on a friend who worked for the newspaper to ask if he knew of a good doctor. The journalist made a quick phone call and gave him a name, and then apologized for not having any more time that day, because Ani Thrinle Chödrön was being brought to Lhasa for her execution. All captured rebels who had been fighting Chinese rule guerilla-style along with her were to be executed simultaneously the next day in Lhasa, Lhokha, Nagchu, and Chamdo. The journalist himself had to go to Lhokha to photograph the execution.

Thrinle Chödrön was a legendary figure of mythic proportions. Although she was a nun (*ani*), in June 1969 she and a band of followers had murdered fourteen cadres and soldiers of the PLA propaganda team in Nyemo, dispatching their victims with appalling brutality; they had burned a few Chinese alive, and had amputated the arms or legs of others.

In the beginning the party had viewed the actions of Thrinle Chödrön's group as "normal" excesses of the Cultural Revolution's work to purge the party leadership of reactionary elements. In fact, the group's true motivations were entirely different. Under the cloak of the officially sanctioned Cultural Revolution, Thrinle Chödrön's rebellion was directed at the occupiers in general, and was developing into a national uprising. She gathered hundreds of supporters in a very short time, rapidly won over eighteen districts, and her support among the general population continued to increase as the revolt took on the form of a millenarian uprising.

Everywhere, bands of Tibetan nationalists began to hunt down Chinese cadres and their Tibetan supporters. In Chamdo, they had cornered a former Tibetan student from Rinpoche's Middle School who was working in the local administration. The murderous crew had already stabbed all of the local officials to death when they trapped him in the storage room where he was trying to hide. In desperation he recited the six-syllable mantra of Chenrezig, and the band spared him. (He faced more difficulties, though, when the army arrived and forced him to explain why he alone had been spared.)

By the time the Chinese finally understood the true aim of the firestorm Thrinle Chödrön sparked, it was almost too late. Ani Thrinle Chödrön had become legend, and there was a rumor that she was possessed by a local protector deity and had magical powers. She was believed to be invulnerable, and stories were told about how she had been put in prison and had escaped by supernatural means. In the end, strong military units were sent to Nyemo and other districts to crush the revolt and she fled to the mountains to continue the guerilla war, but eventually Thrinle Chödrön and fifteen of her followers were captured. Tibet had been on the brink of a nationwide uprising such as the one in 1959, and most people in Lhasa were genuinely surprised at the news of her capture—having needed so desperately to believe in an invincible savior.

On the next day, Chetsang Rinpoche rode to the stadium on a bicycle he had borrowed from some relatives. While the terrible deeds of Thrinle Chödrön and her followers were described in detail over loudspeakers, the newest weapons of the PLA were paraded before the audience: brand-new machine guns and an unimaginably long cannon on a specially built transport vehicle with gigantic wheels that rolled slowly past the astonished crowd. Rinpoche wondered how the Chinese had succeeded in bringing this monstrosity to Tibet without causing a great stir among the Tibetans. The message was clear: you are helpless against an arsenal like this, even with magical abilities. Then the sixteen bound prisoners were driven into the stadium on open-bed trucks and the convoy passed by where Rinpoche was sitting, so he had a good view of their faces. Thrinle Chödrön was looking straight ahead, steadfast and fearless. She reminded him of the heroines portrayed on Chinese Communist propaganda posters, with their proudly resolute poses, utterly determined and seeming to glow from within. Three elderly Tibetan women near him spat at her and pelted her with refuse but Thrinle Chödrön remained unmoved.

The rebels were then driven out of the city to an open space below the cemetery of Drepung. When Rinpoche arrived on his bicycle his view was blocked by trucks full of spectators, but one of the trucks was equipped with a crane on which only one man was sitting. Rinpoche climbed up to join him, high above the huge crowd of civilians and the even greater number of PLA soldiers with heavy artillery. Anti-aircraft guns were pointed at the heavens, as if they were about to be attacked by air. The excessive display of threatening weaponry and the theatrical staging of troops seemed absurd to Rinpoche, like the backdrops and extras in a propaganda film. Then the prisoners were thrown from the trucks, kicked to make them stand up again, and ordered to run. The firing squad lined up and a soldier gave the signal to fire. The crowd surged forward to see the victims and the army almost lost control. Photographers pushed their way through the chaos and took pictures of the sixteen bodies, which were then buried on the spot without ceremony. Rinpoche had climbed down from the crane with shaking knees when two soldiers dragged a young man with a shaved head over to a vehicle, threw him roughly into the back, and drove off with him. Pulled out of his distress by this reminder of the constant need for caution, he hastily left the scene of brutal horror and was relieved when he got back to his room in Thong Ga.

Rinpoche was young and strong and took on the hardest work himself. When the spring labor in the fields was done, he went with three other young men from the People's Commune to procure firewood for the peasants. Wood was scarce in the immediate vicinity, and it was a fourteen-hour trip to where the wood was collected. They started off early and completed the journey in a day, although it should have been a two-day trip. Each man led five donkeys, and on their way out they could at least ride the donkeys.

The strongest donkeys were unruly and stubborn, so his companions only rode on the smaller animals, but Rinpoche did not wish to take advantage of the weaker animals. He tied one hand fast to the saddle and mounted one of the powerful, fractious donkeys that periodically kicked and bucked until its rider was thrown off. But Rinpoche always remounted and tied up his hand even more tightly, riding only the wildest donkeys.

The four young men would reach their destination after dusk. Early the next morning, they left the animals grazing at the campsite, and with long heavy ropes on their backs they climbed the steep mountain flank. In a clearing where the slope was less steep, they laid out their ropes according to a certain system, cut the willow branches with large sickles, packed the branches together in thick, tightly bundled rolls, and sent them flying down the slope with powerful thrusts. The bundles that got stuck in the brush had to be retrieved and rolled down further. Rinpoche could not keep up with his more experienced companions, who could chop off the branches with astonishing speed. In about three or four hours they had tied all their loads into bundles and sent them rolling, and on their own way down they collected dry wood to make a fire for tea. Rinpoche always took longer, finishing the load for his last donkey while the others were already down below, and his companions were usually done with their midday meal by the time he joined them in camp. After their break, they loaded up the donkeys and walked to a village where they spent the night. Thanks to their speedy work they had the next day off; the donkeys grazed the entire day, and Rinpoche and his companions rested up for the difficult return journey, which would be all on foot, ahead of them.

One summer, they went to gather wood from a mountain directly above the monastery of Tsurphu, the main seat of the Karma Kagyupa, and Rinpoche was curious to see what had become of the monastery. He climbed to the summit, from which he could see the monastery, or what was left of it, standing in a field of green grass before a bare mountain slope on the other side. Although it was quite far away, Rinpoche could make out the red and yellow of the wall paintings on the inside of the remains of the walls. For the most part, the rafters and pillars had been dismantled and carried off, causing many of the walls to collapse. On his excursions with the donkeys, Rinpoche occasionally encountered teams of workers carrying long wooden beams that they had dismantled from Tsurphu Monastery to the district capital, to be used for new buildings. Ten men, each shouldering one mighty beam, walked in step to marching songs to ease the transport of their heavy loads.

One time Rinpoche lodged in a house near Ganden Monastery. All of the wood in this house—beams, pillars, doors, and paneling—had come from the monastery, which the local population had completely stripped for use in building houses for themselves. The truly tragic aspect of these events was the fact that Tibetans themselves were the instruments of destruction, although only a few did so freely. In some cases, Chinese propaganda had done its work subtly and with astonishing efficiency, while in others the threat of being subjected to inhumane tribunals—or worse, torture and labor camps—compelled them.

The final truth taught in Tibet's great historic monastic centers was the Buddhist principle that all things arise through causes and conditions, change, and decay in an endless process of transmutation. Some venerable temples had endured for centuries, and all had been expected to endure centuries more, but first they were plundered by the invaders, and everything of value was carried off. Then they were ravaged by the fanatical hordes and terrorized Tibetan accomplices of the Cultural Revolution. As the numerous buildings of the sprawling monastery complexes, some as large as entire cities, stood empty and abandoned without maintenance, they finally fell into decay. No longer treasure-houses of ritual practice and sacred artifacts, the crumbling edifices were now only masses of building materials, and many thought it would be better to take away whatever material was still undamaged and put it to use. When the Tibetans removed the wooden beams from the monasteries, the buildings slowly began to collapse. Buddhist rituals continually refer to this basic process of all existence, the rhythm of creation and dissolution, as when the exquisite mandalas so painstakingly produced with fine particles of colored sand are swept away by the tantric master at the ritual's conclusion.

Thus, over the course of time, monasteries in settled areas completely disappeared from the landscape, and other edifices appeared in their place. The new town of Drikung Qu was constructed on the ruins of the Drikung philosophy school Nyima Changra. Today, a Chinese military camp is located where Yangrigar once stood. Part of a wall of the monastery was spared for a long time, though, as it was regarded as the dwelling place of Achi, the Drikung protector deity, and unexplained deaths occurred among the construction workers involved in the demolition of the building.

Chetsang Rinpoche was an attractive, athletic young man. At meetings of the commune, girls made a point of sitting near him, casting meaningful glances in his direction and engaging him in conversation. He was courteous and cracked jokes, but that was the extent of his interest. His roommate, on the other hand, got married, and Rinpoche had to move into smaller and shabbier lodgings, a run-down storage room with two tiny windows in the upper part of a house where two families were already living. A hill rose at the back, and directly under his room was a sheep pen with a circular roof. Rinpoche closed off the inner door and enlarged one of the windows into a door to the outside so he could enter and leave by way of the roof of the sheep pen, and not have to go through the families' private rooms.

To cook in his dismal chamber he had to make an opening high up in the wall for a smoke-hole. Rinpoche used bricks to make a three-part cooking area; in the middle was an aperture for a large cooking pot, and on each side of this a hole for a smaller one. He placed a stone slab over the openings when he needed a work surface for preparing his meals, and old iron grates served as shelves for his utensils. By this time Rinpoche had acquired two pots, two thermos bottles, and two enamel cups, and had made a ladle by nailing a tin can to a piece of wood. He bought dried yak-dung fuel from nomads who lived a two-day journey from the commune, and stacked his year's supply of yak-dung in a corner behind the door. His furniture consisted of a small table, a battered wooden chest for his clothing, and a bed that was nothing more than a frame, with huge holes in the rotten planks of the base. Rinpoche filled them with flat stones, rags and old shoes, and covered everything with a mattress of yak-hair that Tritsab Rinpoche had given him.

The walls were old, crumbling, and damp, and the house was full of strange insects, but none of this bothered Rinpoche. One frosty winter evening he returned after a hard day's work, lit a fire, pulled a Chinese cotton coat over his shoulders, and leaned against the cold wall to relax. Then he noticed that something very cold was crawling underneath his clothing, down his neck, and onto his arm. He took off his coat very slowly and found a large black scorpion perched on his forearm. What astonished Rinpoche most was how cold the scorpion felt, but he remained completely calm, knowing he must not touch or alarm it. With quiet interest he observed its bizarre form, waited until the arachnid had reached his hand, and then shook it off. The animal came right back to him, but Rinpoche stayed composed, reminding himself that this was an old house and that there was no way to expel the creatures that had taken shelter in it. They would come, and go.

Chetsang Rinpoche's residence had changed many times over: his parents' magnificent manor house, surrounded by devoted servants; his monastery chambers, anxiously attended to and shielded from the ordinary world; his existence as an urban nomad at Tritsab Rinpoche's side in Lhasa; the dormitory of the Middle School; this humble solitary room in a ramshackle building in an agricultural commune. When he thought about it, though, he realized he had been a nomad all his life, since even in Drikung he had changed his quarters every couple of months, with frequent pilgrimages and visits to other monasteries. Seen in this light, the other nomads seemed to have a more stable lot. They changed locations, but not their homes.

A series of small hydroelectric power plants was being built to the west of Lhasa, one of the plants in the Thölung district. The authorities called on officials and public employees to dig a canal for it "voluntarily"—although anyone who shirked would forfeit his career—and without pay, as a service to the country. Among those who came to Thong Ga to help dig the canal was Rinpoche's uncle, Tsering Döndrup Phunkhang. When Phunkhang saw his nephew's desolate quarters he struggled against his tears, stunned that his nephew was living in such squalor. He shook his head sadly, but then became aware of Rinpoche's perfect equanimity and serene smile, and said, "Milarepa lived in comfortless caves and it looks to me as though you are living just the way he did." Rinpoche hardly knew what he meant because he had heard practically nothing about Milarepa, Tibet's legendary Buddhist yogi. The name lit only a tiny glimmer of memory from the long-ago days of his childhood in Drikung.

When a directive to eradicate the *abra* (black-lipped pika, or *Ochotona curzoniae*) was issued, a large-scale extermination was organized in the commune. The Chinese regarded the animals as disease carriers and wrongly blamed them for the worsening condition of the soil. The area was full of abras, and the numerous holes they dug for their burrows were a nuisance for the nomads' horses. All of the workers were ordered to form a chain from the river to the slope of one of the mountains and pour a mixture of barley and poison from a can into each burrow. Rinpoche's can held only barley; he had managed to avoid adding any poison.

Rinpoche had no time for religious practice, nor did he have any texts or ritual objects. But he often performed a tea offering, recited mantras, and began to refresh his memory of the sacred texts he had learned by heart, although he didn't think that the Tibetans would ever be granted religious freedom or that he would return to monastery life. Chetsang Rinpoche's aunt and his cousin Jigme came to visit him one summer and innocently inquired in the village as to his whereabouts, asking for the Drikung tulku. The young people did not know what they were talking about, but the older villagers' eyes shone when they learned that the Drikung Kyabgön Rinpoche was living in their midst. They wanted to know where he was, and if they could see him.

In winter Rinpoche took large loads of hay to Lhasa on a horse-drawn wagon. In exchange he was to bring human manure back for the farm. In Lhasa the courtyards had large latrines that were shared by a dozen or so families. Usually the Tibetans threw ashes from their ovens onto the sewage, to neutralize the odor and soak up moisture, but now there were hardly any ashes and the cesspools were very wet. Rinpoche had to climb down into the pits, shovel the muck into large sacks and heave them onto the wagon. He transported the manure back to the commune, where the villagers added waste from their own latrines to it. The mixture was left to ferment for a few weeks, and then Rinpoche had to climb up onto the gigantic steaming heap and turn it over with a shovel or pitchfork. In spring he loaded up the donkeys with the fertilizer and spread it over the fields.

His physical appearance began to change after a few years of this hard labor, and it seemed to him as though his youth slipped away from him. In his glory days as a soccer player, he had been very fast, nimble, and agile but no longer. Nor was he as flexible as he had been, and his sense of balance had deteriorated. Rinpoche's muscles had stiffened, mostly from carrying heavy loads, especially the wood used for making tsampa.

A particular kind of thorny wood that burned with a very hot flame but was exceptionally difficult to obtain was used to roast the barley. In the region around Thölung the wood grew only in the north, on a mountain near Yangpachen where dangerously strong winds arose in the afternoons. The thorny wood was harvested in two-person teams, and Rinpoche would set off with the strongest man from the commune, starting up a steep path at three in the morning. Wearing thick gloves to protect them against the thorns, the two men cut the long branches into smaller pieces and tied the bundles in a special way to keep them balanced during the descent. The bundles could not always be rolled downhill, they often had to be shouldered and cautiously carried past high cliffs and across stretches of stone and gravel, where they would otherwise start an avalanche and endanger those working down-slope. Carrying these heavy loads on the steep slopes was especially hard on Rinpoche's knees.

Once Rinpoche was late and the afternoon winds were beginning to rise. He tied everything into a single large bundle that weighed eighty to ninety kilograms, heaved it onto his back, and began his descent. Lifting the bundle back onto his back each time he stumbled or lost his balance was a torment, and he slipped under the load several times, falling into the thorny brambles. His whole body ached when he arrived at the foot of the mountain, and he could barely go on. He made his way back home the next day only with great difficulty, and his joints gave him trouble for the next ten years.

11

On the Run, Alone

RINPOCHE COULD SURVIVE on his pay, but he never had anything left over. However, there were Tibetans who were clever at business and who had built up a shadow economy that catered especially to Chinese cadres who received higher wages and had money to spend, and who secretly demanded goods that they could not obtain in China. During the winter, when there was less work in the commune, Rinpoche spent a few weeks in Lhasa with his cousin Tsering Chödrön and her husband Karma Geleg, a sharp-witted fellow who knew many traders and was himself involved in numerous different business deals. One of his former schoolmates had a Chinese friend who wanted to buy a wristwatch, so he asked Rinpoche if he would sell his wristwatch. Rinpoche had received this watch from his father when he was young. It was the only object of personal value to him that he could save when he had to leave the monastery in Drikung. He bargained skillfully and got a good cash price, plus a ration of butter and fuel for an entire year. With the proceeds he was able to purchase a brand-new Swiss watch through Karma Geleg's business connections and still have a solid profit left over. He sold the new watch to his uncle Nyima Sholkhang, a high official in the administration, and thus gradually developed a thriving little business in watches.

After a few years all of his friends had been assigned appropriate employment, but high lamas and the children of noble families were denied better-paid work and forced to continue their drudgery in the fields, on the mountain slopes, and in the latrines of the capital. The only other option open to them was the equally debilitating work in road construction. It became clear to Rinpoche that his life would be squandered this way and he began, meticulously and calmly, to make plans to escape. The greatest hurdle was obtaining information, since it was hard to know who could be trusted in a land crawling with informers, including those who might simply exploit the chance to curry favor with the authorities. But without accurate information, any attempt to flee was doomed to failure.

In 1973 Chetsang Rinpoche was transferred to Chushul, south of Thölung at the confluence of the Kyichu and the Yarlung Tsangpo (Brahmaputra). His main tasks were to prepare translations for the local authorities and to take over the organization of a camp of canal workers. The pay was as miserable as it had been in the agricultural commune, and the work day was no less strenuous. He was lodged in the camp with the canal workers, and when there was not much translating to be done, he helped dig the ditch.

In an austere office in the building of the district administration, Rinpoche translated reports, applications, and documents for meetings of the work units. Many politically charged texts also crossed his desk, such as the detailed accusations leveled by Mao against Deng Xiaoping (1904–1997), and the self-criticism and apology that were forced out of Deng later. One text described Thrinle Chödrön's Nyemo revolt and the uprisings in other parts of the country that had resulted from it. From this, Rinpoche learned that had the army delayed its intervention for even a few days, a war of independence was almost certain to have broken out all over Tibet, including in Lhasa. Chetsang Rinpoche gained insights into the Communist Party's power structures, its apparatus of control, and its methods of repression.

Farmers lived in the valleys and nomads in the higher areas of this large district. Rinpoche was assigned to accompany a Chinese official, the chairman of the department in charge of the creation of communes in Chushul, into the remote areas as translator and cook. More nomads were going to be forced into settled life in communes, and the authorities wanted to increase the productivity of the ones already there.

On his first excursion he was sent to Tsabuna, high on a mountain, to check on the progress of a nomad commune. There Rinpoche met nomads who had been forced into sedentary life. They were very different from the nomads he had encountered with Tritsab Gyabra north of Drikung and in Changthang. At the commune Rinpoche found dejected, apathetic women and men who stared listlessly into the distance, as if the world no longer had anything to offer worth noticing. The Chinese had begun land reform in 1960, distributing to the poor and to former serfs parcels of land that had been owned by the old Tibetan government, the monasteries, and the aristocrats who had fled. Pompous ceremonies had accompanied the transfers, and the peasants were led to believe that this land, and the animals they received with it, was a gift from the Communist Party of China. Ten years later, after their animals had multiplied, their Communist "benefactors" suddenly appeared and took everything away from them. The animals were taken to the commune, and each family was allowed to keep only two animals. Even their cooking utensils now belonged to the commune rather than to the family units.

Now, the authorities had become concerned that the commune nomads were no longer attending to the animals because they did not own them any more, or that they were slaughtering them, which was prohibited. Rinpoche was to investigate, and he found that this was the case. Neglected yaks, *dzo* (a cross between yak and domestic cattle), and sheep wandered around the camp, with no one seeming to feel responsible for them. One depressed old nomad admitted that he had, in fact, slaughtered a yak, and Rinpoche kept that admission to himself.

Rinpoche didn't like his role of trying to explain the government's exhaustively long directives to them. The nomads were unable to adjust to the forced disruption of their traditional way of life, not understanding why they had to give up a system that had always functioned very well in the country's economic structure, and which had also offered a way of life that made them happy, despite its hardship. They could not—and would never—understand this, no matter how anyone tried to explain to them the government's decisions.

Rinpoche intensified his escape preparations as the full realization of his bleak future in Tibet settled on him. He had told one of his few trustworthy friends in Thölung about his intention, and for a while they considered fleeing together, but Rinpoche came to the conclusion that it would be less conspicuous if they went separately. They never discussed serious plans, but only occasionally mentioned their intentions as a vague possibility. In Chushul there was no one with whom he could build up a relationship of trust. Although his trips to Lhasa were now much more infrequent, they were his only opportunities for gathering the information he needed. During the early stages of the Cultural Revolution, the PLA had reinforced its troops in the border regions and saturated the population with informers, but now the situation had relaxed slightly. A few families were permitted to receive visits from relatives in Nepal, and so occasional traders from Nepal began to make their way into Lhasa. Rinpoche encountered them at his cousin's home, where many people came and went. Karma Geleg, her husband, had many diverse contacts, and Rinpoche was able to meet and converse with Nepalese merchants, pursuing his goal methodically and cautiously. He discussed matters of current interest to the traders—the products presently in demand, prices, barter values, sales turnovers, and so on—before deciding whether he might safely steer the conversation in another direction. Knowing that one of the Nepalese merchants spoke fairly good English, he drew him into a conversation about language and semantics, giving detailed elucidations of Tibetan concepts and their Chinese equivalents, and thus innocuously extracted a few useful English expressions from him.

He finally confided in one of the traders, but still said nothing to his relatives, as he did not wish to cause them trouble. He learned that the route to Darjeeling that he had followed on his journey as a young boy was far too dangerous, since there were many army bases on the way and along the border with India and Bhutan. It was best to head for Nepal because the PRC had good relations with Nepal and was now allowing limited trade across that border. The trader advised him to try the route over the pass at Khumbuka La (Nangpa La) in eastern Nepal, a route used by a few of the traders from the border villages who wished to sell their goods on the black market. The way was neither safe nor easy, as it led over a very high pass surrounded by eight-thousand-meter-high peaks, over ice fields and glaciers, and was dangerous without knowing the area. Rinpoche then began to search for maps of the region without drawing attention to himself. He found a few, but since it would be unsafe to possess any of them, he just studied them thoroughly enough to memorize the paths and terrain. His informant told him where along the route the PLA was stationed.

Rinpoche knew that he had to take something with him that would be easy to carry and sell. The traders had told him that in Nepal the pods of the musk deer commanded high prices. An extract from the male musk deer's testicles was an ingredient in expensive perfumes, and in the Far East it was also used in traditional medicine; in Southeast Asia, musk pods were more valuable than gold. The nomads knew how to capture the rare male musk deer, and those in Chushul had no contact with foreign traders, so Rinpoche was able to purchase five of the precious pods from them with the modest savings from his wristwatch business.

One of Rinpoche's friends was a truck driver who occasionally visited his family near Chushul, and met with him there. In April 1975, the truck driver casually mentioned he had an upcoming trip to Nyalam to deliver goods for the celebrations on May 1, and Rinpoche immediately saw his chance. Nyalam was located in the far south of the country, near the Nepalese border, and the road passed through Tingri, the starting point of the path over the Khumbuka La. Rinpoche told him about an imaginary distant relative in Tingri, whom he wished to visit, and his friend offered him a ride on the upcoming trip, saying he could pose as his assistant. Chetsang Rinpoche accepted, and his friend promised to pick him up in Chushul on April 28.

Rinpoche had no idea how long it would take to get out of the country, and he wanted to make sure that no one would start searching for him before he had crossed the border. He sent a letter to his superiors in Chushul claiming that he was sick and that his doctor had urgently recommended he take a long rest; he would return to his job as soon as he had recovered. His leave was granted without any probing questions.

Equipped with only a little clothing, a bit of food, a thermos of tea, a knife, and the five musk deer pods, he left his room at daybreak, just as he did every day when he went to work, and made his way to the prearranged meeting place on the main street. The truck appeared on time and they drove to Shigatse, where they spent the night. On the evening of the second day, they reached Tingri, a small city with low houses on a dreary plain. There were only a few fields along the river, because the soil was swampy and salty. The driver let him out on a small bridge and they agreed to meet there in a few days for the return journey. That was all the time Rinpoche would have to cross the border into Nepal, unless he was lucky and his friend didn't become suspicious, thinking instead that they had simply missed each other.

Rinpoche quickly ducked into a public toilet and changed his clothes to dress like the locals. He had no documents with him because his ID would instantly show that he was far from his assigned work unit and it would be assumed he was attempting to flee. If questioned, he would simply say he wished to visit his parents who lived nearby.

Meeting up with the wrong people posed a greater danger than getting lost. Not only were there plenty of police and PLA soldiers in the area, but Tingri and the settlements near the border were also full of informers; the road, however, was unmistakable, leading straight south through an arid, icy plateau with the peaks of the Everest range shimmering in the distance. He could make out the peculiarly shaped mountain, the Cho Oyu, that his Nepalese informant had said indicated the direction he was to take. Rinpoche waited until night had fallen before setting off on his way in order not to be spotted on the treeless plain.

The full moon was only four days past, and the night was not completely dark. He proceeded at a swift pace, avoiding the few settlements. He did not feel the icy temperatures that had descended over the countryside as darkness fell, nor the pain in his limbs, though they were still strained from his hard labor in the mountains. Every step that took him further away from his homeland brought him closer to his true calling. The Drikung Kyabgön Rinpoche recited the mantras of Chenrezig and Guru Rinpoche as his body seemed weightless to him, with the suppleness of youth, the kind he had rejoiced in as he dashed ahead of the others in the soccer stadium or effortlessly mastered the steepest ascents on the journey to China.

He reached the PLA camp near Dragmar long past midnight. In the distance the buildings were black silhouettes with only one pale light in the window of a guardhouse. Nevertheless, Rinpoche made a wide detour. The ground changed as he approached the moraine of the great glacier. He had to ford an icy brook of meltwater, so he took off his shoes, rolled up his trousers, and found a place where the water wasn't too deep. He rested briefly, and when he set off again, he could vaguely make out a path that branched off to the right. The Nepalese trader had told him that it was an arduous trail that led to the valley of Rongchar Chu and then on to the sacred mountain of Lapchi, where Milarepa had meditated, and then later, Jigten Sumgön had sent thousands of yogis into solitary retreat. But Rinpoche's path now continued straight toward the glacier.

At daybreak he found that he had made considerable headway in his ascent of the mountain, but he was still visible against the endless snowfields, and would be an easy target for any border troops that happened along. The path climbed steadily and Rinpoche could no longer proceed as quickly as the night before. When the first outlying spurs of the Kyetrak Glacier appeared before him, he saw two men far ahead, climbing up the path; he couldn't tell whether they were Chinese soldiers on patrol, Tibetan nomads, or Nepalese traders. He concealed himself as best he could and studied the two men, then quickly but cautiously approached them. They were two Tibetans, an elderly fellow and a younger one, who appeared to know the area very well. The older man and his son intended to visit relatives beyond the border and sell the sheep's wool blankets they carried in their heavy backpacks. Rinpoche was relieved and joined them as they silently accepted their ill-equipped companion who had no baggage and was wearing completely inadequate shoes.

The route became increasingly difficult, and they were forced to trudge through deep snow and carefully inch their way over ice-covered slopes. There was no path here that someone unfamiliar with the territory could follow, and meeting the two men had been an incredible stroke of good fortune. Rinpoche had known that his flight would not be easy before he had set out, but he now realized that without assistance he would very likely have gotten lost in the unforgiving mountains. Once on the glacier, deep crevasses in the ice made every step critical. His informant in Lhasa had warned him about this; the path over the Khumbuka La was an old trade route for yak caravans, but many a trader had met an untimely death in the icy crevasses, even with knowledgeable guides. Rinpoche's companions pulled a long wooden slat out from where it had been hidden under a cliff outcropping. They tied themselves—including Chetsang Rinpoche—together with rope, laid the board over the first fissure, and crossed one at a time over the precarious bridge, held secure to the others by the rope. Then they very carefully pulled the plank across and placed it over the next rift. It was essential that the plank not slip from their grasp and fall into the abyss, thereby stranding them in this great stretch of cleft ice.

The trek over this difficult terrain seemed endless. Icy winds began to blow, dangerously driving particles of snow into the travelers' lungs.

After many hours they reached the high pass, an elevation of 5,716 meters, and Rinpoche could just barely make out the forms of the traditional cairns of piled up stones with prayer flags under a layer of snow and ice, as the wind blasted clouds of white crystals against them. He did not turn around, nor did he cry out "Victory to the gods!" as was the custom when crossing a pass. In Tibet, it was as though all of the old gods had departed. Fortunately the winds died down as they descended, and they made good progress in the calm weather. From the Nangpa Glacier they descended to Khumbu in Nepal, an area replete with legends and home to yeti as well as Sherpas. The Sherpas call the area Belyul Khebalung, "Hidden Valley," and claim it has been blessed by Guru Rinpoche. There are holy lakes and mountains here, including a sacred Spring of Long Life.

That night they found lodging in a nomad's tent in the tiny settlement of Lunak, and they ate a simple meal. Rinpoche gave his companions the rest of his meager provisions and then fell into a deep sleep. He set off alone the next morning, as he wished to put the border region behind him as quickly as possible.

(Much later, when the Drikung lamas living in exile were to hear about the circumstances of his escape, they would be convinced that the appearance of his two companions was a manifestation of the goddess Tara, or the Drikung Protectress Achi, and they were equally certain that the two had simply vanished afterwards, like a mirage. Rinpoche would smile at this interpretation; it is almost certain that his flight would have failed without the help of the two men, and whether one sees it as a lucky coincidence or as the help of the Sublime Ones depends on the point of view and the purity of perception.)

Rinpoche's path took him along a glacial brook to lower-lying regions, where he came upon the first settlements, which he tried to circumvent, as he assumed that border soldiers would be everywhere there. In front of a hut he saw some Nepalese policemen playing cards, but they completely ignored him.

He also encountered Tibetans now and then, but he hesitated to confide in anyone after living for so long among informers and spies. He continued alone and silent until he reached the valley of Tengboche, where he struck up a conversation with a Sherpa whom he heard speaking Tibetan and who seemed trustworthy to him. Rinpoche sold him the musk deer pods for much less than their real value, as he urgently needed Nepalese rupees and less-conspicuous clothing. He bought trousers such as the locals wore and a common black umbrella. He continued through many villages, now eating in roadside taverns, having to trust in the tavern-keeper's honesty as he simply held out some money and took whatever change was given him.

Chetsang Rinpoche crossed the scenic Kosi Valley, but making an effort to ask as few questions as possible, he made a wrong turn in Kharikhola—at the crossroads of various trade routes—thus going too far south. He had to turn back and take the foot path leading to Nunthala after having already been a few days on the road. If it had not been a matter of reaching his destination—one about which he knew nearly nothing except that it was where he could lead a free life—as quickly and as inconspicuously as possible, he might have serenely enjoyed the path crossing over steep meadows and the views of majestic mountains from which the skies sometimes kindly withdrew their cloudy grip. He might have studied the thick layers of lichen and mosses on the tree trunks of the enchanted rhododendron forests with the same fervor with which he studies every blossom and every unfamiliar blade of grass to this day.

At the Lamjura Pass he left the Buddhist Solu-Khumbu region and continued on to Jiri in the Jiri Khola Valley, where the drivable road began, and where he could wait in a tea shop on the side of the road for the bus to Kathmandu. The bus wasn't really comfortable, but after the long days on foot, worrying that he might attract attention and be asked to show his papers, he was finally able to relax a little. Rinpoche took a window seat at the back of the bus. Glowing, emerald-green landscapes reaching up to the skies passed him like slides shot through a projector, one after the other. At one point it seemed to him as though shadowy soldiers were appearing, soldiers advancing with armed force against defenseless civilians, brutally marching them off, soldiers of the People's Liberation Army like those he had seen on his return to Lhasa from Chengdu. But out the window were only densely wooded slopes that dissolved in the dust whirled up from the gravel road. The martial impressions were mere overlays, like transparencies of dreamlike visions ushering in sleep. Rinpoche dozed off into nightmares that had escaped Tibet with him.

Kathmandu was dusty, busy, and loud. Rinpoche found a room in a simple hostel near the bus station. He was still hesitant about going out onto the street, but there were many Tibetan businesses where he would not be conspicuous so he cautiously started to explore. Once he thought he recognized a Muslim woman from Lhasa who used to sell tea. He and his friends had often gone to her shop to drink tea after soccer games. In those days she had been impoverished and ragged, but now she had gained a great deal of weight and was astonishingly well-dressed. He had the impression that she recognized him, too, but they passed each other without exchanging greetings. Another time a young man stared at him as though he thought he knew him. Rinpoche continued past him, but furtively glancing back he saw that the man was still studying him; he quickly ducked into one alleyway and then the next—having come to know the area well—so that the man couldn't follow him. Later Rinpoche found out that he was an informer who worked for the Chinese and filed a report whenever he spotted a possible refugee.

Rinpoche now set about emerging from anonymity with the same premeditation he used for his flight. He did not dare present himself to the Nepalese authorities for fear they would hand him over to the PRC. Rinpoche slowly made the acquaintance of a young Tibetan shop owner who seemed educated and trustworthy, and one day when they were alone in the store, Rinpoche bluntly admitted that he was a son of the Tsarong family and had fled from Tibet. He asked if the shop owner knew how his family was faring; one of the Nepalese traders in Lhasa had said that his parents were running a bus line between Kathmandu and Kalimpong. The Tibetan informed him that they had had such a business years ago, but that they had emigrated to the United States of America, although perhaps a brother was still living in Dharamsala. When Rinpoche asked where Dharamsala was located, his new friend told him that it was the home of the Dalai Lama and the seat of the Tibetan government-in-exile. He suggested to the astonished Rinpoche that he approach the office of the Tibetan government in Kathmandu, writing down the address and sketching a map for him. In Tibet, Rinpoche had heard nothing about a government-in-exile under the Dalai Lama, much less that it maintained an office in Kathmandu.

It was mid-May when Rinpoche presented himself at the Tibetan office, where the skeptical representatives listened to his story. His report seemed unbelievable to them; they couldn't understand how he could have succeeded at crossing the Khumbuka La since the few refugees who managed to escape over that route were local inhabitants who knew the terrain and the weather conditions, and they came in small groups. It had been a long time since anyone from central Tibet had made it across the border. They found it equally improbable that he was Tsarong's son and the Drikung Kyabgön Rinpoche, who had been missing for fifteen years, and had even been once declared dead. Nevertheless, they found quarters for him and arranged a meeting with the home minister of the Dalai Lama's government, Wangchug Dorje, who was visiting Kathmandu at the time.

Remembering the traditions of the old Tibetan government of his childhood, Rinpoche expected the minister to receive him in a brocade robe, with a long earring and an amulet box in his pinned-up hair, and was quite surprised to be greeted by an older gentleman in a Western suit and short haircut. The home minister's presence in Kathmandu was another stroke of luck since he knew Rinpoche's father, brothers, and sisters very well, and after conversing with Rinpoche he was certain that he was no imposter. He told Rinpoche that his sister Namgyal Lhamo was now married to Lobsang Samten (1932–1985), a brother of the Dalai Lama, and that he knew her very well. Rinpoche's older brother, Jigme, was living in Dharamsala. They agreed that it would be better not to inform other members of the Tibetan government-in-exile nor the Nepalese government of his whereabouts or his intention to enter India; relations between the government-in-exile and Nepal had become strained because of the CIA-supported Tibetan guerilla base in Mustang. The minister said that he was experienced in getting people across the border and would take care of things.

One day an employee of the Tibetan secret service in Kathmandu accompanied Rinpoche to a restaurant and introduced him to a foreign-looking man with long hair who said that he would take Rinpoche to his brother in Dharamsala, although he didn't explain how. The next morning at the bus station Rinpoche met his contact man, who had third-class tickets for the Indian train from the border. The third-class train car would be uncomfortable, and as a farewell gift, the secret service man gave Rinpoche a bed sheet to sit on, to protect him a little from the filth.

It was an awful bus, an awful road, and an awfully hot day when Rinpoche and his nameless companion took to the border that day in early June of 1975. The bus broke down twice, once at night, when it took hours to fix. A lamp set up to facilitate the repairs attracted a cloud of extremely large and unpleasant insects, and some unfamiliar animals were making an unbelievable racket nearby. Rinpoche curiously asked his companion if the noise was the braying of donkeys, and was told it was the singing of frogs in a nearby lake. It was hard to imagine that little frogs were able to make such a big noise.

The next day they reached the border town of Birganj. His companion seemed nervous, and transferred documents and letters that he was carrying for the government-in-exile into Rinpoche's pouch, saying that he might be frisked. They each held a new thermos since his business was supposedly selling thermos bottles, and customs allowed only one thermos per person. He emphasized to Rinpoche not to say anything, under any circumstances; he would do the talking. Rinpoche wasn't sure this was such a good idea, considering how agitated his companion seemed, but it also seemed better than trying to speak to the border guards in Tibetan or Chinese.

They climbed into a rickshaw that was to take them to the border crossing at Raxaul, and at ten o'clock in the morning they were waiting in a long line of vehicles as those ahead of them were thoroughly checked. When it was their turn, his companion got out and approached the guards, who, oddly enough, remained seated by their guard house and went on playing their game of cards.

His companion looked confused when he returned. They hadn't wanted to see anything, they had only asked where the travelers had come from and said they could go. This turn of events had unsettled him almost more than his fear of inspection had. It was unprecedented not to be searched, and they hadn't even had to show their papers. They had had unbelievably good luck. The man looked at Rinpoche in his bewilderment, as Rinpoche sat there serenely on the rickshaw bench's torn plastic cover and returned his look with an expression that seemed like a solemn smile.

They had some time to rest at the Raxaul train station, since it would be a while before the train arrived. Rinpoche rested a little with his pouch under his head, but he was uncomfortable in the hot, damp climate, after a life spent high on the plateau. Things became even more difficult in the train car, where they sat on a hard wooden bench and the train grew more crowded with every stop. Foul odors became an unbearable stench in the car's sticky air. Rinpoche suffered, but tried to stay tranquil as every fifteen minutes the train came to a halt and there was a chaotic pushing, shoving, and yelling as a few passengers got off and even more got on. Rinpoche's seat was in one of the first cars, and when he opened the window to let out the stench and the heat, the outside air was no cooler and the hot diesel smoke from the engine blew in. Resigned, he had to shut the window again. The Drikung Rinpoche had crossed frozen rivers in high mountain ranges only lightly clothed, but he was not equal to the oppressive, reeking humidity. He was drenched in sweat and was constantly thirsty.

Rinpoche's companion was alert and sent him hastily to the toilet at the stops where police boarded the train and checked a few passengers. During these breaks Rinpoche turned on the faucet and quenched his thirst in great gulps, which his distressed companion then told him he shouldn't have done, as that water was foul and contaminated. Although he had already drunk his fill a few times, Rinpoche fortunately didn't become sick. Later, his guide obtained clean water for him at the train stations.

The train took a circuitous route, first east toward Katihar in the vicinity of Darjeeling and then back to Lucknow, where they disembarked and spent a night in a simple hotel near the station. The next day they continued by rail to Pathankot, and finally by bus to Dharamsala.

12

The Burden of Freedom

C HETSANG RINPOCHE arrived in Dharamsala on June 6, 1975. He felt better at the higher elevation, even though it was not as high as Tibet. Rinpoche was greeted by Kungo Depön Phuntsog Tashi, whose motorcycle had caused such merriment among the nomads at that long-ago reception for the Dalai Lama. Phuntsog was now the government-in-exile's minister of security. Rinpoche was going to be given accommodations in a small house in the Tibetan Children's Village, where all newcomers were first brought, but when the Gyalyum Chenmo, the mother of the Dalai Lama, and her daughter, Jetsun Pema, heard that he had arrived, they invited him to lunch and to spend his first night in Dharamsala in their home.

Jetsun is an honorific title for a highly esteemed teacher, or in the case of a woman, a revered nun. An old nun, Jetsun Kusho, had lived in the house of his aunt Taring, and so Rinpoche expected to be lodged in the home of elderly women with shaved heads. The image of the wrinkled little old nun was before his eyes as he went up to the house and knocked on the door. A pretty, elegant young lady greeted him and introduced herself as Jetsun Pema. Rinpoche was astonished and amused at the tricks the human mind can play. Another dignified lady appeared behind him, wearing glasses. "Don't you recognize me?" she asked. He did not. It was the Gyalyum Chenmo, the Dalai Lama's mother. She examined Rinpoche's mysterious companion and said that his face did not look Tibetan, and she wanted to know who he was. Rinpoche's nameless companion excused himself and left without revealing his identity.

There were many delicious dishes to enjoy at lunch. Rinpoche, who hadn't eaten so well in many years, was very happy to be served Indian curry with mutton, lentils, and potatoes, and he enjoyed the first taste of mango in his life. After Rinpoche had spent a few nights in a guest room of the Gyalyum Chenmo's home, his brother Jigme returned to Dharamsala; he had heard that Rinpoche would be traveling through Delhi and had gone to meet him there. Jigme had graduated from the University of Indiana and worked for a bank in New York for a while before moving to Dharamsala with his wife, Yangzom Dolma Döndrup, a daughter of Gyalo Döndrup, one of the Dalai Lama's brothers. He was currently the director of the Tibetan Medical School and lived on the same property as the Gyalyum Chenmo. They were like strangers to each other when Rinpoche embraced his brother for the first time in eighteen years; they had been children the last time they had seen each other, and even then they had been together only seldom. In the United States their parents had heard the first reports of their son's escape from Tibet. They couldn't believe it and suspected a hoax—only a telegram from Jigme, who had seen their long-lost son in person, brought them certainty. Dundul Namgyal immediately booked a flight to Delhi.

Jigme recounted the family's tale. Their parents had first lived in Kalimpong after their flight, and their father had worked for the Dalai Lama's government-in-exile in Delhi, Calcutta, Mussoorie, and then Dharamsala. Together with Wangchug Deden Shakabpa (1907–1989) he built up the Central Social Welfare committee that facilitated the integration of the Tibetans into their Indian exile. Dundul Namgyal Tsarong and Gyalo Döndrup were in charge of selling the Tibetan gold and silver reserves and art treasures that had been deposited in Sikkim, and of investing the proceeds in the stock market in India. The war between China and India in 1962 had triggered a stock market crash, and the Tibetan government lost a great deal of money that was urgently needed for the support of the Tibetans in exile. Part of the proceeds from the sale of the Sikkim reserves had also been used for the construction of an iron and steel factory in Bihar, and Tsarong was essentially the factory's sole director, as Gyalo Döndrup, the official director, spent most of his time at the CIA-supported Tibetan resistance camp in Mustang.

Tsarong urgently wanted to be relieved of this responsibility, but the government insisted he remain. He was a mild and gentle man, and no match for the hard-nosed tactics of Indian business. The losses on the stock market made it difficult to obtain credit, and he struggled just to pay his factory workers, continuing in this unpaid volunteer position for years while fighting for the factory's survival. His own family lived on the proceeds from the sale of his wife's jewelry, and in addition to their responsibility for their own children, the Tsarongs had taken on the obligation of sponsoring the education of two Tibetan orphans. Tsarong's work-related stress and their private difficulties had worn out both of them, first his wife and then Dundul Namgyal himself, until he finally became severely dyspeptic and was forced to retire from public office. No physician could help him in India, so he went to Switzerland, where his daughter Namgyal Lhamo and her husband, Lobsang Samten, were living. Medical treatment there also failed, and in 1970, on the advice of his doctors, he and his wife moved to the United States for further treatment, at first living in New York with their younger daughter, Norzin, who had married Tsering Wangyal Shakabpa, a son of Tsipon Wangchug Deden Shakabpa.

His Holiness the Dalai Lama wished to see Chetsang Rinpoche, and they spoke for a long time. The Dalai Lama naturally wanted to know what life was like under the Chinese, what he had endured, and how hard he had been forced to work, and asked to see his hands, which bore the signs of heavy labor. He also wished to know if he could write Chinese. The Dalai Lama was considering all options, his mind open to all possibilities. Rinpoche could lead the life of a layman, he could assume leadership of the Drikung lineage, or he could become a much-valued employee in the government-in-exile. The Dalai Lama advised him to first go to the United States and spend time with his family; distance would provide him with the detachment he needed to make decisions about his future. He appreciated Rinpoche's alert intelligence and the way he answered all questions promptly and thoughtfully, and so in parting he also recommended that Rinpoche take up his responsibility as throne holder of the Drikung lineage, although he could take his time before beginning. The Dalai Lama could see that the unadulterated spirit of the Dharma was still alive and strong in him, and as symbols of the manifestations of the body and mind of the Buddha in the Kagyu tradition, the Dalai Lama presented him with a statue of Milarepa and Gampopa's famous text *Jewel Ornament of Liberation* (*Dagpo Targyen*), which he recommended warmly.

Chetsang Rinpoche's passport photograph taken in 1975
in Dharamsala after his escape from Tibet.

Rinpoche did not wish to make a decision right away, as he had gone through too many radical changes recently and needed some time to take stock of his situation and consider his options. The one thing he knew for sure was that he wanted to travel to the United States to see his family. Everything else would come in due time.

Some Drikung lamas who had fled in 1959 had begun a modest reconstruction of their religious life in exile. Ontul Rinpoche was building a small monastery on Lake Tso Pema near Rewalsar in northern India, and Ayang Rinpoche was in the process of constructing another monastery in the Tibetan colony in Bylakuppe in southern India. Lamkhyen Gyalpo Rinpoche, whom Rinpoche had met as a boy in Drikung, had given up his ordination and was the chief secretary of the Tibetan government-in-exile's home department. A few influential members of the Drikung lineage were living scattered throughout India, but they were not organized. Many followers did not even know where the Drikung Rinpoches were.

An unbroken Drikung tradition still existed in Ladakh, where Togden Rinpoche was responsible for three major monasteries and about fifty smaller ones. They were poorly funded and at odds with each other, and only a few monks and tulkus had the necessary transmissions and were still familiar enough with the tradition to try to preserve the long-established rituals, ceremonies, lama dances, musical forms, academic studies, and esoteric meditation practices. Even for native-born Indians there were enormous bureaucratic hurdles to overcome in order to visit Ladakh, and there was very little communication between the Tibetans in India and the Ladakhis. Overall, the Drikung lineage had suffered a great deal, and there wasn't much left of its former grandeur and importance. There were no great centers of study, fewer and fewer knowledgeable lamas, and even the traditional rituals and ceremonies were gradually being lost. The Drikung tradition was in danger, and many tulkus and lamas were turning to other schools, primarily the Karma Kagyu and the Nyingma, whose scholarly and ritual traditions had suffered less in the diaspora. Nonetheless, there were still devoted disciples, monks and laypeople, who were electrified by the news that their Kyabgön Rinpoche had arrived in the free world.

Konchog Samten, the former drönyer, and Chösjor, the former solpön, the men who had tried to secure Rinpoche's escape while he was at Drikung, were very excited. They had been sure that the Chinese must have killed the two Kyabgön Rinpoches in 1971, and there had even been serious discussions about beginning searches for their reincarnations. Samten and Chösjor arrived in Delhi on July 3, intending to travel on to Dharamsala at once to see Rinpoche, but they learned that Rinpoche was on his way to Delhi. In the afternoon, they went to the Delhi Tibet House to meet someone else, but when they entered the office of the head secretary—she was Rinpoche's aunt Tsering Dolma—they saw Dundul Namgyal Tsarong and his son, the Kyabgön Rinpoche. Chösjor was speechless and Konchog Samten wept uncontrollably, stammering "*Yishin Norbu, Yishin Norbu!*" ("Wish-Fulfilling Jewel") over and over again, and prostrated to him. Rinpoche helped Konchog Samten up and guided the trembling man to a chair. He was profoundly happy to see his faithful companions alive and well after such a long time.

Samten asked Rinpoche in detail about his studies, the course his life had taken, and above all about his ethical and moral conduct, and

Rinpoche answered each question patiently, thoroughly, and honestly. Seeing so much compassion in Rinpoche's heart made Samten realize what an extraordinary being he was for neither his personality nor his moral conduct to have suffered under the rule of the Communists, self-avowed enemies of spirituality. He saw a noble being, and was filled with renewed hope.

The Drikung lamas were distressed when they learned of Rinpoche's plans. Many of them assumed as a matter of course that Chetsang Thrinle Lhundrup would stay in India and take charge of the Drikung lineage. Without giving much thought to his current state of mind after the arduous times he had so recently emerged from, they decided to perform a second enthronement. Konchog Samten proposed the Ladakhi colony in Delhi, but Gyalpo Rinpoche was strictly against this, insisting that such an important event had to take place in Dharamsala. When they realized that Rinpoche was planning to travel with his father to the United States they were afraid the experience of freedom and luxury after the years of oppression and deprivation would distract him from his role as Drikung Kyabgön, his responsibilities to the lineage, and his mission as a tulku.

But not all were anxious to see the Drikung Kyabgön resume his position. In the fragmented situation some had improved their own stature, and they were unwilling to give up their positions and return to their former places in the reinstated hierarchy. Of course this kind of jockeying for status had been an ever-present aspect of the monastic social structure in all lineages, and was especially visible during periods of regency, but the disarray of the diaspora and most Westerners' egalitarian insensitivity to traditional hierarchy had provided opportunities for a more serious reshuffling of the traditional order. There was no open opposition, but a political tug-of-war was beginning behind the scenes. Rinpoche himself, however, had had enough of politics and would be very happy to leave it all behind.

Meanwhile, a delegation of Drikung dignitaries visited the Dalai Lama. Togden, Ontul, and Ngagchang Kunsang Rigzin wanted at least some indication from the Kyabgön Rinpoche that he would commit himself, and they urged the Dalai Lama to confer the novice monastic vows on Chetsang Rinpoche. The Dalai Lama responded that he did not want to pressure him. It was, after all, a weighty matter, and even more so where such a high incarnation was involved. Rinpoche had heard practically nothing about the Dharma since the age of fourteen. He had been under constant pressure from the Communists, who had condemned religion as poison and as a means of exploitation, and who regarded lamas and monks as the main enemies of their ideology. He had been continually exposed to bad advice and indoctrination, and a clear and deep understanding of the outer and inner meaning of the Dharma would be necessary to discard these views. It would be neither prudent nor appropriate for Chetsang Rinpoche to take these vows merely at the behest of the desperate rinpoches and monks. Furthermore, since he was going to the United States for an indeterminate time, there was no guarantee that he would keep his vows, and if he broke them, it would be much more difficult to renew them. "In Tibet," said the Dalai Lama in conclusion, "I cut his hair when he was a small boy, but he did not take vows from me at the time. Nonetheless, he has kept his moral discipline intact. That is an excellent sign, and there will be no problem with his taking his vows when he returns, even if he were not to keep his moral discipline in the meantime."

The Drikung lamas were suffering, because just when they had regained their precious throne holder, he was to be snatched away from them again. They felt cheated and bereft at not being able to give him an official reception in the form of an enthronement according to the Drikung tradition. The Dalai Lama sympathized with them and agreed to a more modest ceremony, a symbolic act of accession to the throne, as a sign that the throne holder was present and would return.

In Delhi, Gyalpo Rinpoche convinced Chetsang Rinpoche and his father of the significance of this ceremony. They also requested that he shave his head for the occasion as an outward sign that he intended to remain a monk. The father was somewhat annoyed at the pressure being put on his son, but Rinpoche calmly allowed the brother of Rigyal Tulku to cut his hair, which Gyalpo Rinpoche took, and has kept to this day. Rinpoche then returned to Dharamsala, accompanied by his father and his sister Norzin.

On July 16, an astrologically auspicious day, many Drikung followers assembled in Dharamsala to see the throne holder, including Togden, Ayang, Ontul, and Gyalpo Rinpoches. Togden was overjoyed to see Chetsang Rinpoche again after twenty years, and in the changed physical form he saw the same character: Rinpoche radiated the same harmony and peace he had shown as a small child. A procession of Drikung dignitaries led Rinpoche into the great audience hall where the Dalai Lama was seated. Rinpoche took his seat on the throne opposite that of the Dalai Lama, and a long-life mandala was offered him according to the Drikung tradition.

The next day the department of religion and culture of the Tibetan government-in-exile held a great ceremonial reception for him and the Dalai Lama, attended by delegates from the various schools of Tibetan Buddhism and the different areas of Tibet. A Gelug representative performed the mandala ceremony. Then the Drikung Kagyu representatives performed a mandala offering for the Dalai Lama, and carried out the symbolic enthronement of Kyabgön Rinpoche Thrinle Lhundrup with a long-life mandala according to a treasure text discovered by Rinchen Phuntsog. It was a glorious day for the Drikungpa, a kind of resurrection of the school beginning to rise like a phoenix from its own ashes once again.

In India Rinpoche had the status of a refugee, and to travel to the United States he had to acquire an Indian registration certificate, and then an identity certificate. The process first required exhaustive interrogations by the secret services, and every day he met with members of various intelligence organizations, one of which seemed to be specifically concerned with Tibetan matters, while another was active in international espionage. They wanted to know in detail about the political situation in Tibet, about the strength of the Chinese army, their camps, how informers were recruited, and so on. A third group from the domestic secret service wanted to know how Rinpoche had succeeded in escaping, and especially how he had managed to enter India without being noticed. Rinpoche mentioned nothing about the help from the Dalai Lama's office in Kathmandu or his mysterious traveling companion. He simply hadn't been checked at some border crossing; he couldn't remember its name. It was the truth.

The interrogations in New Delhi were conducted where Rinpoche was staying, in the home of his aunt Tsering Dolma and her husband, Gelek Rinpoche. Chetsang Rinpoche remembered seeing Demo Rinpoche, Gelek Rinpoche's father, hounded across the Barkhor and vilified; to him, it all seemed like yesterday. Gelek Rinpoche was the director of the

Dundul Namgyal Tsarong, Chetsang Rinpoche, Lama Lobsang, and Gelek Rinpoche (from left) in front of the Ladakh Buddha Vihara.

Tibetan section of All India Radio and was well acquainted with many officials, and so was of tremendous help in shortening the lengthy process he had to endure.

The chairman of the Minorities Commission and member of the Indian parliament, Bakula Rinpoche,[1] who had held some of the highest offices in the Indian government, also assisted Chetsang Rinpoche to the best of his ability during the endless interrogations. Bakula had met Rinpoche once in Tibet, and soon after Rinpoche's arrival in Dharamsala, he invited him to tea and informed him that in India he could expect an intimidating bureaucracy with many questions and even more problems.

Lama Lobsang, a member of the Indian government's Scheduled Castes and Scheduled Tribes Commission, also supported Chetsang Rinpoche with all of the resources at his command. In India, stacks of documents tended to gather dust on the desk of a bureaucrat until, one by one, each file was slowly passed on to the next civil servant, and placed at the bottom of his tall stack of documents. Only a bribe would help a file move from the bottom of the stack to the top.

Gelek Rinpoche always seemed to find a way to keep Chetsang Rinpoche's files moving through this labyrinthine sequence of bureaucratic offices. He placed phone calls, sometimes arranging small perks for the bureaucrats, and sometimes applying pressure. As soon as the file moved to a new office, Gelek Rinpoche would find out where it was and he would pay a call on the departmental director in charge. The meetings with the section heads were yet another kind of amazing new experience for Chetsang Rinpoche. No one ever turned up for work on time, and when they did appear they had lengthy conversations with their subordinates in the office, ordered tea, and debated endlessly with friends and acquaintances. Around noon they would disappear for an extensive lunch, then return to continue chatting, and they were always the first to leave the office at the end of the day. Gelek Rinpoche tracked and pushed Chetsang Rinpoche's files for three months, handing out banknotes to lower, middle, and high-ranking officials, to keep the files moving on to the next office. Finally, Chetsang Rinpoche got his refugee identity certificate.

He had mixed feelings when he called on the American embassy, dreading the thought of another bureaucratic process, but all he had to do was to swear formally that the information on his identity certificate was true and accurate and submit to a medical examination. In the embassy he was handed a thick, sealed envelope that he was not allowed to open, but was to hand over to the authorities upon arrival at the airport.

In the fall of 1975, Chetsang Rinpoche and his father disembarked at Newark Airport in New Jersey. An Immigrations official helped them fill out the confusing forms and guided Rinpoche to a separate room, where he handed her the envelope he had been given in Delhi. While his father waited outside, Rinpoche sat on the sofa and examined the many unknown things in his new surroundings—an air-conditioner, a vending machine, and a color television set broadcasting a baseball game with the sound turned off—until a friendly-looking police officer

Lobsang Samten (the brother of the Dalai Lama), Chetsang Rinpoche,
Dundul Namgyal Tsarong, and Namgyal Lhamo in New Jersey.

appeared and handed Chetsang Rinpoche a green card still warm from
the printing machine. Rinpoche's father shook his head in disbelief; he
had had to wait three years to get his green card. Rinpoche accepted it
with equanimity, accustomed to having obstacles suddenly melt away
before him.

His sister Namgyal Lhamo and her husband Lobsang Samten picked
them up at the airport. They drove to Namlha and Lobsang's home
in Scotch Plains, New Jersey, one of the many indistinguishable sub-
urbs of New York. Namlha could hardly believe that her brother had
escaped; it had been so completely improbable they had given up all
hope, and now he was there, standing before her. The Mongolian Geshe
Ngawang Wangyal, who lived nearby and had gathered many disciples,
was visiting just then. He was a straightforward, openhearted lama who
had known Chetsang Rinpoche's grandfather well. He embraced the
Kyabgön Rinpoche warmly and pressed a hundred-dollar bill into his
hand in greeting. Rinpoche did not want to take it, but Geshe Wangyal

insisted, saying that his grandfather Tsarong had often helped him and his family, and it was the least he could do; he also invited Rinpoche to come and visit him any time.

In the days that followed, Rinpoche had to get used to the fact that there was no one here who gave orders and no place where he had to appear and submit reports; the unaccustomed freedom was disconcerting. In Tibet, he and others of his class were treated with condescension and contempt. Rinpoche had been able to avoid some of the worst of it, mainly because he had heeded Gochok Rinpoche's warnings and stayed in school, but he had still been subjected to malice and hostility, and he had been compelled to constantly monitor what he said and did. Now he began to see his experiences in a new light, and he realized how productive they had been for the practice of patience and compassion.

His parents owned a large, attractive house not far from Namlha, but it had been rented out because they had moved to Texas, where his mother anxiously awaited his arrival. His younger brother, Paljor, was studying anthropology in Wisconsin. After spending a few days with Namlha and Lobsang Samten, Chetsang Rinpoche traveled on to Texas and moved in with his parents in an apartment near Galveston, not far from Houston. Wanting to put some weight on her emaciated son, Rinpoche's mother happily dragged him from one restaurant to the next.

In the winter of 1975, Rinpoche took his first extended trip with his mother. They went by Greyhound bus to visit Paljor and his Brazilian wife, Sara, in Minneapolis, where Paljor was attending the University of Minnesota for a semester. Rinpoche was absorbed by the many and varied landscapes they traveled through, and the dismal roadside restaurants where the bus stopped also made an impression. The icy wind blowing in Minneapolis was even colder than a Lhasa wind when Rinpoche met with his younger brother, each of them trying to connect the young man now before him with the brother in his childhood memories. As an anthropology student, Paljor had many questions about what Tibet was now like, and Rinpoche provided detailed answers.

His parents also hoped that their son would tell them about his time in Tibet, but didn't press him, as they had no idea what he might have gone through. Perhaps they also feared they might hear things they would rather not know about. Rinpoche felt no urge to go into detail about the past right away—he wanted to explore and enjoy his freedom instead. His parents drove him many places to visit their Tibetan and American friends, and in the evenings his father taught him the basics of English. Rinpoche gradually began to tell his father about Tibet under Chinese Communist rule, and his father was outraged that, as he saw it, Tritsab Rinpoche had treated him so badly. But Rinpoche never spoke with bitterness or blame about the terrible events of his youth; he maintained a compassionate tone in all that he related, whether about narrow-minded monastery administrators, Tritsab Gyabra, or their Communist rulers. He always took their positive efforts and intentions into account, their fears and worries, and the limitations of their understanding.

His parents had moved to Houston because his father had become involved with the Chakpori Ling Healing Foundation, run by an unusual man who called himself Norbu Chen and who claimed to be a Tibetan lama. Norbu Chen was a small, effervescent American whose real name was Michael Alexander. He had studied Tibetan Buddhism and had caused a considerable stir as a healer, thanks to financial and social support from tobacco heiress and billionaire Doris Duke and several other minor celebrities. He was a controversial figure and many wild rumors about him were in circulation, some of which he himself had started. Despite his flamboyant claims, there was no scarcity of people who were convinced that Norbu Chen had healed them, including Dundul Namgyal Tsarong, who had finally been relieved of the chronic problems that had defeated Indian, Swiss, and mainstream American doctors.

Chetsang Rinpoche's brother Paljor came to Texas during summer vacation and taught him to drive. On Sundays they cruised around the extensive parking lots in front of the shopping centers. Soon, Rinpoche was steering the car down side streets with little traffic, then on the busy highways. Driving itself was not a problem, but the written exam presented a major obstacle, because Rinpoche still knew very little English. After he failed the written exam, Paljor had a brilliant idea. They drove to a small town outside of Houston and the two brothers registered for the exam separately and sat down far apart in the small, bare room. Rinpoche just checked the boxes of the multiple-choice test at random and they surreptitiously exchanged their answer sheets while standing in line to hand them in. Rinpoche got his license. (When he tells this story, he laughs and adds, "Paljor flunked!")

His parents soon began pressuring him to improve his English. His father and his brothers and sisters spoke excellent English, and his mother also had a good command of the language. For a while, Rinpoche attended an intensive course at an international language school at the University of Texas in Houston. At first he took the bus to the school very early in the morning, but when his father bought a new car Rinpoche drove his parents' old Toyota to class. He only attended the school for five months, though, because the course was designed for much more advanced students who could already read and write fairly well. He wasn't even familiar with the Roman alphabet and needed a more basic introduction to English. Rinpoche's knowledge of the Chinese and Tibetan writing systems were of no help, and despite his quick intelligence and extraordinary memorization skills, the course material was not very useful to him.

When he was taking morning English classes he had nothing to do in the afternoons, and he disliked inactivity. He first tried to get a job as kitchen help at a Chinese restaurant near his parents' apartment, but when the owners were reluctant to hire him, his brother helped him apply at a McDonald's restaurant in the neighborhood. Despite his poor English, the manager hired him on the spot, and the job was better than the Chinese restaurant, where he would only have spoken Chinese. From then on, he worked at the McDonald's every afternoon. The restaurant was popular, and he had to work briskly and without interruption. During his first week he had considerable difficulty keeping all of the orders straight, working the machines and finishing all of the hamburgers quickly enough. But soon he had mastered the routine and could perform all of the tasks smoothly.

His work in the restaurant gave him great pleasure. He marveled at the contrast between his improvised hearth in Thong Ga and the fast-food restaurant's kitchen. All the appliances in the kitchen were machines, and everything was subject to continual innovation, presenting him with a drastic example of the fundamental Buddhist principle of impermanence and change in all things. Each week, something was altered or improved, the chairs were replaced, or the decoration was modified.

The level of activity and efficiency was incredible and ceaseless. Rinpoche had never seen anything like it, either in Tibet or in India. He began to think that people in the West were not just materially advanced, but more intellectually advanced as well. He was most impressed by the specialization of labor, which was completely different from the way work was performed in Tibet. He began to think about the importance of education, and he noticed that specialized knowledge in diverse areas was what made it possible for the West to take the lead in many fields. But in spite of the deep impression these advanced techniques made, he was certain that they had produced a perilous disequilibrium by focusing exclusively on the technical, material aspects of life. The Tibetans, on the other hand, were far more advanced in terms of spirituality. They had harnessed all of their intellectual energy to spiritual progress, and their material wealth was also dedicated to this purpose, as texts were written in gold on the most expensive paper available and bound in book covers that had cost artisans weeks of intensive effort, costly statues were produced, stupas were built, and temples were magnificently endowed. The challenge was to bring both spiritual and technological development into a harmonious relationship with each other, integrating both aspects, the material and the spiritual, without prejudice.

The Tsarong family changed lodgings frequently in the greater Houston area, and when they were about to move yet again, the McDonald's manager tried to keep Rinpoche by offering him a promotion. He would gladly have stayed because he enjoyed the work there, but he had to relocate to Arlington with his parents. Norbu Chen had moved to Arlington and Chetsang Rinpoche's father wished to follow in order to keep working for him. Furthermore, Norbu Chen had fallen seriously ill and Rinpoche's father was determined to take care of him.

Chetsang Rinpoche had had his driver's license for two months when they moved to Arlington. His parents drove off first, and Rinpoche followed in his father's old car. Just before Dallas, the highway divided behind a wall of huge traffic signs. At the last moment Rinpoche's father noticed that he had to turn off, but there was too much traffic for Rinpoche to make the exit and he drove on straight toward Dallas. Yangchen Dolkar and Dundul Namgyal were distraught; it seemed that it would be impossible to find their son, or for him to find them again in that confusion of unfamiliar roads and people. Although it seemed hopeless, Rinpoche's father drove back to the place where they had lost sight of him and searched vainly for the Toyota for a long time. Suddenly, out of the corner of his eye, he saw Rinpoche's car turning into

Chetsang Rinpoche in front of the White House in Washington, D.C.

a gas station. Rinpoche got out of the car with an impish smile, as if it were just another adventure. He had driven to Dallas and then back in the direction of Fort Worth to turn off at the exit for Arlington, and so they met in the midst of that massively congested area, in a tangle of highways, like two needles meeting in a haystack.

Later, Rinpoche simply got into his old Toyota and explored the United States on his own. Although his parents had lived in America for six years by then, they still had difficulty finding their way, hesitated to drive to unfamiliar areas, and felt like uncertain strangers. Rinpoche, however, simply got into his car and took off on solitary tours, without any particular destination, for days, sometimes weeks at a time, taking in a multitude of details in that new world.

After the move to Arlington, Rinpoche went to the library at a nearby college every morning for six months to study on his own to improve his English. In the audiovisual section he could watch videos and slides with accompanying narratives. Not surprisingly, he especially enjoyed the programs about animals and their behavior. Slides about the yeti amused him, because he was convinced that in reality the yeti was a very large bear. Occasionally, colossal bears appeared in Tibet, even larger than yaks. Rinpoche himself had once seen the skin of one of these monstrous creatures in a house in Tibet. It lay spread over a huge double bed, and still covered part of the floor. The fur of such a bear was very short and shiny, with a long white stripe. Only a very few people in remote settlements had ever seen one of these huge animals, and thus the myth of the yeti had arisen. In Arlington Rinpoche also worked in a restaurant again, this time in a steak and ale house, first as a dishwasher, then as a kitchen helper, mostly frying potatoes and looking after the salad bar.

He had now lived almost two years in the United States, and although he had seldom thought about it, he had never doubted that he would eventually return and take his place on the throne of the Drikung lineage. He had ignored the Drikung lamas' beseeching letters that came during the first months after his arrival in the United States, but now he began to speak with his father about returning to India, telling him that there had never been any other option. Rinpoche had brought two sets of monks' robes to the United States, one from the Dalai Lama and the other from Chönyi Dorje, the Rani of Bhutan. He had given them to his mother and requested that she take good care of them, as he would need them.

At the end of 1977 Chetsang Rinpoche decided to move in with his sister Namlha in New Jersey, packed his things in his car, and drove off. Lobsang Samten had grown up with rinpoches, and three of his brothers were high incarnate lamas: the Dalai Lama, Taktser Rinpoche (Thubten Jigme Norbu), and Ngari Rinpoche (Tenzin Chögyal). When Rinpoche arrived unannounced on their doorstep, Lobsang said to his wife, "That is certainly a rinpoche! He is a stranger in the United States, knows hardly any English, and just drives all the way from Texas to us on his own. And on top of everything, he arrives without letting us know beforehand!"

A short time before moving to New Jersey, Rinpoche had received a package from Tsondu Senghe, a learned monk from the Drikung monastery in Tso Pema in India. It contained a copy of a very rare Tibetan text on the history of the throne holders of the Drikung order, written by the Fourth Chetsang Rinpoche, Peme Gyaltsen (1770–1826). He had composed this history of the lineage and the life stories of the lineage holders (*denrab*) in the early nineteenth century and entitled it *The Golden Garland of the Throne Lineage* (*Denrab Chöjung Serthreng*). His sources were chronicles and works by earlier Drikung lineage holders as well as the Dharma history of Pawo Tsuglag Threngwa (1504–1564/66). As was the case with all historical writing in Tibet, Peme Gyaltsen had difficulty identifying precise dates if only a year's zodiac sign was specified without indicating the corresponding element and sixty-year cycle (*rabjung*). Rinpoche was fascinated by this document and decided to turn his attention to the study of the history of Tibet, of Drikung, and of his own previous incarnations as written down by Peme Gyaltsen.

Although Peme Gyaltsen had gone to great pains to verify the dates of particular events by comparing them with Tibetan annals, Rinpoche took on the even more daunting task of ascertaining the exact chronology in terms of Western calendar dates. The project's difficulty lay in the extraordinarily complex astronomical calculations used to construct the Tibetan calendar for each year, one in which days—or even entire months—could either be skipped or repeated. Every day Rinpoche took the bus to New York City to comb through literature on this topic in the New York Public Library, and he was surprised to discover how many Tibetan works, on the most varied subjects, were available in the library. In the reading room he met Shakabpa, his sister Norzin's father-in-law and author of the well-known historical work, *Tibet: A Political History,* published in 1967. Shakabpa was now working on a new book, and they found themselves caught up in lively discussions about the history and politics of their homeland. Rinpoche closed in on his difficult task methodically until, after exhaustive research, he succeeded in unequivocally fixing a date from Jigten Sumgön's times. He had drawn up a concordance of the Tibetan rabjung cycles with the Gregorian calendar, starting in 1975 and working backwards in time until he found a correspondence with the date he had ascertained in Jigten Sumgön's era. He checked some of his dates with those in other historical works, and when he found that they corresponded with his system, he began to delve into the contents of Peme Gyaltsen's book.

This work was a source of a profound understanding for Chetsang Rinpoche, and he became familiar with the origins, significance, and history of the lineage he was to lead. At the same time, his study of the text inspired a broad perspective on the Tibetan past, the spiritual roots of the Drikung Kagyupa, and his own mind-stream, since his own incarnation lineage was intertwined with the unfolding history of the order, and on a larger scale, the country. He was a manifestation of this history; he was the result of these historical events.

He gained insight into the development of the Drikung lineage within the unfolding of epochs, into his spiritual genealogy, and into a history filled with tales of heroism and villainy; purity, corruption, and intrigue; weakness and power; war and peace. This was a history of an epic struggle to manifest goodness in the world, to bring about the spiritual perfection that would ultimately defeat all suffering and affliction. This was a history of which he himself was an integral part.

13

Spiritual Genealogy
The Throne Holders of Drikung

T HE FIRST DISSEMINATION of Buddhism in Tibet, the *ngadar,*
took place during the seventh and eighth centuries, and was followed by an epoch of decline. The Buddhist renaissance was initiated
by Rinchen Sangpo (958–1055), who was regarded as the first great
translator of the *chidar,* the "second diffusion" or "later spreading of the
Dharma," and his activity was crucial to the revival of cultural exchange
between Tibet and India. The renowned Bengali monk Atisha went to
the kingdom of Guge in Western Tibet, where he reformed Tibetan Buddhism, translated numerous texts into Tibetan, and introduced the tantra most recently disseminated in India, the Kalachakra, which became
the basis for a new calendar system in Tibet. The Kadampa order arose
on the basis of Atisha's reforms, and in the eleventh and twelfth century
many famous monasteries emerged in the wake of this Buddhist renaissance, among them Drikung Thil in 1179.

Marpa Chökyi Lodrö (1012–1097) of Lhodrak was another important translator. He had obtained many precious religious manuscripts
in India, among them the *Six Yogas of Naropa,* which has become a
fundamental work of the Kagyu school. The compilation of all known
Tibetan translations of Buddhist works in the monastery of Narthang,
near Shigatse, marked the triumphant flowering in Tibet of the Buddhist seeds that had been transplanted from India. The form in which
the great historian of Tibetan Buddhism, Butön (1290–1364), cast the
Kangyur and the Tengyur is considered authoritative to this day. During

this period the Sakya school of scholarship and transmission lineages was preeminent in Tibet.

The Kagyu tradition of Tibetan Buddhism originated with the Indian Mahasiddha Tilopa (988–1069), who had received the Dharma in a direct spiritual transmission from the Primordial Buddha Vajradhara.[1] His disciple Naropa (1016–1100) passed on the teachings to the Tibetan Marpa, who had traveled to India to seek the teachings. After he had returned to Tibet with the teachings, Milarepa (1040–1123) became Marpa's most important disciple, who, after an angry and adventurous youth, dedicated his life to meditative practice in the solitude of mountain caves. His renown as a realized yogi spread throughout the Land of Snows, and it was from Milarepa's disciple Gampopa (1079–1153), a physician from Dagpo, that the first Kagyu schools originated: the Karma Kagyu, Tselpa Kagyu, Barom Kagyu, and Phagdru Kagyu. Of these, only the lineage of the Karma Kagyu exists to this day.

The founder of the Phagdru Kagyu was Phagmodrupa Dorje Gyalpo (1110–1170), one of Gampopa's most important disciples. His spiritual lineage split into various branches that carried different names, but the Phagmodrupa name continued in history as his clan played an important role in Tibet's secular government in the ensuing epoch. Of the lineages founded by Phagmodrupa's main disciples, only three are still extant: the Drikung Kagyu, Taklung Kagyu, and Drukpa Kagyu.

Phagmodrupa's Heart Son, Kyobpa Jigten Sumgön ("Protector of the Three Worlds") (1143–1217), took over the throne of the Phagdru in Densa Thil for three years after his teacher's death (1177–1179). He then founded his own lineage and monastery in the area of Drikung, as Phagmodrupa had predicted. In 1167, Minyak Gomring, a disciple of Phagmodrupa, had built his little hermitage in Drikung, and Kyobpa Jigten Sumgön chose this site for the construction of the monastery of Drikung Thil.

Jigten Sumgön's main practice was that of the *yidam* Chakrasamvara, conqueror of Shiva.[2] The wrathful, worldly god Shiva and his demons had taken possession of twenty-four places on the earth, and the transcendent Vajradhara manifested as Chakrasamvara, defeated Shiva and his army of demons, and transformed the twenty-four places into sacred Buddhist sites, dwelling places of Chakrasamvara. Jigten Sumgön recognized a cliff near Drikung Thil, called the Lion's Shoulder, as the mandala of Chakrsamvara, and founded a monastery and built a stupa

Drikung Thil Monastery.

there. When the Karmapa Dusum Khyenpa (1110–1193), founder of the Karma Kagyu lineage, came to Drikung Thil, he recognized the entire area as the mandala of Chakrasamvara and saw Jigten Sumgön as the Buddha, and his two main disciples as Shariputra and Maudgalyayana, the two main disciples of the Buddha.

Jigten Sumgön attained great fame and people flocked from all parts of the country to receive initiations and teachings from him. He placed particular emphasis on meditative practice, and he sent practitioners to three especially sacred mountains, Kailash (Gangri Tise), whose form corresponds to the body of Chakrasamvara; Lapchi in the present-day border area between Tibet and Nepal, the site of the speech of Chakrasamvara; and Tsari, the site of the mind of Chakrasamvara. He first sent eighty *ripa* (practitioners who engage in meditative retreat) to the three sacred mountains.[3] His second delegation consisted of nine hundred ripa, and in 1215, before his final passing away, he sent three groups of 55,525 ripa each to Kailash, Lapchi, and Tsari, each led by one of his three most important disciples.

As the order grew and spread, Drikung monasteries arose in lands far from the main monastery, near Mt. Kailash, in Ladakh, in Kongpo, and in Kham, the founder's homeland. Jigten Sumgön's great-grandmother, Achi Chökyi Dolma, had come from Drikung. She moved to Kham and married a yogi from the Kyura clan, thus producing Jigten Sumgön's line. In later times she came to be known as the spiritual protectress of the Drikung order. As was the custom in many schools of Tibetan Buddhism, Jigten Sumgön chose his successor from among his relatives, and in the beginning all but three Drikung Kagyu throne holders came from the Kyura clan, although there was no set rule of succession.

From the very beginning there was no real hierocracy in Drikung, as is often claimed with respect to the Tibetan form of rule. Powers were shared; spiritual leadership was the responsibility of the *denrab*, the throne holder, while secular matters were under the governance of a *gompa*, a civil administrator. Both usually came from the Kyura clan.

Several of the early Drikung throne holders attained prominence, among them Chenga Drakpa Jungne (1175–1255), a Heart Son of Jigten Sumgön, who was entrusted with the leadership of Phagmodrupa's monastery, Densa Thil. He led that monastery to a new period of flowering and then took over the throne of the Drikung Kagyu in 1235. When the Tibetans stopped paying tribute to the powerful and militant Mongolians, Ogodei (1186–1241), the son and successor of Genghis Khan (1162–1227), ordered punitive action, and in 1239 Mongolian troops burned down many monasteries, among them Reting, where they slaughtered five hundred monks before moving on toward nearby Drikung. The secular leader of Drikung opposed them and was captured, and it is said that stones rained down from the skies when Drakpa Jungne hastened to the Mongolian camp, although perhaps it was just a strong hailstorm. In any event, his courageous intervention resulted in a peace settlement with the Mongolians, and Drikung rose to become a major power in central Tibet.

Meanwhile, the Tibetan aristocracy sent Kunga Gyaltsen, later known as Sakya Pandita (1182–1251), as chief negotiator of a delegation of Tibetans to Godan Khan, Ogodei's general. Kunga Gyaltsen made a pact in which Tibet accepted Mongolian suzerainty and agreed to pay tribute, although many Tibetan noblemen continued to object to the demands for tribute until Mongolian troops put an end to their resistance with a bloody and crushing defeat in 1251.

The Sakya school's amicable relations with the Mongols ensured their position of political leadership in Tibet. Kunga Gyaltsen didn't succeed in converting the Mongolian ruler to Buddhism, but his nephew and successor, Phagpa Lodrö (1235–1280), was more successful. Phagpa became the spiritual teacher of Khubilai Sechen, who became Great Khan of the Mongols in 1259, but had to deal with competition from the Second Karmapa, Karma Pakshi (1204–1283), who attempted to expand the influence of the Karma Kagyu order among the Mongols. Legend has it that Phagpa Lodrö won this spiritual contest through a magical display. The Khön Clan of the Sakya throne holders originated in Brusha, in the vicinity of Gilgit in the Hindukush, a place that is closely associated with Padmasambhava and was regarded as a land of witches and warlocks, and Phagpa was also initiated in the magic of Brusha. Thus, he was said to have created the illusion, in front of the entire Mongol court, that he had dismembered his own body and transformed the pieces into the five buddha families, out of which his body was then reassembled. This performance is said to have cemented his unchallenged position as spiritual master and teacher.

More likely, Karma Pakshi lost all influence because of a political blunder. He had snubbed Khubilai Khan (1215–1294), a grandson of Genghis Khan, by refusing to remain in his tent camp and becoming court lama to the Great Khan Möngke. When, four years later, Möngke died and Khubilai rose to become the Great Khan, he refused his protection to the Karmapa and his school, and gave Phagpa Lodrö the provinces of U and Tsang, as well as Kham and Amdo in 1275 as feudal fiefdoms. When Khubilai became emperor of China in 1279 and founded the Yuan Dynasty, he conferred on Phagpa Lodrö the title of Imperial Preceptor, and, for the first time in Tibet, the hierocratic form of government was constituted in a relationship of patronage between the emperor and his spiritual teacher.

Resistance to this transformation of the country into a series of feudal fiefdoms began to stir among the Tibetan aristocracy, especially in the provinces that were closely connected with the Drikung, Phagdru, and Karma Kagyu. Drikung had risen to great power by this time, and it is reported that even as early as the rule of the fifth throne holder, Chung Dorje Drakpa (1210–1278), great numbers of monks filled the Drikung monasteries. At the same time, the Mongolian tribes were engaged in struggles over leadership and landed estates among themselves, and after the death of the Great Khan Möngke in 1259, Hulagu (ca. 1217–1265),[4] Khubilai's brother and rival, positioned himself in Tibet by declaring himself the powerful protector of Drikung, and he sent a small Mongolian unit to the Drikung Kagyu for their safety and security.

The dispute between rival Mongol groups that was played out on Tibetan soil would go down in history as a war between Drikung and Sakya. It was not a feud between two schools of Tibetan Buddhism, as is often claimed, but rather a few provinces' attempt to make alliances that exploited Mongolian rivalries in order to overthrow the suzerainty of Khubilai. The actual local conflict centered on disputes concerning the line of succession in Phagmodrupa's monastery of Densa Thil, where one branch was supported by the Sakyapa (and their Mongolian allies, followers of Khubilai), and the other by the Drikungpa (and their Mongolian allies, followers of Hulagu). The war broke out at the time of Drikung's seventh throne holder, Tsamche Drakpa Sönam (1238–1286), and in 1290, during the time of his successor, Nub Chögo Dorje Yeshe (1223–1293), Drikung Thil Monastery was devastated by Mongolian troops. Unfortunately for Dorje Yeshe, as he was not a member of the Kyura clan but of the Nub clan, he lacked popular support in those difficult times.

Drikung Thil was rebuilt under the ninth throne holder, Chunyi Dorje Rinchen (1278–1314), with support from the emperor of China and the Sakyapa, but the powerful political influence that the monastery had exercised for decades in Tibet was gone. Dorje Rinchen turned his focus to monastic instruction and instituted an annual cycle in which Drikung philosophical texts and the fundamentals of Mahayana Buddhism were taught in spring and autumn, teachings on the *Fivefold Path of Mahamudra* were given in summer, and, wearing only light clothing, Dorje Rinchen taught the *Six Yogas of Naropa* on the great terrace outside the main temple of Drikung Thil in winter.

Although the Phagdru Kagyu order was in a state of decline in the fourteenth century, the rulers of the Lang clan that was closely associated with it assumed secular leadership in central Tibet. The central figure of this epoch was Jangchub Gyaltsen (1302–1373), who was both a skillful politician and a monk of the Phagdru Kagyu. He led the country to greater independence and created a new system of administration by dividing the land into districts that were administered by dzongs (fortresses), with the stronghold commanders as district governors (*dzongpön*). But Jangchub Gyaltsen's reforms worsened relations with the newly strengthened Drikung, and thus Drikung became embroiled in armed conflicts with the Phagmodrupa. After some initial successes, the Drikungpa suffered a few painful defeats on the battlefield and were forced to accept the rule of the Phagmodrupa in northern U, but toward the end of Jangchub Gyaltsen's life the Drikungpa succeeded in reestablishing the autonomy of their lands. This coincided with a larger shift in the balance of power, the fall of the Yuan Dynasty and the ascent of the Ming Dynasty (1368–1644), but the Mongols still remained a powerful influence in both Tibet and Ming China.

In the midst of this political turmoil, Chenga Chökyi Gyalpo (1335–1407), the eleventh throne holder, remained focused on spiritual issues, and had the Kangyur of Narthang and the newly edited version of the Tengyur copied. Tsongkhapa (1357–1419), the founder of the Gelug school, came from Amdo to Drikung in 1373 and became a disciple of Chökyi Gyalpo. His family settled in a village about forty kilometers away from the monastery. Tsongkhapa received the Drikung teachings on the *Six Yogas of Naropa* as well as all of the outer and inner texts by Jigten Sumgön.[5]

The Drikungpa gradually strengthened their position, and in the fifteenth century, the Ming Dynasty recognized their renewed and increasing influence and granted the throne holder the honorific title, *Ch'an chiao wang,* conferred on the heads of the eight most important schools or monasteries. At the close of the fifteenth century, the dzongpön of Rinpung, the protector of the Karma Kagyu, overthrew the Phagmodrupa, who had become entangled in internal conflicts, but then in the second half of the sixteenth century the Tsangpa wrested power from the Rinpungpa. Shigatse, in the province of Tsang, was the center of power in Tibet for two hundred years, first under the rulers of Ringpung (1436–1566), and then under the Tsangpa (1566–1642). Since both noble families supported the Karmapa, the Karma Kagyu was the most influential school of the epoch.

Two outstanding personalities on the throne of Drikung left their marks in the beginning of the sixteenth century: Gyalwang Kunga Rinchen (1475–1527) and his successor Gyalwang Rinchen Phuntsog (1509–1557). Kunga Rinchen was regarded as the reincarnation of Jigten

Sumgön. He aspired to improve the quality of spiritual life and dedicated himself intensively to giving transmissions and teachings, and he also worked to revive the tradition of hermitage retreats. He sent many of the disciples who came in droves to Drikung into retreat at Gangri Tise, Tsari, and Lapchi, and fifty new meditation huts were built at Drikung Thil Monastery. The Kangyur and Tengyur were copied on indigo paper in gold and silver script, and two hundred scribes were involved in the production of the complete texts of the Drikung lineage.

Rinchen Phuntsog, the seventeenth Drikung throne holder, was a great reformer. After receiving transmissions from various lineages, he integrated many doctrines, rituals, and meditation practices, mainly from the Nyingma order, into the traditional teachings of the Drikung Kagyu school. Rinchen Phuntsog discovered the treasure text *Gongpa Yangzab* in the Kiri Yangdzong Cave of Terdrom Valley, and he later gave teachings in the cave and had the hermitage of Yangrigar expanded into a monastery. He was a prolific author whose writings were also taken up by the Nyingma and included in the collection of Nyingma tantras.

Rinchen Phuntsog's only son, Chögyal Rinchen Phuntsog (1547–1602), used the monastery of Drikung Tse that had been founded in 1560 as his primary residence. He was the twenty-first on the Drikung throne when Altan Khan (1507–1582), the powerful ruler of the Tumat Mongols, entered into the alliance with Sönam Gyatso (1543–1588) of the Gelugpa school that was to direct the course of Tibetan history. The Mongolian ruler conferred the title of Dalai Lama on Sönam Gyatso and accorded him extensive privileges.[6]

Drikung was located in the corridor of the repeated Mongolian invasions, so that whenever the Mongols moved into central Tibet to fight on the side of one faction or another the region was subjected to devastation. At the end of the sixteenth century the Drikungpa had become so weakened by the many armed conflicts that Chögyal Rinchen Phuntsog had the Drikung Dzong complex reinforced and expanded into a fortress.

The succession of throne holders based on the family line ended with the sons of Chögyal Rinchen Phuntsog. His eldest son, Naro Tashi Phuntsog (1574–1628), called Naro Nyipa ("the Second Naropa"), succeeded to the throne, while his second son, Garwang Chökyi Wangchug (1584–1630), was recognized as the Sixth Shamarpa.[7] During Naro

Tashi's rule numerous armed conflicts took place with the Mongols, who had allied themselves with the Gelugpa against the Tsangpa kings. The Mongols were fighting to shift power decisively to the Gelugpa and the nobility loyal to them, especially since a great-grandson of Altan Khan had been brought to Lhasa as the Fourth Dalai Lama (1589–1617).

Chögyal Rinchen Phuntsog's two youngest sons, Gyalwang Konchog Rinchen (1590–1654) and Kunkhyen Rigzin Chödrak (1595–1659) became the last biological heirs to inherit the throne of Drikung; the Kyura lineage died with them. After the death of Konchog Rinchen the Drikungpa began to seek the reincarnations of their throne holders, and a system of two lineage holders, the elder (Chetsang) and the younger (Chungtsang) brother, was established. Konchog Rinchen became the first Chetsang Rinpoche and Rigzin Chödrak was the first Chungtsang Rinpoche.

The First Chetsang, Konchog Rinchen, was born prematurely, and it was feared that he would die in infancy. But he survived, and is said to have spoken, when he was still a child, about his past lives. When he was three he was considered the most likely candidate for being the reincarnation of the recently deceased Third Dalai Lama, but the Mongol Yonten Gyatso was recognized as the Fourth Dalai Lama and Konchog Rinchen remained in the Drikung lineage. During his time on the Drikung throne he had to resolve numerous quarrels within the order, and he renewed the Drikungpa's ties with the Mongols when he became a Mongol chieftain's spiritual teacher. He received transmissions of various treasure texts in visions, including transmissions from Milarepa and Guru Rinpoche.

Meanwhile, the Tumat Mongols were claiming rights to Tibetan lands and properties, as the Fourth Dalai Lama was a descendant of the Tumat clan, and the Drikung again found themselves embroiled in armed conflict. The fortress of Drikung Dzong fell to Mongolian troops and the entire region of Drikung lay in such ruin that Konchog Rinchen was unable to live there for a long time. When the Tsangpa king Phuntsog Namgyal succeeded in driving back the Mongols, Konchog Rinchen quickly rebuilt Drikung Dzong in 1624. He named the new building Namgyal Chödzong.

But the warfare continued. The king of Tsang Karma Tenkyong Wangpo (1605–1642) was forced to hold his ground against both Gushri

Khan, the ruler of the Khoshuud and a powerful ally of the Fifth Dalai Lama (1617–1682), and the king of Ladakh, who was threatening his domains from the south. When Gushri Khan's troops defeated the king of Tsang, the Gelugpa, with the Dalai Lama as their supreme head, gained sovereignty over the entire country. The Gelugpas enforced their supremacy over the other schools of Tibetan Buddhism, proceeding with special severity against the Karma Kagyu. Monasteries and noble residences fell to the depredations of the Mongolian army, including the recently rebuilt Namgyal Chödzong. In Drikung, nothing remained of many villages but their names.

Only two years after the enthronement of the Fifth Dalai Lama as ruler of Tibet in 1642, the Manchu, or Qing, Dynasty (1644–1911) took over rule in China. The Dalai Lama lost no time in securing the emperor's support, and the Manchus resumed the formal relationship, which had lost importance during the era of Ming rule, between the Fifth Dalai Lama and the emperor as spiritual master and patron, respectively.

In the midst of this epoch of depredation and ruin, Drikung became famous, and was both admired and feared, as a center of magic. Konchog Rinchen's brother, the First Chungtsang Rigzin Chödrak, attained mastery in the areas of astrology, divination, geomancy, and palmistry, and founded an important school of astrology and divination in Drikung. He is said to have magically caused *champaka* flowers with sparks of flame to appear on a mountain,[8] and also to have averted a threatened Mongolian attack. The Dalai Lama esteemed him highly, while governing circles feared his magical powers to such an extent that he was compelled to swear he would never employ magical arts against the central government. Rigzin Chödrak was reported be able to cause a person's death by writing his name on a piece of paper and grinding it in a mortar consecrated to Yamantaka. He also attained mastery in medicine and founded the Drikung system of medicine, one of Tibet's four medical traditions. Among his works are texts on Yamantaka practice and an Achi practice for divination with dice. Following a disastrous cold wave and famine in central Tibet in 1643, many believed that Rigzin Chödrak's rituals averted catastrophe in subsequent years, and they called him the "Lama Who Provides Precious Tsampa."

Konchog Rinchen died in 1654 while attempting to mediate in a dispute that threatened to escalate into civil war. In 1658, a year before his own death, Rigzin Chödrak saw the reincarnation of his elder brother, the Second Chetsang Rinpoche, in a vision and had him brought to Drikung.

Under the Second Chetsang Rinpoche Konchog Thrinle Sangpo (1656–1718) the tradition of first enthroning the Kyabgön Rinpoches in Drikung Tse Monastery was introduced. Thrinle Sangpo was an excellent thangka painter and devoted to the arts, founding one of the four great schools of painting in Tibet, the Driri school of Drikung. He was also highly intelligent and able to solve difficult philosophical problems with ease. In the Snake Year of 1677 he began the tradition of Snake Year Teachings on the threshing ground of Drikung Tse, where he gave initiations and teachings on the Chakrasamvara and Guhyasamaja tantras. In 1681 he had Yangrigar Monastery, which had been largely destroyed by the ceaseless warfare, completely rebuilt, and is now considered the monastery's founder. For a long time he guided the lineage alone, because the reincarnation of Chungtsang, recognized by the Tenth Karmapa, died in a smallpox epidemic before he could be brought to Drikung, and it wasn't until 1704 that Chungtsang reincarnated as Thrinle Döndrup Chögyal (1704–1754).

"The Great Fifth," as the Fifth Dalai Lama is called, introduced the office of *desi*, a viceroy who was responsible for the secular aspects of government and who would hold his regency until the next incarnation of the Dalai Lama had come of age. Three years before his death, he entrusted Sangye Gyatso (1653–1705), rumored to be his son, with this office. Sangye Gyatso kept the Dalai Lama's death in 1682 and the discovery of his reincarnation in 1688 secret for many years, and during this time he pursued a policy of harsh repression against the other schools of Tibetan Buddhism, confiscating many Nyingma and Kagyu monasteries.

The Qing Emperor K'ang-hsi (1662–1722) was furious when, after the enthronement of the sixteen-year-old Sixth Dalai Lama (1683–1707) in 1697, he learned of Sangye Gyatso's deception, and he gave his support to the Khoshuud ruler Lhabzang Khan's (1697–1717) efforts to seize power in Tibet and depose the Dalai Lama. Lhabzang Khan attacked Lhasa in 1705, killed Sangye Gyatso, and took the Dalai Lama prisoner. Although the young Dalai Lama was more interested in worldly love and poetry than in spiritual leadership, the high clergy opposed his removal from office. The Sixth Dalai Lama died on the way to exile in China, perhaps at the hands of an assassin.

During that era the power of the Gelugpas was far from being firmly established. Conflicts between the Dzungar and the Khoshuud, two tribes of the western Mongolian Oirates, offered the Tibetan nobility an opportunity to insist on a secular government in Tibet. The Dzungars did not wish to hand over supreme power in Tibet to Lhabzang Khan, and the Manchus were also attempting to break the Mongols' hold in Tibet. Two Tibetan aristocrats, Pholhane (1689–1747) and Khangchenne (murdered in 1727), now seized their opportunity.

Meanwhile, the central government had confiscated Drikung Dzong during Rigzin Chödrak's lifetime, and Thrinle Sangpo negotiated its return to Drikung hands in 1715. Not much was left of the formerly magnificent monastery by then, as costly roofs and expensive building materials from Drikung Dzong had been carried off to the capital to build up the area around the Barkhor. Rebuilding had just begun in 1717 when the Dzungars invaded Tibet, overran Lhasa, and assassinated Lhabzang Khan, and the construction work on Drikung Dzong was halted because, although the Drikung region was spared this time, the overall situation was unpredictable and dangerous. The Dzungars were devoted to the Dalai Lama and, blaming the Nyingma school for the alleged heretical tantric practices of the Sixth Dalai Lama, they burned and plundered numerous Nyingma monasteries.

But their merciless rampaging cost the Dzungars whatever popular support they may have had. Pholhane appealed to the Manchu Emperor K'ang-hsi for aid, and in 1720 K'ang-hsi had the young Seventh Dalai Lama (1708–1757) seized in Lithang and taken to Lhasa with a military guard of four thousand troops. The Dzungars were forced to retreat before these superior numbers, and the emperor secured the good will of the Tibetans with a triumphal enthronement of the Dalai Lama in Lhasa. His soldiers remained in Lhasa as a permanent garrison under the control of *amban*s, the emperor's newly installed civil representatives in Lhasa. The office of desi was abolished and a cabinet (Kashag) was created, with Khangchenne as the first prime minister.

During the time of the Second Chungtsang Thrinle Döndrup Chögyal, Pholhane, who was attempting to set up a secular government with the help of the Chinese Imperial Court, had wood prints, based on the old Narthang manuscripts, of the Kangyur produced in 1732, and of the Tengyur in 1742. Döndrup Chögyal founded several new monasteries, and also became known under the name Drikung Bhande Dharmaraja. In his work *Jewel Treasury of Advice* he summarized the entire structure of the Buddhist path according to both Sutrayana and Tantrayana.

The Second Chetsang Rinpoche's reincarnation, found in 1720, was the son of the great treasure-finder Chöje Lingpa, but he died in infancy and was therefore never officially confirmed as the Third Chetsang Rinpoche. The Chinese Imperial court attempted to push through its own candidate, but a boy seen in a vision by Chungtsang Döndrup Chögyal was brought to Drikung and enthroned. When the Third Chetsang Rinpoche Konchog Tenzin Drodul (1724–1766) was still very young, his previous incarnation's sly nephew claimed that his own son was the true Chetsang Rinpoche reincarnation, thereby producing discord in the order. To put an end to the quarrels, Döndrup Chögyal performed a divination in the Jokhang, together with Pholhane, the highest-ranking government official, that unquestionably confirmed Tenzin Drodul. But this did not completely dispel the disputes in his monasteries, and Chetsang Rinpoche Tenzin Drodul was plagued by bad omens, ceaseless quarrels, malicious attendants, and vicious gossip. He withdrew from active participation in the lineage and spent almost his entire life in meditation. Tenzin Chökyi Nyima, the Third Chungtsang (1755–1792), son of a noble family from Jangyul, also failed to make much headway against this state of affairs, although he made every effort to renovate the monasteries and purify discipline.

Under the Seventh Dalai Lama, the Gelugpa began to regain the upper hand in Tibet, but the Manchu emperors manipulated the government by gaining control over the Gelugpa regents who ruled between one Dalai Lama's death and his successor's enthronement. The Eighth Dalai Lama (1758–1804) had no interest in secular matters and left government business to a regent, and of the four Dalai Lamas who followed him, none lived past the age of twenty-one, apparently all murdered. Thus, Gelugpa regents, rather than a Dalai Lama, governed Tibet for a period of 140 years, from the death of the Seventh Dalai Lama to the enthronement of the Thirteenth Dalai Lama in 1895.

The situation began to improve in Drikung with Tenzin Peme Gyaltsen, the Fourth Chetsang Rinpoche (1770–1826), who was born in Kongpo, the son of a yogi. When he observed that ethical discipline had deteriorated badly in Yangrigar, he had all monks who did not live according to the precepts, thus bringing the monastery into disrepute, perform punitive labor, and he gained fame as the author of *The Golden Garland of the Throne Lineage*. When the Fourth Chungtsang, Tenzin Chökyi Gyaltsen (1793–1826), died in the same year as Peme Gyaltsen, it became necessary for the second time for a regent, Lhochen Chökyi Lodrö (1801–1859), to guide the lineage.[9] The Kyabgöns' reincarnations were found and brought to Drikung in 1832.

Konchog Chönyi Norbu (1827–1865), the Fifth Chungtsang, and Konchog Thukje Nyima (1828–1885), the Fifth Chetsang Rinpoche, were enthroned at the same time on Jigten Sumgön's red earth throne near Drikung Thil. When Yongzin Konchog Jönten Jungne died in 1840, turf battles over the best positions in the monasteries broke out, and shortly thereafter, the Sikhs under Gulab Singh conquered Ladakh and occupied the three provinces of Ngari. The Drikung monasteries in Ladakh and near Mt. Kailash suffered severe damage during these conflicts, and although the Sikh warriors were successfully driven out, mostly thanks to extremely cold weather conditions, the ensuing period of peace was short-lived. During this period the Opium Wars in China (1839–1842 and 1856–1860) coincided with skirmishes in Sikkim and in southern Tibet as the Montawang tribe that lived near Bhutan was being driven out by the British.

The Drikung lineage was in full blossom, but success and admiration brought envy and jealousy in their wake; Drikung was accused of wishing to rival the Potala with its impressive dzong, the golden roofs of Thil and the palatial edifices of Tse. Thukje Nyima was an exceptionally learned man, particularly expert in medicine, and became known as the "Medicine King Thukje Nyima." Malicious monastic officials slandered him, and a Gelugpa-controlled government delegation sent to investigate the accusations found Chetsang Rinpoche Thukje Nyima guilty and forced him to abdicate the throne in 1854. As punishment, the golden roof of the temple in Drikung Thil was removed to Lhasa, and some Drikung estates were confiscated, resulting in acute food shortages. Thukje Nyima set off in secret on pilgrimages to Kailash from his exile in Tsang, and gave teachings and empowerments in other locations.

Drikung monasteries always feature two separate thrones for Chetsang Rinpoche and Chungtsang Rinpoche, before which *tsog* offerings and bowls with sweet rice are placed on special occasions. After 1854 it was forbidden to lay such tokens of devotion before the throne seat of Thukje Nyima, but during the New Year's celebrations of 1859 a monk of Yangrigar believed that bad luck would ensue if he did not stack up the traditional offerings on both the Kyabgöns' tables. At Mt. Kailash, Thukje Nyima saw this with his psychic vision and decided that it would now be safe to return to Drikung. He went to Tsang, where he did in fact receive permission from the Tibetan government to return to Drikung.

Great joy reigned in Drikung when the two lineage holders were finally reunited, and the next year they journeyed together to Lhasa for the enthronement of the four-year-old Twelfth Dalai Lama, his predecessor having been assassinated at the age of twenty-one. In 1863, during the Pig Year examinations of the yogis, Chungtsang Chönyi Norbu was appalled at their poor performances; they showed off with imposing hair knots, yet were unable to recite even the most basic prayer of supplication by heart. To remedy this disgraceful situation he instituted a stringent regime of discipline and study, to be enforced through rigorous examinations. Chönyi Norbu died in 1865, and Thukje Nyima recognized the reincarnation of Chungtsang Rinpoche in a vision at Lhamo Latso.

Shortly thereafter, monastic officials again began intrigues against Thukje Nyima, seeking to provoke a dispute between him and the new Chungtsang Rinpoche. For the second time Thukje Nyima was forced to leave his position in Drikung Thil, and this time he withdrew to Trolung for the rest of his life. Many of his followers fell into deep despair, while he accepted all obstacles with a wide-open heart and deep serenity.

The Sixth Chungtsang Tenzin Chökyi Lodrö (1868–1906) was born in Olkha in Lhokha and the reincarnation of the Sixth Chetsang Rinpoche Tenzin Shiwe Lodrö (1886–1943) from Daghla Gampo was found in 1891 and brought to Drikung in the following year. Chökyi Lodrö wrote two comprehensive guidebooks for pilgrimages to holy places, Mt. Kailash and Lapchi, which offer insight into the meaning of sacred geography in Tibetan Buddhism. During his stay in the Kailash region he founded the monastic community of Phuntsogling in eastern Ladakh and appointed the eighth reincarnation of Togden Rinpoche as the religious head of the Drikung monasteries in Mangyul (Ladakh).

When the two Kyabgöns visited Lhasa in 1893 they received various initiations from the Thirteenth Dalai Lama, who also bestowed upon them the title of hotogthu. Since that time, they have always worn the golden hotogthu hat on official journeys, in accordance with an ancient prophecy of the First Chungtsang Rigzin Chödrak that in the future he would wear a golden hat.

At the beginning of the twentieth century, as tensions between the British and Tibet were increasing, Chökyi Lodrö undertook his second great pilgrimage to Nepal and Lapchi, and in 1906 he became seriously ill and died. A letter to Shiwe Lodrö, composed as an acrostic in which he requested Chetsang Rinpoche's permission to depart, was found under his mattress.

Rinpoche Shiwe Lodrö was then enthroned as the thirty-fifth lineage holder. He had received all of the important empowerments and teachings of the Drikung lineage as well as the *Kagyu Ngag Dzö* at an early age, and he transmitted them to Tritsab Gyabra, who would later become regent. Shiwe Lodrö traveled to Kham and received many empowerments there, and he also visited the Thirteenth Dalai Lama in Lhasa in 1912. He was distantly related to the Dalai Lama, and they became such close friends that some believed they were brothers.

 Shiwe Lodrö recognized the Seventh Chungtsang Tenzin Chökyi Jungne (1909–1940), who was enthroned in 1914. The following year Shiwe Lodrö published the collected works of Jigten Sumgön in five volumes. In a small meditation hut in Drikung Thil he devoted himself to the practice of *Mahamudra* and the *Six Yogas of Naropa,* mastered the generation and completion stages of Tantrayana, and attained insight into higher dimensions of knowledge. His main interest lay in integrating meditative practice with philosophical study, as these were the main pillars of education and training in the Drikungpa tradition.

Shiwe Lodrö renovated Yangrigar and introduced a committee in Drikung Thil to improve the monastery administration, but the poor educational level in his monasteries was his greatest concern. He found a sponsor, an aristocrat named Khyungram, who provided financial support and in 1932 he established the Nyima Changra Academy of Higher Buddhist Studies.

At this time, Yangrigar and Drikung Thil were engaged in an ongoing conflict. The Seventh Chungtsang Tenzin Chökyi Jungne lacked authority, although he had attained great mastery in scholarship, and his failure to successfully mediate between the monks of Yangrigar and Drikung Thil in 1932 during the Monkey Year Teachings in Drongur eroded his authority even further. He was also troubled by intrigues that attempted to pit the two Holinesses against each other. Shiwe Lodrö's strong personality was unaffected by all of this, but the sensitive Chungtsang Rinpoche suffered from it. After losing Rigzin Chödrak's magic horn during a rain ceremony at Medro Sijin Lake, he became seriously ill. As he was not given good medical care in the monastery, he went to the home of Khyungram in Lhasa, but just then Khyungram fell into disfavor and was deported from Tibet. Chungtsang Rinpoche's servants fled, the house was sealed shut, and Chungtsang Rinpoche, severely ill, was locked in alone for three days.

Saddened by his own fate and the internal conflicts of the lineage, he wrote many letters to Shiwe Lodrö, whom he missed greatly, but the messengers misappropriated them. His depression and sense of having been abandoned deepened and he began to wish for death. Shiwe Lodrö intended to pay him a visit on his way to Drikung Dzong in 1940 but his servants prevented him from doing so, and Chökyi Jungne was mockingly informed that Chetsang Rinpoche was on his way to Drikung Dzong but had not stopped by to see him. That evening his sorrow was so great that he passed away.

Chungtsang Chökyi Jungne's death left Shiwe Lodrö bereaved and heavy-hearted, and soon after, on a journey to Kham, he suffered a stroke from which he did not recover. He then spent most of the time before his death in meditation, and in 1942 he suddenly announced that Chungtsang Rinpoche had been reincarnated, but then slipped into another level of consciousness without giving any details as to the location of the rebirth. Shiwe Lodrö finally passed away in 1943.

Then, for the third time in the lineage's history, a regent—Tritsab Gyabra—was responsible for the fate of the lineage, and under his leadership, the current reincarnations of the Chungtsang and Chetsang Rinpoches were found and enthroned.

14

A Noble Being's Promise

W HILE CHETSANG Thrinle Lhundrup studied the history of
Tibet and the Drikung order, lineage lamas tried again to persuade him to return to India, and Lobsang Samten came back from a
visit to India with a message from Ling Rinpoche, the senior tutor of
the Dalai Lama, requesting him to take up Buddhist studies and attend to
the needs of the Drikung lineage. His followers were happy to learn what
he was studying, although they weren't able to answer all of the questions
he was beginning to ask. Rinpoche requested information about the
earlier incarnations of the Chetsang and Chungtsang Rinpoches from
Konchog Samten, who wrote back that he did not know all that much
about them. There were too few among the Drikungpa who possessed
well-founded historical knowledge, so Rinpoche sought out learned Tibetan masters in New Jersey, meeting often with Geshe Wangyal and
inviting him to his sister's house. Ngawang Wangyal (1901–1983) was
a Mongolian of Kalmyk descent. In 1958 he founded the first Tibetan
Buddhist Dharma center in the United States in Howell, New Jersey,
and his students included Jeffrey Hopkins, Robert Thurman, and Joshua
Cutler, who would later become eminent scholars of Tibetan Buddhism.
Wangyal belonged to the generation of the Thirteenth Dalai Lama but
advocated progressive ideas for integrating Tibetan Buddhism into
Western society. Rinpoche enjoyed the company of this open-minded,
educated, and cheerful man who never tried to give him any advice, at
least not directly.

In the beginning of 1978, Sakya Trizin, the throne holder of the Sakyapa, visited the Tibetan community in Manhattan, together with his
teacher Dezhung Rinpoche (1906–1987), and Lobsang Samten invited

the two Rinpoches to lunch at his home. Dezhung Rinpoche, an erudite and important master, had settled in Seattle in 1960. Rinpoche insisted on chauffeuring Dezhung Rinpoche personally, as he was known to be very knowledgable about the history of Tibet. After a few minutes in the car, Dezhung Rinpoche broke the silence: "These days the world is really topsy-turvy, that's obvious; His Holiness the Drikung Kyabgön is my driver!"

During their meal Rinpoche put many questions to Dezhung Rinpoche, who was pleased, and said that only someone who asks lots of questions would come to understand things deeply. At that time Rinpoche was studying the history of the Panchen Lama, and Dezhung Rinpoche had detailed answers to all of his inquiries.

During that period Rinpoche often spent time with Tenzin Tendong, the Dalai Lama's representative in the United States, who was another relative and who was living in New York. Rinpoche sometimes accompanied him to his office and spent the night in his apartment. They had many discussions about Tibetan politics, and Tendong encouraged him to gradually emerge from anonymity and to write down his memories of life under Chinese occupation. He also organized interviews and lectures for him.

In America Rinpoche had become acquainted with the importance of advertising, and he thought that the Drikung lineage needed a little advertising, as it was practically unknown outside of a small circle. He assumed that some sort of a logo, an easily remembered symbol, would be helpful, and the ancient seal of the Drikungpa had simply consisted of the syllable HUNG in a unique form. Rinpoche had a rather precise idea of how the new symbol should look—simple and clear, and at the same time multileveled in its symbolic expressiveness, a HUNG in the center of a sun and moon disk. A Tibetan graphics designer who worked for Tendong helped finalize the design.

The Drikung Kyabgön Rinpoche was ready to go, he had spent three years in America and did not wish to lose any more time; the flights were booked, and Tenzin Tendong had organized lecture-engagements for him in Canada, London, and Switzerland on his way to India. He now had a residency permit for the United States, but he needed to renew his Indian Refugee Identity Certificate, which would involve a time-consuming process. But when his paperwork from the Indian embassy failed to arrive, Tendong suggested he apply for a reentry permit, as this was said to be easier to obtain. At the Indian embassy Rinpoche stated that he needed the reentry permit very urgently, as he would have to leave the country in two days. When the official became very upset and asked him how he could take on such an obligation if he still had no travel documents Rinpoche merely answered, "I have to go." She then meekly inquired if he had written invitations and he was able to hand her a thick file full of letters. Rinpoche received his reentry permit.

Chetsang Rinpoche was well aware of the consequences of his decision. The Drikungpa expected him to take on the leadership of an organization that was in danger of disappearing, just as several other Kagyu schools had already, and lead it to renewed flowering. There were many obstacles to overcome. The Drikung order now only consisted of a handful of dedicated practitioners and a couple of monks. There were large village communities in Ladakh that were traditionally connected to the lineage, but the people were desperately poor and couldn't even provide for the urgently needed repairs to the decaying monasteries in their own region, much less establish new monasteries and institutions elsewhere. Qualified teachers were in short supply everywhere. While his devoted followers were sure that miracles and the blessings of the lineage would solve all their problems, Rinpoche could see that qualities such as business administration, negotiating skills, and diplomacy would be necessary.

As to his Buddhist studies, he was still where he had been when he had left the monastery twenty years before—at the beginning. He would need not just a broadly based course of study in Buddhist philosophy, empowerments, and transmission of the tantras, but also years of intensive practice in secluded retreat. Somehow Chetsang Rinpoche would have to be a manager and a hermit, teacher, and student, everywhere and all at once.

Chetsang Rinpoche arrived in Delhi in early September 1978, greeted by delegates of the Drikung monasteries and communities, representatives of the Dalai Lama in Delhi, Lama Lobsang, Bakula Rinpoche, his aunt Tsering Dolma and her husband, Gelek Rinpoche. Gyalpo Rinpoche went to Tibet House on the evening of his arrival, where he was allocated a storeroom to sleep in. He had to move some of the piled-up packages of books to make a little more space and, curious, he opened one of them and withdrew an edition of the *Achi Beubum,* a collection of texts on the

Drikung protectress. The packages of the texts had simply lain forgotten in the storeroom. His surprise turned into amazement when he saw that the books had been printed on the same day that Chetsang Rinpoche had fled from Tibet. Gyalpo saw this as a sign that Achi had guided the Kyabgön Rinpoche from Tibet to India, and had now brought him back from America.

The next day there was a formal welcoming ceremony with a mandala offering for the Kyabgön Rinpoche at the Ashoka Hotel. The lamas urged him to take the vows of a fully ordained monk (*gelong*), and Chetsang Rinpoche tried to pacify the insistent lamas. As throne holder he would have to see to the reconstruction, preservation, and strengthening of the Drikung lineage, and the time for the gelong vows was not yet ripe. In response they begged him to at least take the novice (*getsul*) vows. Ahough he had always maintained perfect ethical discipline without the vows, to dispel their anxiety Rinpoche agreed, and a few days later he received his novice vows from the Dalai Lama in Dharamsala. The Dalai Lama handed him a statue of Amitayus to express his wish that Chetsang Rinpoche live long, and a statue of the Buddha for pure moral and ethical discipline. He was also given Milarepa's *Vajra Songs* as symbolic support for the aspect of speech, and a vajra and bell as support for the mind in tantric practice. Finally, the Dalai Lama gave him much advice and encouragement on his new responsibility. Many ideas had already begun to take shape in Rinpoche's mind, such as a Buddhist educational center with a substantial library, perhaps something along the lines of the Library of Tibetan Works and Archives in Dharamsala.

From Dharamsala he set off for Ladakh. It was like returning to Tibet, even like a return home to Drikung, because the order had been deeply rooted in Ladakh for centuries. In the early sixteenth century Rinchen Phuntsog had sent Denma Kunga Drakpa to Mt. Kailash. This realized master became the root lama of the king of Guge and of the provincial governor of Purang, and under his influence the Drikung monasteries near Kailash rose to new heights. His fame spread to Mangyul (Ladakh) to the northwest, and Kunga Drakpa accepted an invitation from the king of Ladakh, Tashi Namgyal (1555–1575).[1] His departure meant a bitter loss for spiritual life at Kailash, but a great gain for Ladakh. Kunga Drakpa founded the monastery of Phyang, and in all likelihood, the

Chetsang Rinpoche taking the novice vows before the Dalai Lama in Dharamsala.

Kadampa monastery of Lamayuru was transferred to the guidance of the Drikungpa during his lifetime.

The sixth reincarnation of Togden Rinpoche, Tenzin Chödrak, renewed the influence of the Drikungpa in Ladakh in the eighteenth century. He was the first tulku of his reincarnation lineage to leave central Tibet, and he settled in Phyang Monastery for a long time, where he became the teacher of two kings of Ladakh. The Eighth Togden Ngawang Lodrö Gyaltsen, a son of Jigme Kunga Namgyal, a prince of Ladakh, received his monastic training at Yangrigar Monastery and renovated the monasteries of Phyang and Lamayuru after his return. The present Ninth Togden Konchog Tenzin Thubten Tenpe Gyaltsen, born in 1938 in Dorkhul, a small village in eastern Ladakh, is one of the most learned and influential men in the Buddhist intellectual life of Ladakh.

In 1978 there was no civil air traffic to Ladakh yet, and an army transport plane took Chetsang Rinpoche from Chandigarh to Leh on October 1. Everyone of rank and importance had assembled to greet him, from the Maharani and the district military commander to the leaders of all the local religious groups and the village headmen. Rinpoche rode in an open Jeep, escorted by over twenty vehicles, and after a breakfast reception in the village temple of Kelsang Ling, he was guided to the main temple of Leh, the Jowo Tsuglagkhang, while thousands of people lined the streets and greeted him with cheers.

After the welcoming ceremonies, Rinpoche turned to the crowd to thank them for their sincere and open-hearted welcome, and expressed his joy at the fact that in India the lights of the Buddha's teachings were shining so brilliantly, while in Tibet they were being extinguished by the Chinese. He then went to Sarkar House, the government's house for guests of state, where he was able to discuss his plans and visions with the district administrator and other leading politicians. The next day he went to take up residence in Phyang, the main Drikungpa monastery in Ladakh, visiting the revered throne of Kunga Drakpa in Men Khang on the way. The monastery of Tashi Chödzong was built in 1515 on the hill of Phyang in one of the monastic land grants made by the king of Ladakh to Kunga Drakpa; it has come to be known as Phyang. A few of the wall paintings in the monastery's shrine rooms date from the time of the monastery's founding.

When the Kyabgön and entourage arrived in Phyang there were days filled with the traditional ceremonies, receptions, lama dances, mandala offerings, protector rituals, and speeches, the rituals and atmosphere of the ancient monastery bringing Rinpoche's childhood memories to life. Afterwards, Rinpoche traveled the region for two months, visiting many villages associated with the Drikung lineage and the local monasteries, and he and Togden began to make plans for the preservation of the monasteries. This was the first time a Drikung Kyabgön and a *chöje* had guided the spiritual activities of the Drikung Kagyu order in Ladakh.[2]

The monastic educational system in Ladakh was inadequate, offering little opportunity for a classical Buddhist education. Rinpoche was dismayed to see that there were no young students at all, because instead of receiving training, the monks had to perform hard physical labor to provide for their upkeep. Joining the army or some other occupation was more appealing to most young men.

There was a small retreat center near Sharchukhul, and a second one was built near Lamayuru Monastery. All that was lacking was a school for higher Buddhist studies, and Rinpoche aspired to create one immediately, and also a meditation center. But it would entail more than just the construction of a school building; the potential students had to be convinced of the value and necessity of a good education. Rinpoche found an ally in Khenpo Togdrol, who had taught at the Nyima Changra in Drikung and now wanted to establish a college of philosophy using Shiwe Lodrö's great academy as a model. Now, with the help of Shiwe Lodrö's succeeding incarnation, Khenpo Togdrol felt he could start work with confidence.

There was no financial support, as the offering boxes in the monasteries yielded only tiny sums, but Khenpo Togdrol was able to recruit many of his relatives for carpentry and masonry. With Rinpoche's active involvement a modest building was constructed and instruction began in July 1979, with eleven students. Togdrol was not discouraged by the small scale and took on about ten other school projects in Ladakh. A small school was also established at Lamayuru, where Togden Rinpoche was one of the teachers, although he was not very optimistic about the project, and problems soon arose. There sometimes wasn't enough food for the students because the local villages didn't understand the purpose of the institution, and thus didn't provide adequate support. Rivalries among the teachers also created trouble, and Togden's misgivings were well founded; only a handful of students completed their studies and the school closed its doors after seven years.

The old role of the monasteries was obsolete. In the past they had provided the farmers and nomadic herders with loans and credit, and with monks who worked for their spiritual well-being with prayers and rituals in exchange for the food and other daily necessities that were provided. But now banks provided loans and credit, taxes were paid to the state, and income was generated by paid work, particularly in the military or the tourist industry.

Rinpoche decided to lease the monasteries' lands in exchange for a fixed percentage of the harvest, but this approach also encountered difficulties, as some farmers were reluctant to cultivate the fields of a

monastery for fear of being attacked by the protector deities. However, Rinpoche slowly succeeded in leasing out all of the major monastic lands, so no monks would have to work in the fields. As a second
source of income, simple buildings were erected at advantageous locations along the main roads and rented out as businesses and roadside
restaurants, and further income was generated by charging tourists for
admission to the monasteries. Monks' families no longer had to support
them, as the monasteries began to provide room and board, as well as a
good education.

After Phyang and Lamayuru, Sharchukhul (Sharkhul Phuntsog Chöling) was the third-largest Drikung monastery in Ladakh. A special
permit from the Indian government was required to visit it, because it's
located in a restricted military zone on the border with Tibet. Chenga
Sherab Jungne had come to this area from beyond Pangong and founded
the first branches of the Drikung lineage here in the thirteenth century.
It became the original center of dissemination of the Drikung order in
Ladakh.

A little before Rinpoche arrived at the remote monastery at the end
of October 1978, the Dralha Wangchug came to greet him. Wangchug,
a fierce-looking older man with a face lined with deep wrinkles, was
the medium of a *dralha* oracle, a local warrior deity dedicated to defeat-
ing the enemies of the Dharma. The Dralha had been very famous in
eastern Tibet in earlier times, and this medium cut an impressive figure
here as well.

A few days later, when Rinpoche and his entourage arrived at Sharchukhul Monastery, Wangchug was dressed in his striking oracular
vestments and a mighty crown sat heavily on his head. With dramatic
gestures he described a vision, full of auspicious omens, in which he
had seen Rinpoche to be of inestimable benefit to the Dharma, and
then continued with a long-winded lecture about the vows he had
taken in past incarnations and in this one to act as a protector of the
Dharma, and in particular as the protector of the throne holders of the
Drikung lineage, and he prophesized that there would be no obstacles in
Chetsang Rinpoche's life or in Chungtsang Rinpoche's. He also guaranteed that Chungtsang Rinpoche would come to India one day, and the
Holinesses would meet again.

Chetsang Rinpoche suspected that Wangchug was putting on a show, since an oracle's trance normally involves trembling, convulsions, and speaking in a hissing, barely understandable voice, and it only lasts a short time. But the Dralha Wangchug was apparently in trance for hours conversing with many people, intelligibly and at length, and then he later demanded all sorts of privileges. Of course, oracles were a peculiar lot, but Rinpoche remained skeptical, and would never consult oracles in the future, preferring to rely on his own intuitive and divinatory abilities.

That evening the Dralha Wangchug took gracious leave from Rinpoche with the advice to note his dreams that night. Rinpoche dreamed that he was flying a kite, a much-loved pastime in Tibet. The kite strings were coated with ground glass and competitors would try to saw through the string of an opponent's kite. In his dream Rinpoche was about to lose his kite battle when he noticed an old man sitting next to him and smiling. It was the Dralha Wangchug, who skillfully assisted him in steering his kite to cut his adversary's kite string. Rinpoche revised his assessment of the oracle somewhat, and the next day he made an offering to the Eight Protectors of the World and composed a long-life prayer for the oracle.

Chetsang Rinpoche returned to Leh in early November for discussions with Bakula Rinpoche, directors of government agencies, and other public figures. Then, after visiting Atitse, a sacred place associated with the Mahasiddha Naropa, he settled in the remote monastery of Yungdrung Tharpaling, known today as Lamayuru. According to legend, it was built on the site of a long-ago lake, although the region is bare and desolate today. Naropa meditated in a cave here in the eleventh century and Rinchen Sangpo, the great translator, built many temples and stupas in the area as his Kadampa teachings began to flourish. The monastery was later passed on to the Drikungpa and given the name Yungdrung Tharpaling. Rinpoche decided to do his traditional three-year retreat (which actually lasts three years, three months and three days) at Lamayuru.

One year after Rinpoche had departed for the United States, delegates from Drikung monasteries had assailed the Dalai Lama with requests to persuade the Kyabgön Rinpoche to return to India. They were terribly afraid that he would never leave the United States, that he had abandoned them to their fate. The seventh-century Buddhist scholar Dharmakirti wrote in one of his seven treatises on logic, the

Pramanavarttikakarika (*Commentary on [Dignaga's Compendium of]* *Valid Cognition*) that noble beings never make great pledges, but when they do make a promise it is as if it were engraved in stone. They would keep it even at the cost of their own lives. Now it was obvious that Rinpoche had given the promise of a noble being even before he went to America, and the Drikungpa were ashamed of their pusillanimity, their lack of trust, and their blindness to broader contexts and perspectives. A noble being's intentions never change. It was only their own ignorance, attachment, and self-centeredness that had caused them to fear that the Kyabgön Rinpoche would never return. But he had not only renewed his vows and immediately begun dealing with the dismal situation of the Drikung monasteries, he had now decided to do his three-year retreat in the ancient and crumbling monastery of Lamayuru, lacking even the most basic modern comforts and conveniences, and where it was not even possible to obtain good food. The monks were astounded. There was no doubt that Chetsang Rinpoche did not simply intend to take on his role as a figurehead, but would strive to personally embody and further enhance the spiritual heritage of the lineage.

15

Absorption and Withdrawal
Dreams, Studies, and Retreats

K YUNGA SODPA GYATSO (1911–1980), from Kham, was
regarded as a realized master. He was a man of indomitable character, strong and strict like Marpa, and had spent thirty-five years of his
life in retreat. Kyunga became Drikung Thil's meditation master and
Shiwe Lodrö later sent him to Lapchi as *dorzin*.[1] There, he directed retreats in the Dudul Cave ("the Cave Where Evils Are Defeated"), one of
the four major caves of Lapchi, for seven years. After making a few pilgrimages he withdrew to a sacred place associated with Guru Rinpoche
for fifteen years, and he fled before the Tibetan national uprising and
worked with other Tibetan refugees on road construction in Sikkim.
The Karma Kagyu master Lama Sansang happened to pass the road crew
and recognize his former teacher, and thus the dorzin emerged from
anonymity. Togden Rinpoche learned about him through Druk Tuktse
Rinpoche (1915–1983), and he was installed as meditation master in a
monastery near Sharchukhul. There Kyunga directed the first three-year
retreat with nine students under very primitive conditions in 1974.

Drubwang Kyunga had been humble and undemanding all his life.
He had married while still in Drikung, and in Ladakh he lived in a tent
with his family, even during the winter months. He had practically no
personal possessions, savings, or provisions, and never made use of donations for himself; when his followers brought food for offerings, he
gave it to his students and kept none for himself.

In autumn of 1978, the second three-year retreat under Kyunga's guidance began in Lamayuru and included the Drikung Kyabgön Rinpoche

as a participant. Before the retreat, Khenchen Konchog Gyaltshen gave Rinpoche teachings on Nagarjuna's *Letter to a Friend* and Gampopa's *Jewel Ornament of Liberation,* the text that the Dalai Lama had presented to him after his escape from Tibet, and Kyunga gave him the transmissions and instructions on the two fundamental texts of the Drikung tradition, *Gongchig* and *Tenying (Thegchen Tenpe Nyingpo).*[2]

Buddhist practice entails conscious confrontation with and mastery over unwholesome habits of the mind. Deeply ingrained habitual ways of reacting constitute the greatest obstacles to spiritual progress. Without continually overcoming these habits the mind cannot be prepared for true openness. Only a consciousness that has been purified through specific practices can generate an awakened mind, the mind of enlightenment. For this reason, the so-called "preliminary practices" are given highest priority at the start of a retreat.[3] These practices consist of the Four Thoughts That Change the Mind as the general outer preliminaries: reflections on the precious human body, on impermanence and death, on the cause and effect of karma, and on the shortcomings of samsaric existence. The special inner preliminaries are the practices of refuge and bodhichitta (including full prostrations), Vajrasattva recitation, mandala offering, and guru yoga; they are called the "Four Times Hundred Thousand Practices" because each practice is repeated one hundred thousand times.

Taking refuge is the means by which the mind is directed toward the Dharma, prostrations serve to overcome pride and to lessen clinging to the ego, Vajrasattva practice purifies the practitioner of negative karma, the practice of mandala offering is a training in generosity and accumulates merit, and guru yoga leads to a deep unity with the mind of the teacher, which is inseparable from the mind of the Buddha. Above all, these are practices for overcoming laziness and sloth, and counteract a relapse into the old behavior patterns that have kept all beings ensnared in the cycle of rebirths since beginningless time.

In Tibetan Buddhism, wholesome new habits are inculcated artificially at first, but through continual practice they become completely natural, and undisguised awareness arises. Insights into the true nature of mind remain inconsequential impressions unless they are maintained and transformed into a permanent state of mind. This is a task that demands courage, strength of will, and trust, both in the liberating teachings of the Buddha and in the Buddha who appears in the form of the spiritual teacher.

Gelek Rinpoche escorted Chetsang Rinpoche to where he would begin his retreat, and when he saw the humble hut in which Rinpoche would spend the next few years, he wished to spare him the ordeal of a complete traditional retreat. He tried to negotiate with Drubwang Kyunga, saying, "Rinpoche is the rebirth of your root lama Shiwe Lodrö. He is no ordinary being, but a true *mahasiddha* who has reappeared in samsara. He had to endure so much suffering in occupied Tibet! Please permit him to do fewer prostrations as a special consideration, and grant him the transmission of the complete practice of the lineage quickly!" But Kyunga adamantly refused. He did not make any exceptions, but on the contrary replied, "He is the incarnation of His Holiness Shiwe Lodrö, and therefore he must practice more than others, to give proof of his qualities." After his return to Dharamsala a disheartened Gelek Rinpoche told the Dalai Lama about this discussion. The Dalai Lama was extremely pleased and replied, "Kyunga Rinpoche is a true guru!"

Kyunga told Chetsang Rinpoche that it was not important how much time he needed for them, but that he must do full-length prostrations. Kyunga was as immovable as a mountain in his meditation practice, and Rinpoche would not have accepted special treatment in any case. Within forty days he had completed the hundred thousand prostrations, sleeping only five hours a night. He had to pause now and then when he developed circulatory problems or had to vomit. His knees had scrapes and cuts, and occasionally his forehead bled, but Rinpoche was not content, and did an additional two hundred thousand prostrations.

His retreat room was on the top floor of the monastery, a small Spartan chamber with a floor of stamped earth, a narrow bed, and a traditional low reading table. The practitioners were thankful for even a thin blanket. The monk Konchog Sempa was assigned to Rinpoche as his personal assistant, and still is to this day. He planted potatoes and sold them to the Indian army to support Rinpoche during his retreat, and the Kyabgön Rinpoche's diet consisted almost exclusively of potatoes and turnips. It was bitterly cold in winter when the monastery was cut off from the rest of the world by massive snowdrifts, so Konchog Sempa had to trudge through the snow for three hours to obtain firewood from the villagers in Kaltse.

The preliminary practices lead to a certain degree of control over the aspects of body and speech. The difficult part is when, after the mind has attained one-pointed concentration, it is further reconfigured by a cycle of tantric practices involving subtle energies and complex meditation techniques. In the Drikung tradition, this is accomplished through reliance upon the practices of the *Six Yogas of Naropa* and the *Fivefold Path of Mahamudra*. The *Six Yogas of Naropa* are the generation of inner heat (*tummo*), the experience of one's own body as an illusion (*gyulu*), dream yoga (*milam*), the apperception of the clear light (*ösel*), the teachings on the intermediate state (*bardo*), and the transference of consciousness (*phowa*). These are complex psycho-physical practices that induce a profound transformation in consciousness and the accompanying subtle energy processes.

Mahamudra is considered one of the supreme Vajrayana teachings. Its goal is insight into the unity of emptiness and clarity as the true essence of primordial awareness. In meditation, all perceptions are transformed into their qualities of emptiness and clarity by means of the practice of calm abiding, and then transferred into the experience of the nature of reality, free of any exertion, through special insight.[4] The result is a freedom of mind that transcends all conventions. Tilopa said in his oral instructions on Mahamudra, "A mind free of reference points, that is Mahamudra."

During the second year of the retreat, Kyunga died from the delayed consequences of untreated internal injuries he had suffered in a bus accident a few years previously. Before his passing, he exhorted his disciples not to leave the retreat under any circumstances, and the next day Kyunga spoke with Rinpoche. With a weak voice he said, "If you are the reincarnation of Shiwe Lodrö, I never want to be separate from you. I pray for this. I have cut through space with a sword. A sword finds no obstacle in space, it is absolutely free." He ended the interview with the words, "In the past, you were unable to leave Tibet, and I was worried about you. After you fled, you went to America, and I was worried about you. Now you are in India and are perfecting your studies and your practice, and I am no longer worried about you. So I can die with a quiet mind. All dharmas are impermanent. You are responsible for the Drikung Kagyu lineage. It is a difficult task; it is good that you have accepted it. Go back to your retreat." Lama Sönam Jorphel took his place as retreat master.

Chetsang Rinpoche interrupted his retreat in the summer of 1979 for a ceremony at Phyang Monastery that he had already planned while in the United States to mark the eight-hundredth anniversary of the founding of Drikung Thil Monastery (1179), and hence of the Drikung lineage. Before leaving the United States, Rinpoche had met Warren Scott, a wealthy entrepreneur who supported his plans, and whose son, a filmmaker, was enthusiastic about producing a documentary film about the festival in Ladakh and the Drikung lineage. He came to Ladakh and filmed *Drikung — A Faith in Exile* during the ceremonies. Heinrich Harrer also came from Austria and was happy to meet up again with his old friend Dundul Namgyal Tsarong, who told him about his son's life and daring escape. Harrer later published a volume about the ceremonies in Phyang, richly illustrated with photographs.[5]

The sky was cloudless as the guests began arriving, but the monastery was framed by a rainbow. It was a moving ceremony, intended to mark a significant turning point in the history of the order. There wasn't enough room in the monastery for the great numbers of people, and they spread over the entire hill; this event celebrated the return of the Kyabgön Rinpoche as well as the founding of the order. Chetsang Rinpoche gave a long-life initiation, and on July 27 a huge newly completed thangka, a gigantic piece of cloth rolled around a wooden beam, was carried through the main gate. Although it had been hot and dry for months, raindrops fell from the nearly cloudless sky just at that very moment, which was considered a sign of the blessing of the lineage lamas. The beam was lifted along the front elevation of the monastery and the magnificent sixteen-meter-high appliqué thangka of Kyobpa Jigten Sumgön was unrolled to symbolize the Drikungpas' renown, reaching far and wide, that Rinpoche intended to rekindle.

Lama dances were performed according to ancient tradition in the courtyard below the colossal image of the lineage founder, who seemed to gaze far beyond Ladakh. Rinpoche sat on his throne under an honorific golden parasol and consecrated the thangka, and behind him sat the crowded rows of delegations from numerous Kagyu monasteries, from the Indian government, from the kingdom of Nepal, the army, Hindus, Christians, and Moslems, guests of honor and the members of his family, all facing the enormous image. It was Drukpa Tseshi, Chetsang Rinpoche's birthday, and the day commemorating the first teaching of

Chetsang Rinpoche leading the eight-hundred-year celebration of the Drikung lineage at Phyang Monastery in Ladakh.

the Buddha. To conclude the ceremony, Rinpoche gave a phowa transmission to a gathering of twenty thousand people and then returned to his retreat in Lamayuru.

Toward the end of his retreat, Rinpoche had a few significant dreams. In one of them he was on a pilgrimage with two monks to see the relics of the Buddha. They arrived at a large cemetery and a building with a temple roof, but when they entered, the situation changed and suddenly they were standing in front of a house with an office. They didn't know where the relics were and asked in the office where the relics of the Buddha were to be found. A man took out a catalog, leafed through the thick volume without finding anything, and finally went to ask someone else. Rinpoche now realized that they must be in a Muslim cemetery. Someone pointed to a dark area and said that the relics were there. Rinpoche was disappointed, because it was a cowshed. He sent the monks to dig in the dung. A huge Tibetan mastiff was lying beside the cowshed, and Rinpoche had the strange feeling that the dog might be Mahakala or some other protector. He protested to the Muslims that it was impossible to leave the relics of the Buddha there, because people all over the world wanted to see them, and they must be stored with appropriate dignity. Rinpoche mounted a nearby platform to watch the monks at their digging, and the man who had gone to ask about the exact location of the relics returned and said angrily, "You already know where they are, why do you ask me?" Rinpoche looked at him incredulously, and the man responded, "They are right behind you, just where you are standing. Turn around." Behind him was a wooden panel with a Tibetan window with cloth stretched over it, and Rinpoche was able to look through a slit, but could recognize nothing. He pulled the window open and was immediately engulfed in a cloud of dust and something fell on his head. He reached for it and saw that it was relics. He saw a marvelous, round, red mandala, and at that very moment his entire body was flooded with a stream of bliss, as if he were being filled with the relics. Feeling that he had been profoundly blessed, tears flowed down his cheeks.

He then awoke and still felt a prickling over his entire body like the physical reaction to a blessing. It was early morning, and the air was filled with the vibrant songs of a flock of birds. Rinpoche felt perfectly happy and wished to tell Khenpo Togdrol about his dream immediately, but he was so overwhelmed by this intense sensation that he neither could nor wanted to move. He fell asleep again, and another dream began right away.

He crossed some wide, elevated terraced fields and descended into a valley together with a large group of people. On the way he encountered an old monk who was sitting on a dried-out tree trunk. When he approached the monk he saw that it was the eighty-year-old Lama Konchog from Lamayuru. The monk greeted him and handed him a gold coin. "This is for you," he said. It was many-sided rather than round. Rinpoche refused, but the monk insisted that he keep it, as he had another one. He opened his *chuba* and revealed a second gold piece. Rinpoche took the coin with the words, "I shall keep the gold piece, and if you need it, just ask me." When he put the coin in his pocket he noticed that he was wearing a shirt and trousers instead of monastic robes. Rinpoche then went farther down the slope and came to a large building that he had to go around. As soon as he had passed it, he found that he was wearing his monk's robes again. He was carrying a briefcase and thought that he should put it aside, as it was not suitable for a monk. He proceeded slowly, and a little boy approached him who appeared to recognize him;

Rinpoche did not know who he was, perhaps someone from Lhasa. He did not wish to meet the boy, and simply turned a corner and found himself standing at a great fair full of noisy, laughing people. There was also a restaurant where a few monks from Phyang Monastery were sitting. He felt uneasy there, went in another direction, and came upon a market stand full of delicious fresh fruits. As he was buying some fruit, he awoke.

Rinpoche understood the general meaning of these dreams, but not all of their details, and Khenpo Togdrol's explanations did not completely satisfy him. He later told these dreams to Garchen Rinpoche, one of the great realized masters of the Drikungpa, who said they were easy to understand. Thrinle Lhundrup had already recognized the nature of mind; all he was lacking was trust in his own insight. The gold was a sign of attainment of highest realization, the extraordinary *siddhi*.[6]

Archetypal dreams such as these yield their meaning on many levels. The symbols in both dreams speak of upheaval and a new chapter in Rinpoche's life, a period of personal change. The dream images are reminiscent of the symbolic language of the alchemists, whose goal was the transformation of the ordinary human being and the liberation of the highest spiritual potential from its entrapment in the material body. The alchemists spoke of finding the highest good in filth. It was discovered exactly where one would least expect to find it. Gold, the highest form that matter could take, was potentially present in the basest metals—it only had to be extracted from them, just as the purest and most subtle form of the mind is present in deluded, unawakened consciousness.

All sentient beings possess buddha nature, the *tathagatagarbha*, the "seed of the Perfected One," but the obscurations of ignorance and confusion prevent them from recognizing it. Buddha nature is concealed in each and every being, yet it is also what embraces each and every being. Tantric practice involves working an inner alchemy through subtle-energy processes until buddha nature is revealed and primordial wisdom manifests itself.

Now the archetypal symbols in the dreams unfold their many-faceted meanings: the highest is concealed in what is lowermost; the buddha nature residing in all sentient beings is entangled in the delusion of samsaric existence; the cemetery is a place of transformation and a symbol of the impermanence of human existence, of emptying oneself of the world and of ego-attachment. At the same time there was an experience of becoming imbued with genuine life, which was open, free, and inexpressibly immense, and which permeated Rinpoche with a bliss that transcended the realm of human experience. At the moment of transformative experience the image of the circular mandala, the symbol of wholeness, appeared. Islam is the religion that drove Buddhism out of India, the land of its origin, and has played the role of opponent of the Dharma. Even in the midst of enemies, buddha nature, the seed of awakening, is present. The platform represents the elevation that Rinpoche was experiencing through his practice, and also the exaltedness that has always befitted him as the incarnation of the Kyabgön Rinpoche. By virtue of this exaltation the window into another reality opened up, the passageway to awakening. The intensity of his dream experience was underscored by his feeling of peace and fulfillment, as well as by the accompanying bodily sensations upon awakening.

His second dream was a variation on and continuation of the same theme. It speaks of bringing realization into the world: after a life as a layperson (his layman's clothing), Rinpoche has cultivated fertile soil (the terraced fields) through his practice and realization (the gold piece). Here, too, the insight that primordial wisdom is present in us finds expression. The highest inborn insight cannot be described or discovered outside of ourselves. It can only be pointed out, and the old monk who indicates what *is* present and always has been is a symbolic representation of the Buddha, the one who points out Mahamudra. Everyone possesses this piece of gold, but only those who have been on the path a long time, like the old monk, understand this. Rinpoche wishes to safeguard the gold piece; it is still imperfect, not yet round, and not yet entirely his own. His path is to return to monastic life (his monk's robes), as it will lead him to the "golden state," to the realization of buddha nature, and then from the heights of realization already attained down into the banality of ordinary life (the fair). Chetsang Rinpoche's task will be his activity *in* the world, but it seems that in this phase of his life he is not yet prepared to embrace it fully, as he still does not want to face the frenzy of worldly activity without reservation, although he has already reached a stage at which his practice is bearing rich and abundant fruit (the market stand with the fruit).

. . .

In the years that followed Chetsang Rinpoche single-mindedly pursued the path that had been pointed out in his dreams, and when his retreat was concluded he began a period of intensive study of philosophical texts and tantra. He chose Phyang Monastery as his official residence, but spent three winters in the Drukpa Kagyu monastery of Sangnag Chöling in Bhutan, where he studied Shantideva's *Bodhicharyavatara,* Chandrakirti's *Madhyamakavatara,* and the *Uttara-Tantra,* and received a few important transmissions of the general Kagyu tradition and the special teachings of the Drukpa Kagyu on Mahamudra. His teacher was Khenpo Noryang, the abbot of the main Drukpa Kagyu monastery in Darjeeling. Noryang was a wonderful teacher with an extraordinary mind who looked like an ordinary, poor monk; his robe had been washed so often that it had almost completely faded, and his shoes were old and worn out. Kyabje Tuktse Rinpoche was ashamed of his khenpo, who appeared in such clothing even on official occasions, and was constantly giving him new things, but Noryang never wore them.

Khenpo Noryang was a scholar in practically all areas of knowledge. Although he had not studied any philosophical texts since 1959 because he had been entrusted with the construction of the monastery and administrative duties, he had forgotten nothing. He never looked at notes when he summarized and explained philosophical texts but brought only two small slips of paper to class, and taught without referring to them. In Tibet it was said that those who reach a certain level of spiritual development possess "the memory that never fails" because everything remains available in the mind, and Khenpo Noryang was one of them.

He was never at a loss for a precise answer, penetrating to the essence of the question without beating around the bush. Although he was gifted with immense knowledge, he never flaunted it, and whatever was irrelevant to an answer remained unmentioned. Druk Tuktse once told Chetsang Rinpoche, "The higher one goes with him, the more energy he generates." Rinpoche developed a very close and fruitful relationship to Noryang, and the monks in the monastery were pleased when he requested teachings from him, because it gave them the opportunity to benefit from his great wisdom too.

Once, in teachings on the ninth chapter of the *Bodhicharyavatara,* which deals with the perfection of wisdom, the khenpo expounded upon a common simile, that the fundamental nature of mind is like free, open space. It is unstained, transparent and clear, naked and undisguised. Just as space is featureless and cannot be seen, the mind has no characteristics and cannot know itself. What one sees are objects in space, what one knows are thoughts that arise in the mind.

Buddhist logic invites dissent, as it deals with such indescribable topics. It operates with concepts designating referents that are incomprehensible on the conceptual level, an exciting but ultimately hopeless undertaking for rational thought. Rinpoche became involved in a heated discussion with Noryang on exactly this point—he took a cloth and held it in front of his eyes, claiming that he could very well disguise space, because he now could not see the khenpo. Noryang took the cloth and moved it a little. Where had the space gone when the cloth had moved from one spot to another? Noryang asked. And what happened to the space on the other side of the cloth—wouldn't it have to be empty? Empty of space? Something in Rinpoche was touched in a way that went beyond rational understanding. Suddenly, all questions had disappeared, and later on, he understood that this was the beginning of his awakening to the ultimate nature of mind. He had to laugh at the thought that this experience beyond conceptual thought had happened right in the middle of a lesson in Buddhist philosophy.

Chetsang Rinpoche learned with ease, as if he were only refreshing his memory of something already familiar, and the 1980s were years of intensive study, transmissions, and empowerments. Tibetan biographies of lamas always include lists of the initiations and transmissions they received, as this forms the "inner biography," and illustrates the continuity of the unadulterated and unbroken lineage transmission. A Tibetan master has traditionally been judged more by the lineage transmissions that he holds than by his knowledge of particular works, but listing all of the empowerments and transmissions that Rinpoche has received would go beyond the scope of this biography, as it would not be very meaningful to most readers. However, a few of his teachers, and the initiations and instructions he received from them, were of particular importance, and should be mentioned.

When he was very young, he received the complete transmission of the Drikung Kagyu and the Nyingma treasuries from Tritsab Gyabra, as well as the *Rinchen Terdzö* (*The Great Treasury of Precious Termas*) from Nyidzong Tripa. The latter set of transmissions was compiled by Jamgön

Chetsang Rinpoche with the Sixteenth Karmapa at Rumtek Monastery in Sikkim.

Kongtrul Lodrö Thaye, one of the most prominent figures in the intellectual and spiritual life of Buddhism in Tibet.[7] Rinpoche now received the Milarepa empowerment and the *Six Yogas of Naropa* from the Sixteenth Karmapa in Rumtek, and Druk Tuktse conveyed a series of teachings to him, including all of the texts of the Drukpa Kagyu tradition on Mahamudra and the *Six Yogas of Naropa*. He acquired the complete Taklung Kagyu teachings from Taklung Shabdrung (1915–1994), the *Northern Treasures* from Taklung Tsetrul, and the initiations into the Kalachakra, Chakrasamvara, and Yamantaka tantras from the Dalai Lama.

Drikung Rinpoches and khenpos conferred all of the lineage transmissions on him: Togden Rinpoche gave him the teachings of Gampopa, Phagmodrupa, Jigten Sumgön, and Kunga Rinchen; Khenpo Togdrol passed on the Madhyamaka teachings to him, as well as the *Achi Beubum* and the *Mani Kabum*.[8] He also received further Drikung empowerments from the meditation master Drubwang Konchog Norbu (1921–2007).

After passing away in 1988, Pachung Rinpoche appeared to Garchen Rinpoche during an experience of clear light in meditation and instructed him to pass on all of the Drikung teachings. Garchen Rinpoche

Chetsang Rinpoche (right) with Garchen Rinpoche,
in Kathmandu (ca. 1990).

did not wait; after more than two decades in Chinese imprisonment, he was able to travel to Kathmandu to meet the Drikung Kyabgön, and Rinpoche received all of Jigten Sumgön's teachings and transmissions from this highly esteemed master. He had already had the teachings, but there was a special blessing that could only be obtained through the lineage transmission from Garchen Rinpoche, the embodiment of one of the most important incarnation lineages of the Drikungpa. Garchen Rinpoche and Chetsang Rinpoche have a relationship of deep mutual veneration and respect, as both of them have endured very difficult periods in this lifetime, without the opportunity to study the Dharma for many years, but nonetheless they both possess the highest qualities in the form of spontaneous wisdom, as high-ranking lamas of all schools never fail to point out.

The meeting with Garchen Rinpoche renewed an inner tie that has connected the lineages of the Chetsang and the Garchen Rinpoches over many lifetimes, and when they were together Garchen Rinpoche had many extraordinary visions and dreams of Chetsang Rinpoche. On a pilgrimage to Nepal together they went to visit the temple in Patan where the Jowo Ukhangpa is kept, a famous crowned statue of the Buddha that is taken out from the temple only once a year in a solemn ceremony. Garchen Rinpoche and Chetsang Rinpoche had no idea when this took place, but just as they were crossing the street to enter the temple, the gates opened and the Buddha came out to them.

In Pharping, a place sacred to Padmasambhava and Marpa, a very special, ancient statue of Dorje Phagmo (Vajravarahi) is venerated and kept strictly locked away.[9] The figure exhibited is not even an accurate copy, and when a visitor paid fifty rupees and requested to be allowed to see the original statue, with a show of secrecy another counterfeit Vajravarahi would be brought out and presented as the genuine statue; no one was allowed to see the original. But when the two Rinpoches visited the temple the supervisor happened not to be there and they spoke with his wife, who innocently opened the secret room for them, and they were blessed with the sight of the genuine statue of Dorje Phagmo. This figure was unusual in that the dancing Dorje Phagmo did not hold her right leg bent with the foot on her left thigh, as is usual, but had dramatically cast one leg high up over her arm.

In November 1981, Chetsang Rinpoche journeyed to Rumtek Monastery in Sikkim for the prayer ceremonies for the Sixteenth Karmapa, who had died in the United States. Dilgo Khyentse Rinpoche, the renowned Nyingma lama, also attended the rituals. Khyentse Rinpoche was considered one of the most outstanding teachers alive, revered by all who had the good fortune to meet him. The Dalai Lama counted him among his most important gurus, and especially appreciated his nonsectarian point of view. During the event Dilgo Khyentse Rinpoche made use of every free moment to impart teachings, going on until late at night, and in the morning, even before dawn, he was ready to start teaching again. With his penetrating gaze, he taught effortlessly, clearly and calmly, as if he were reading from an invisible book, and at the same time always taking the capacities of his listeners into account. In private conversations he could open up a completely new dimension of insight with only a few words.

Chetsang Rinpoche wished to approach him, and he suddenly appeared. Dilgo Khyentse Rinpoche held all of the Dharma transmissions of Tibetan Buddhism, but Rinpoche was too humble to request specific instructions and simply asked that Khyentse Rinpoche impart those teachings that he thought appropriate for him.

Chetsang Rinpoche with Dilgo Khyentse Rinpoche at
Phuntsogling Palace in Bhutan.

Two years later Rinpoche was staying with his aunt Tsering Dolma while on business in Delhi, and he had a strong wish to receive the precious transmissions of the *Dam Ngag Dzö,* a collection of teachings of all schools of Tibetan Buddhism, from Khyentse Rinpoche. When a Western nun who was visiting him mentioned Dilgo Khyentse Rinpoche's name in passing, Rinpoche was overwhelmed by a desire to see him. It turned out that Dilgo Khyentse Rinpoche was then staying in Delhi as a guest of Gene Smith, the field director of the Library of Congress in India, and they arranged a short meeting at which Rinpoche asked him for the transmission of the *Dam Ngag Dzö.* Khyentse Rinpoche consented, and they agreed on Bhutan as the location, and winter as the time.

The teachings began in January 1984 in the Phuntsogling Palace in Bhutan. Dilgo Khyentse Rinpoche arrived late at night a few days after Chetsang Rinpoche, and early the next morning, Chetsang Rinpoche was woken and told that Khyentse Rinpoche was on his way to see him. When the majestic Khyentse Rinpoche appeared in the doorway, he laughingly demanded to know who the fat Drikung lama he had met in Gangtok in 1959 had been. Chetsang Rinpoche answered this could only have been Tritsab Gyabra, the Drikung regent and his teacher, and Khyentse Rinpoche told him that Tritsab Gyabra had asked him to give the two Drikung Kyabgöns the empowerments and teachings of the *Dam Ngag Dzö* back then, but a date had not been arranged because he had been forced to flee. Chetsang Rinpoche was glad about the quarter-century delay, as his understanding of the Dharma was now far more profound and his mind was now better prepared to accept the precious teachings of this incomparable teacher.

The *Dam Ngag Dzö* is extraordinarily rich in profound teachings and pith instructions. The text itself states that the teachings should only be given in a land where the Dharma is flourishing, to avoid obstacles. Bhutan, where Tibetan Buddhism, transmitted by the Drukpa Kagyu school, had flourished for centuries without decline, was surely the right location. About fifty lamas and tulkus took part, along with more than five hundred monks and nuns. In addition, laypeople from remote regions were brought in by bus. Wealthy sponsors not only provided meals for the crowds of participants, but hundreds of local poor people were also fed during the three-month-long event.

Khyentse Rinpoche was tireless, and in the evenings after the teachings on the *Dam Ngag Dzö*, he gave talks on the *Guhyagarbha Tantra* according to the Nyingma tradition, and Rinpoche also received private instructions on the nature of mind from him. Later, in Kathmandu, Rinpoche received from him further important instructions on works that Jamgön Kongtrul had compiled or composed himself, such as the *Gyachen Kadzö* and the *Kagyu Ngag Dzö*, and the transmissions of numerous other works from the many different traditions, among them the *Nyingtig Yashi*, one of the most famous collections of Dzogchen teachings.[10]

16

Concentration and Development
Realizing the Visions

ESTABLISHING GOOD educational facilities for young people was one of Chetsang Rinpoche's top priorities in Ladakh. He explained to the villagers that a vacuum would arise in the community's spiritual life unless sufficient young people were given a classical Buddhist education, and encouraged each family with several children to send one child to a monastery. He promised that he would see to their education, and it would cost them nothing. He convinced them, and thirty young men from the village of Phyang alone donned monastic robes.

When Rinpoche received the minister of culture of the Indian government in his chambers in Phyang Monastery, the minister was impressed by the monastery's cultural treasures, statues, paintings, and books. Rinpoche regarded him calmly and said, "You are right. But we still do not know who will inherit all of this in the future. The Tibetan language is hardly spoken any more, and is taught only in a few schools. The monasteries are growing empty, and the culture of the entire Himalayan region is in the process of disappearing. How to paint a Buddhist painting or make a statue—all of that is written in Tibetan, and if the language dies out, the culture will die out. What use will all these texts be if they can't be read?" The conversation made an impression, and about a year later the ministry of culture was allocated a sizeable budget for improving traditional education, and all the monasteries in Ladakh and India, not just those of the Drikung, benefited when the funds became available for educational projects and the creation of libraries.

It was clear to Rinpoche that the educational system in Ladakh was only a beginning; the monasteries were too isolated, the general mindset was too archaic, and there were too few teachers and pupils to usher in the renaissance in Buddhist learning that he envisioned. All the same, there were many young tulkus in Tibet in even more desolate circumstances who wrote desperate letters in search of an appropriate education, and Drikung monasteries in Ladakh took in a dozen rinpoches from Tibet. Their educational level was shockingly low, but this made their motivation that much stronger. Chetsang Rinpoche had discussed his idea of building a new monastery with Dilgo Khyentse Rinpoche during the first teachings in Bhutan; he dreamed of a monastery that would be a center for both a traditional Buddhist education and would at the same time meet modern needs.

But just the process of founding a nonprofit association as an umbrella organization for the Drikung lineage turned out to be a complicated issue, as many already-established lamas did not wish to be subordinated to a central authority that would control all of the lineage monasteries and institutions. But this was exactly the type of structure, and problems, Chetsang Rinpoche wanted to avoid, and he emphasized that he would not allow a central headquarters to hold the strings of power, as this would only lead to political manipulation, resentment, and resistance. He had seen that other orders administered by an authoritarian centralized management with strict hierarchical structures had run into severe organizational problems. Therefore the Drikung organization would be decentralized, with the centers retaining administrative autonomy, each with its own nonprofit association to obtain subsidies from the state and from private sponsors.

Rinpoche did not want an umbrella organization in an administrative sense, but rather in a spiritual one. His basic idea was radically simple, but difficult to implement: act according to the Buddhadharma, do good, and earn people's respect. He recognized that rigid hierarchical structures were completely counterproductive to spiritual development, as they shifted the focus from practice to politics and position.

Using the logo that Rinpoche had designed in the United States would identify the diverse institutions as belonging to the Drikung order. He hoped that inwardly they would all cultivate and perpetuate the lineage's traditions and teachings. Ultimately, all schools of Tibetan Buddhism pursue the same goal, but each has its own precious and unique tradition of irreplaceable teachings that are transmitted within the lineage. Rinpoche initially proposed a three-year rotation in which the headquarters of the umbrella organization would move from one monastery outside Tibet to the next, but this system could not be adopted for legal reasons. Therefore, the Drikung Charitable Society would be housed in the monastery Rinpoche was planning. Until that was ready, Ayang Monastery in southern India was chosen to function as the main Drikung Kagyu monastery, and the Society was registered with the local authorities in Bangalore.

Meanwhile, the Drikung lineage had been given a house steeped in history in Almora, in the foothills of the Himalayas. Lama Anagarika Govinda (1898–1985), the famous German Buddhist philosopher, monk and artist, had lived there for two decades beginning in 1955. Govinda had received the remote property from the distinguished anthropologist W. Y. Evans-Wentz (1878–1965), and had later left the house to his Tibetan assistants, who then donated it to the Drikung Kyabgön Rinpoche. Almora is located at an elevation of two thousand meters, amidst a forest of majestic pine trees and lush vegetation. Belligerent monkeys, occasional snow leopards, and multitudes of brilliantly colorful birds could all be seen near the house. Rinpoche thought that perhaps this place, which might foster both activity and tranquility, the creative urge and contemplation, could become the site for the monastery he was planning.

After the Tibetan New Year festivities of 1983, Rinpoche gave the Pig Year Teachings at Ontul Rinpoche's monastery in Tso Pema. During a general assembly of the Drikung lamas one evening, he unexpectedly requested Lamkhyen Gyalpo to retire from his post in the Tibetan government-in-exile in order to become general secretary of the Drikung lineage, and Gyalpo Rinpoche accepted the challenge. A few days later they decided to found their new headquarters in Almora, and transfer the venue of the Drikung Charitable Society from southern India to Almora, but it turned out that there were problems with the papers for the land in Almora and the change of venue could not be authorized. Therefore, a new nonprofit organization had to be established, the Drikung Kagyu Institute. Meanwhile, they decided to generate some income by starting a small carpet factory at Almora, as Gyalpo Rinpoche was experienced in this business, having served as director of the Tibetan handicrafts center in Shimla.

As long as Chetsang Rinpoche remained occupied with his own education and training, the Drikung Kagyu Institute lacked the personnel and financial support to begin the projects he had in mind. Gyalpo Rinpoche wished to do something meaningful and decided to visit the field office of the Library of Congress in Delhi, where Gene Smith was collecting, evaluating, and publishing documents brought by Tibetans as they fled their homeland. This office was scheduled to be closed down soon, and Gyalpo Rinpoche searched the collections for works from the Drikung tradition, discovering more than four hundred Drikung texts.

Gyalpo Rinpoche politely, but also firmly, pointed out all of the disadvantages to making Almora the center of the lineage. Almora was very far from Delhi, there was hardly any running water, in summer the monsoon rains washed away the roads (which were always in bad shape anyway), and it would be inconvenient and expensive to supply. Finally Chetsang Rinpoche accepted his secretary's misgivings, although both agreed that finding a permanent seat for the Drikung Kyabgön in India was urgently necessary, as Drikung monks coming into India were drifting away to other schools of Tibetan Buddhism. Gyalpo Rinpoche was thus given the task of finding an appropriate piece of land in a suitable area with the necessary infrastructure.

Gyalpo Rinpoche found what they were looking for in Dehra Dun, a city six hours by car north of Delhi, while Chetsang Rinpoche was receiving the *Dam Ngag Dzö* transmission from Dilgo Khyentse Rinpoche in Bhutan. Located in the foothills of the Himalayas, Dehra Dun enjoyed a pleasant climate and had once been a favorite retirement area for pensioned British army officers. It was best known for its numerous elite schools, and the atmosphere was very conducive to educational projects. Furthermore, there was an old and established community of Tibetan emigrants in Dehra Dun, and with Sakya Center, Sakya College, and Mindrolling Monastery, both the Sakyapa and the Nyingmapa had main seats there. There was also great deal of land then available for purchase in Dehra Dun. (Later, in 1999, it became the capital of the new Indian state of Uttaranchal, and since then the city has grown considerably.)

Gyalpo Rinpoche discovered a piece of land covered with thick brush in a northern part of the city, and white cranes descended and settled themselves while he was inspecting the place. The purchase price was modest at that time, although in India a price could change from day to day at the owner's whim. Gyalpo Rinpoche had only been sent to search for land, not to actually buy it, since neither he nor Chetsang Rinpoche, nor the Drikung Kagyu Institute, had the capital to do so. But the price was so tempting that he concluded a preliminary contract and went to Dharamsala at once to borrow money from the Tibetan government and send a report to Chetsang Rinpoche in Bhutan. The Kyabgön Rinpoche agreed to the purchase and Gyalpo Rinpoche was able to obtain credit from the private office of the Dalai Lama.

The transaction was concluded in mid-March of 1984. The Drikung Kagyu Institute acquired the land for thirty thousand rupees, a very low price by Western standards, but the Drikung lamas had no money at all. The loan from Dharamsala was for sixty thousand rupees, leaving them thirty thousand for construction. In October, after an Achi retreat in Ladakh, Chetsang Rinpoche conclusively decided to establish his monastery and study center in Dehra Dun. The center would be named Drikung Kagyu Institute, and the monastery was to have the same name as the main seat in Drikung Thil, Jangchubling.

Gyalpo Rinpoche began by constructing the access road and laying down water mains, which exhausted most of their financial resources. In February 1985, Chetsang, Gyalpo, and Ontul Rinpoches, as well as Drubpön Sönam Jorphel and Lama Tsulwang, went to Dehra Dun for the consecration ceremony of the land. According to old customs dating from shamanistic, pre-Buddhist times, the local deities had to be placated and measures had to be taken to assure that the project would thrive. The small group carried out the necessary geomantic calculations on the cleared land, and in the place indicated by their calculations they buried a vase containing rolls of mantras, incense, and semiprecious stones as offerings. They also performed rituals to request the local deities for their permission and for the peaceful completion of their project.

Just as they were beginning construction work in summer of 1985, they received news that Chungtsang Rinpoche was coming to visit them. The Kyabgön Rinpoche had spent twenty-three years in Chinese prisons and labor camps, working under inhumane conditions, often to exhaustion, and sometimes to the limits of endurance. He was released in the course of the political liberalization of 1983 and given a leading position in the department of religious affairs of the Tibet Autonomous Region. Being assigned this position gave him a place in society, although it didn't truly provide an opportunity to work for the restoration of religious life in Tibet. The sole function of the department of religious affairs was still just to enforce ideological conformity by controlling all forms of religious activity. The office's employees were all rinpoches and high-ranking lamas only because they guaranteed public acceptance of the department's authority. Monasteries were compelled to accept external administrations imposed upon them by the department, thus preventing them from regaining any real power. Reincarnations could only be confirmed by the department, and had to be sent to China for education and training.

At least Chungtsang Rinpoche could now visit his relatives in India and Bhutan. In July 1985 Chetsang Rinpoche welcomed his spiritual brother in Ladakh, at the Leh airport, in the presence of numerous guests of honor. His childhood playmate's face still bore its serious expression, his character as reserved as ever. In Phyang Monastery the "Eastern Holiness" and the "Western Holiness" sat on their thrones, side by side again, and for the Drikungpa, the sun and the moon had conjoined. At the end of August, the two journeyed to Dehra Dun and visited the land on which the Drikung Kagyu Institute was rising. Chungtsang Rinpoche gave Chetsang Rinpoche his support in the effort to set up a viable educational system based in the lineage's traditions. He said that the Tibetan monastic tradition was reaching the end of a devastating epidemic, and observing ethical discipline should now take priority. Study and practice should go hand in hand, and if an appropriate education could not be provided, it wouldn't matter if a monastery had a thousand monks—they would all be useless as far as the survival and transmission of Tibetan Buddhism was concerned. Good education was essential, and the rinpoches and lamas in Tibet and abroad would have to take a common stand on this issue.

Chungtsang Rinpoche continued his journey on his own and Chetsang Rinpoche went with Gyalpo Rinpoche and Lopön Tenzin to Gangtok to receive empowerments and teachings from Taklung Shabdrung. At the end of October they journeyed to Bhutan to a further cycle of teachings given by Dilgo Khyentse Rinpoche. The daughter of the king of Bhutan requested Chetsang Rinpoche to give an initiation, and he therefore bestowed the phowa transmission in Paro Dzong at the end of November to a huge crowd of people. From Bhutan Rinpoche set off directly to Bodh Gaya, the site of the Buddha's enlightenment, where the Dalai Lama was going to give the Kalachakra initiation. There, on December 11, 1985, Drikung Kyabgön Thrinle Lhundrup took the vows of a fully ordained monk from the Dalai Lama. The Dalai Lama's chief secretary provided him with the necessary equipment: a begging bowl, the yellow monastic robe, and a *kharsil,* the staff of a wandering Buddhist monk.

Two kinds of teaching are indispensable for the survival and dissemination of the Dharma; teaching through realization and teaching through words. Now the time of teaching through words had come for Rinpoche. After ten years of studying intensively and working to physically and spiritually expand the Drikung lineage, Chetsang Rinpoche decided to go on a world teaching tour. He also had to find sponsors for his Dehra Dun project.

In exile the Buddhist schools were forced to create a completely new support structure as the basis for the survival of the monastic tradition and of Tibetan Buddhism in general. The economic foundation of the monasteries had once been guaranteed by the social and political conditions in Tibet, but this situation had changed, and financing could now only be guaranteed if potential sponsors and contributors were convinced of the necessity of support. The Tibetan people could no longer fund the monasteries alone, as they were now also just trying to survive in the radically new conditions. This contributed to many schools of Tibetan Buddhism founding branches in various countries, beginning in the 1960s and 1970s. In industrialized nations, the Dalai Lama raised public awareness of both the plight of the Tibetan people and of the great value of the teachings of the Buddha, and eminent masters of the Nyingma, Sakya, Kagyu and Gelug schools were able to found centers and obtain the urgently needed support. It was as though the Vajrayana, the final elaboration of the Buddha's teaching, had concluded its centuries-long retreat on the high plateau in the heart of Asia, and was now sharing its accumulated strength and wisdom with the rest of the world. The exodus of the bearers of spiritual life in Tibet was perhaps a historically unique opportunity to save the treasury of their teachings from oblivion.

Although many other schools of Tibetan Buddhism had become established in countries around the world, such a global infrastructure was as yet out of reach for the Drikungpa. Ayang Rinpoche was the only Drikung teacher who had traveled to foreign countries and was well-known; Chetsang Rinpoche had given him the task of establishing one or two centers abroad, and the first Dharma center, Drikung Ngaden Choling, was founded in Medelon, Germany.

The schools of Tibetan Buddhism did not arise through disputes over doctrine, orthodoxy, or heresy, as is often the case in other religions. Rather, they are different branches that arose as the various lines of transmission of the Dharma introduced subtle variations in emphasis on certain elements of doctrine and practice and different traditions of interpretation. Such a system harbors the danger of sectarianism, but also the opportunity for mutual enrichment, for increasing spiritual abundance by drawing from the wealth of diversity of traditions. But history shows that the concept of entirely peaceful coexistence among the Tibetan Buddhist schools has so far been only an ideal. Sectarianism and rivalry has often led to conflict; particularly after the political ascendance of the Gelug, the appropriation of monasteries increased in frequency—and not only when they were in material or spiritual decline.

Thus it was no surprise to Chetsang Rinpoche when he met with some opposition from the Karma Kagyu school before his journey to the West. Among the Karma Kagyu were some who claimed exclusive authority over the entire Kagyu lineage, an attitude that completely disregarded the autonomy of the Drikung, Drukpa, Taklung, and the other Kagyu schools. After the death of the Sixteenth Karmapa a dispute arose in Dharamsala because the department of religion and culture of the government-in-exile asked the Kagyu schools to select an official representative for dealings with the government and, apart from the Karma Kagyu, the other Kagyu schools said that they did not want a common representative, as each school had historically had its own representative. They published their decision in the government-in-exile's newspaper, *Sheja*, and the Karma Kagyu regarded this assertion of independence as an affront. On top of this they had problems within their own school when two competing factions supported different candidates as the authentic successor to the deceased Sixteenth Karmapa, a dispute that ultimately led to the enthronement of two Seventeenth Karmapas.

Rinpoche traveled to Europe in autumn of 1986 and planted the seeds for further Drikung branches that would arise in the years that followed, primarily in Germany. At the end of October, he went to the World Day of Prayer for Peace in Assisi, Italy, when for the first time in history, the heads of twelve world religions gathered in one of Christianity's most important churches to pray for peace.

From Germany, Rinpoche and Gyalpo traveled to the United States in December. Khenchen Konchog Gyaltshen had founded the first Drikung center in Washington, D.C. in 1982. The Drikung name was completely unknown at the time, so he named it the Tibetan Meditation Center. Eight years later, the center moved to a spacious and beautiful piece of land in Frederick, Maryland. Khenchen spoke very good English, organized the trip, and served as Rinpoche's interpreter.

Rinpoche gave teachings and initiations at a tireless pace, in Washington, Florida, and Chicago. He became acquainted with Swami Shambhavananda and his wife, Faith Stone, who attended a Chakrasamvara initiation in Washington. They invited him to Boulder, Colorado, where Rinpoche went immediately after his program in Chicago. Swami, the son of Italian immigrants, had been a student of the American Swami Rudrananda, who had popularized Shaivite teachings in the United States during the 1960s.

Rinpoche gave a spontaneous Avalokiteshvara initiation at Swami Shambhavananda's ashram in Boulder. Like the Dalai Lamas, the incarnations of the Chetsang Rinpoches are considered emanations of Avalokiteshvara, the bodhisattva of limitless compassion. Rinpoche briefly stayed with Swami and his wife, shared their lives and even helped to milk their cow and feed the goats, and he cooked Tibetan dumplings for everyone in the ashram. He enjoyed driving a Jeep on rainwashed tracks into the mountain woods, studying unfamiliar plants and trees, and collecting some seeds that he would later plant in Dehra Dun.

Rinpoche traveled on to New Mexico, Arizona, and various centers in California, and then to Hawaii, where he taught at Nechung Dorje Drayang Ling, a Buddhist temple and retreat house. Spring had come, and although Rinpoche was as fresh as he had been on their first day, Khenchen Konchog Gyaltshen felt a need for rest and recuperation after the months of exertion, and didn't join Rinpoche on the trip to Hawaii. Instead, Khenchen Gyaltshen accepted an invitation to teach for a few months at Prescott College in Arizona, before returning to Washington, D.C. to make arrangements for the arrival of the Dalai Lama, who would visit the Drikung center there in the fall.

Chetsang Rinpoche continued on from Hawaii to give an initiation in one of Thrangu Rinpoche's centers in Hong Kong in early May. Interest in his teachings and empowerments was particularly strong in Southeast Asia, and over two thousand people came to receive the Medicine Buddha initiation in Singapore, and even more crowded into the hall for the long-life empowerment.

He was back in Dehra Dun in mid-June 1987. Before his departure he had wanted to purchase an additional piece of land adjoining the property where his monastery was being built, to become the site of a school for higher Buddhist studies to be constructed at a later date. He had urged Gyalpo Rinpoche to borrow more money, convinced that he would be able to collect enough donations on his teaching tour around the world, but Gyalpo Rinpoche had gotten cold feet and had not dared to burden the Drikung Kagyu Institute with more debt, and the property had been sold before Rinpoche returned with the funds. A Christian college would later be built there.

But the seeds that Rinpoche had sowed during his long journey were beginning to sprout as Drikung centers arose everywhere. The new sponsors Rinpoche had won on his world tour were crucial to the progress of his construction plans, since the available capital had all been spent on building the main kitchen. Now, with his return, construction of additional buildings could begin. As soon as a small section on the ground floor was finished, the first ten young monks from Drikung monasteries in Ladakh arrived in Dehra Dun and instruction began on *Lhabab Duchen*, the anniversary of the Buddha's return to earth after teaching in Tushita heaven, in an improvised classroom on the construction site. One year later, a further section was complete and a second classroom had been started. At this point the educational center was officially inaugurated by Sakya Trizin, and from then on a new class entered each year.

Since Gyalpo Rinpoche went to Tibet in 1987, and was then sent by Rinpoche to establish Drikung centers in Taiwan, Lama Tsulwang took over the task of supervising construction; he had gained the necessary experience during the construction of Ontul's monastery in Tso Pema.

Chetsang Rinpoche with a model of the temple, overseeing construction
of Jangchubling Monastery, Dehra Dun.

Rinpoche obtained state subsidies for all the building materials through the support of Lama Lobsang in the government of India in Delhi, and Rinpoche himself was the architect. He designed all of the traditional Tibetan buildings himself: the offices and living quarters right behind the main gate, the large U-shaped edifice with monks' cells and classrooms around a spacious courtyard, and the central temple. An engineer was needed only to calculate the statics. Rinpoche went to the steel factory in person with sketches and plans in hand, and had the required parts made according to his specifications, and when time allowed he sat in the shade of a tree with a cardboard model of the temple at his side and a stack of plans on his table, studying not the floor plan, but rather Tibetan texts. Rinpoche has an infallible eye for proportions and measurements, and he often amazed the construction workers when he noticed faulty dimensions just by looking. When the measurements were checked his visual estimates always turned out to be correct.

One day, a minister of the Tibetan government-in-exile came to visit. Rinpoche was living in a small monk's cell with bare walls and a cement floor, and only a simple bed, a little table with a chair, and a modest shrine. When the minister was shown in to him, he was incredulous.

"What sort of a bed is that, and what a shabby room!" he exclaimed. Compared to his dwelling in Thong Ga, Rinpoche thought this accommodation seemed perfectly comfortable, and he needed nothing more. Lama Tsulwang, who had brought in tea, felt ashamed; the monks knew that Kyabgön Rinpoche placed no importance on beautiful and expensive accoutrements, but they feared that the minister would scorn them for not taking proper care of their Rinpoche and allowing him to live in squalor. After their august visitor had departed, Tsulwang urged that the dismal room be refurbished—or at least that a carpet be laid over the bare floor. Rinpoche refused, but when the monks insisted, he allowed them to purchase a very simple, inexpensive rug.

He had far more need for a car. The property was some distance from the city center, and every simple purchase presented a logistical problem. Most motor vehicles were extraordinarily expensive in India, so he wanted to buy a used Ambassador, the first Indian car ever built, and the only one that was more or less affordable. With the help of an Indian friend of Ayang Rinpoche in Delhi he soon found a suitable car. The main road leading from Delhi to Dehra Dun was well-constructed according to Indian standards, but it was full of huge potholes, and crowded with all kinds of motor and animal-powered vehicles. There were large sugar factories and brickyards, and cars had to share the road with convoys of brightly painted trucks with towering loads of sugar cane, improvised vehicles towing loads of bricks, rusty buses and rickshaws, slow-moving water buffalo pulling tree trunks, herdsmen driving their animals ahead of them, and people on wobbly bicycles.

Rinpoche did not want to drive the car back to Dehra Dun by himself, so his cousin Tenor Taring, who worked for All India Radio in Delhi, took a few days' leave to accompany him. No sooner had they put Delhi behind them than the gas pedal broke. It was quickly fixed at one of the many improvised repair shops along the main road, and their journey continued. An hour later, they had to stop because the motor was overheated, and this time the gas pump had to be replaced at another repair shop.

By now, the sun was setting and Rinpoche turned on the headlights, but they gradually dimmed and then went out altogether; the generator was malfunctioning. They found yet another repair shop to take care of this problem and continued. Then, after stopping for a short break,

The temple at Jangchubling Monastery in Dehra Dun, India.

the car failed to start. They tried to push-start it, but instead of starting the Ambassador emitted an ear-shattering noise, and looking under the chassis, Chetsang Rinpoche and Taring saw that the rear axle was broken. It was past midnight, but they found an open tea shop and Taring, who spoke a little Hindi, found out that the local mechanic lived ten kilometers away. They set off on foot; a few motorcycles rattled past them, but no one stopped until they came upon a man with a bicycle. Taring was able to borrow it for a small sum, and ride to the mechanic's house. He knocked so long and loudly that the entire village was soon awake and wanting to see what was going on. The sleepy mechanic was persuaded to tow away the Ambassador and replace the axle.

At sunrise the mechanic had finished and the rest of their journey proceeded uneventfully. It was obvious that the car had needed a complete overhaul, and it had now had one, in bits and pieces along a memorable journey. Since then, it has functioned without any problems and is still in use at the monastery.

With luck and the support of generous friends, the Drikung Kagyu Institute, including Jangchubling Monastery, was completed in five years. The Drikungpa state with pride that a Tibetan monastery had never been built so inexpensively.

Good education is of central importance, but that alone does not suffice as a complete foundation for the Buddhist path. Academic knowledge provides essential concepts, but their true depth can only be revealed through practice. In addition to providing the experience necessary to realize what cannot be grasped intellectually, practice is essential to generate the kind of energy necessary to be of true benefit to others. The Drikung lineage is a practice lineage, in which truth is sought in immediate experience and wisdom rather than in philosophical analysis.[1] Thus, Rinpoche would have to find a place where the monks of the Drikung Kagyu Institute could undertake secluded retreats.

Rinpoche took his dog and explored the largely unpopulated surrounding areas, searching for a suitable place. He would have preferred to build a retreat center high up on the mountain, where the road winds its way up to Mussoorie, and where the Dalai Lama had first stayed after his escape from Tibet, but it was much too noisy for the contemplative stillness needed in retreat. On one of his hikes he came across the simple hut of one of the monastery's construction workers, where he was offered a bowl of milk. Speaking no Hindi, Rinpoche drank the milk and thanked them with a blessing and by later sending them a crate full of clothing. One of the family's sons now works as a gate-keeper in Jangchubling, and the other as a driver for the retreat center.

As Rinpoche left the humble dwelling, he immediately saw what he was looking for, a large piece of untilled land down in the valley, not far from his monastery, and between two settlements lying far apart from each other. That surely was the most secluded place to be found in the area, and he was able to acquire the property in 1989 and begin construction of the retreat center. It soon became clear that a nunnery was needed, too, as increasing numbers of nuns were escaping from Tibet, among them many who belonged to the Drikung order. Rinpoche decided to build a nunnery next to the retreat houses, and it was named Samtenling.

At the end of August 1990, a man appeared in Ladakh with a supposed letter of authorization from the Dalai Lama that said he was the true reincarnation of Drikung Chetsang Rinpoche. He was Lobsang Chödzin of Lhasa, a former monk who had spent a few years in Yangrigar and Drikung Tse in his youth and had then lived in the Gelugpa monastery of Ganden with Song Rinpoche. After his escape he rejoined Song Rinpoche for a while in his exile monastery in Mundgod in southern India, then he disrobed and married. He had some contact with Ayang Rinpoche's nearby monastery through his earlier relationship with the Drikungpa, and so once met Kyabgön Chetsang Rinpoche there. He bewailed his fate to Rinpoche, who listened patiently to everything and even helped him out with some money.

Later, Lobsang Chödzin moved to Ladakh and set up a lucrative business as a fortune-teller in Leh. In the front room, his wife would pump the unsuspecting supplicants for information about their families and problems, passing the information to her husband, who then performed a traditional divination and delivered predictions based on the information his wife had extracted. He quickly became a local celebrity and made enough to build a house and inflate his opinion of himself. One day he decided to present himself as the true Drikung Chetsang Rinpoche. He obtained an audience with the Dalai Lama, in which he served up fantastic tales and presented counterfeited documents about his supposed divinatory abilities. He impudently claimed to have been one of the candidates at the selection of the Chetsang Rinpoche reincarnation in Tibet, and through this fraud he obtained a general letter of support from the Dalai Lama.

Back in Ladakh, he posed as the true Drikung Chetsang Rinpoche and placed posters of himself with the Dalai Lama in all of the Drikung monasteries. He presented the letter to Togden Rinpoche, who felt it best not to respond, and Chetsang Rinpoche himself was unperturbed by the incident, seeing it as nothing more than the play of samsara. Where there is much light, the shadows are deep, and mental poisons cause flowers of greed, envy, and jealousy to bloom. Rinpoche paid little attention to the outraged protests of the Drikung monks, preferring to concentrate on the tasks he felt were truly important.

But Lobsang Chödzin was planning to go abroad and make his fortune by means of this fraud, so representatives of the Drikung monasteries prevented him from receiving an exit permit and obtained a court inquest into the authenticity of the letter. When the Dalai Lama was informed of this insolent fraud, he was indignant, and he was even

Chungtsang Rinpoche (left) with Chetsang Rinpoche during the 1992 Monkey Year Teachings in Dehra Dun.

more outraged at the brazenly false misrepresentation of his letter. At the end of October he clarified his position with an official statement that he had never said that Lobsang Chödzin was the true reincarnation of the Drikung Chetsang Rinpoche. He had written that it was *possible* that he was the reincarnation of a rinpoche, not that he *was* one. In his letter, the Dalai Lama used a Tibetan expression (*'os pa*), signifying a person who might be appropriate or suitable for something. The term does not indicate that he *was* a true tulku, and certainly not the Drikung Chetsang Rinpoche. The wording was clear and unambiguous; one could not interpret it arbitrarily. The true Drikung Chetsang Rinpoche Tenzin Thrinle Lhundrup was beyond doubt the reincarnation recognized by Taktra Rinpoche in 1950 and enthroned in Tibet. The Dalai Lama followed with praise of Chetsang Rinpoche. He criticized Lobsang Chödzin sharply, forbade him to continue spreading such false allegations, and ordered him to return his letter of support. The Dalai Lama did not mince words; he said this imposter was behaving like a vile and wicked demon (*rakshasa*) pretending to be a human being. Subdued, Lobsang Chödzin dropped out of sight.

After the Monkey Year Teachings in the summer of 1992 in Ladakh, the great ceremonial inauguration of Jangchubling Monastery and its affiliated educational center, the Drikung Kagyu Institute (DKI), followed in November. The conditions could not have been more auspicious. Construction of the nunnery and retreat center, Samtenling, had been concluded the year before, the oldest class of students of the DKI had completed their basic course of study and were ready to move on to a school for higher Buddhist studies, and Chungtsang Rinpoche had obtained permission to travel outside of China for the second time. The Dalai Lama performed the inauguration during a magnificent ceremony, and the Monkey Year Teachings that followed were held under the guidance of both Kyabgön Rinpoches. At the same time, the PRC permitted the teachings to be given at their traditional location in the valley of Drongur for the first time since 1956, when the young Holinesses had made their appearance at the Monkey Year Teachings. The authorities did not expect the teachings to receive very much attention, and perhaps permitted them only because Chungtsang Rinpoche was in India and therefore not participating, but thousands of Tibetans from remote regions made the renowned pilgrimage to receive the phowa blessings from the high-ranking Drikung lamas who remained in Tibet.

17

Master of Dependent Arising

THE FOUNDING OF THE Jangchubling Monastery and Samtenling Nunnery did not mark the end of Rinpoche's activities, but
rather established the foundation for accomplishing his vision of preserving and renewing Tibet's cultural and spiritual heritage. Rinpoche's
objectives do not focus merely on the transmission of his own tradition, or even just on the teachings of the Buddha. Through recognizing
the interconnectedness of seemingly isolated issues, he identifies what
needs to be done, and the most effective way of doing it. His spiritual
mastery allows him to view from an all-encompassing perspective the
ways in which the Dharma is interwoven with social and scientific developments in the modern, globalized world, as well as with the cultural
heritage of Tibet.

Awareness of a historical context is of central importance to Rinpoche.
Growing up in Communist Tibet, he was exposed to the effects of intensive ideological indoctrination, which have helped him recognize the
necessity of in-depth historical study, both to understand the heritage of
the Tibetan people and to plan for the future. His own experience during this period of his life was itself a drastic teaching on the necessity of
historical consciousness.

Only those who know their own history and are able to observe it
from a critical standpoint are equipped with the knowledge needed to
shape the future meaningfully. Research on Tibetan history is of particular significance because Tibet played an important role in central
Asia, primarily in terms of cultural history, but also in the region's political history. King Songtsen Gampo was of fundamental importance to
the development of culture and of the Dharma in Tibet, but knowledge

about his times is still limited, as the original sources have not been ade-quately analyzed and the old Tibetan chronicles are fragmentary and in-accurate. Rinpoche is working on cross-checking the old Tibetan texts, against the far more precise Chinese chronologies, and he is also work-ing to illuminate the even less-known epochs before Songtsen Gampo. This early period of the Pugyal or Yarlung Dynasty, associated with what are known as the "Heavenly Kings," is mostly still veiled in the clouds of myth. Tibet's history reaches even farther back, but all archeological evidence that might have shed light on the country's prehistory and early history has been distorted to conform to the political and ideological agenda of the Chinese authorities. Many discoveries have been dated to periods far more recent than they in fact are, since the official view does not allow any suggestion of a Tibetan culture not directly linked to that of Han.

Tibet did in fact possess a rich treasury of historical works: annals, clan genealogies, family and royal chronicles, and works documenting the dissemination of Buddhism, some dating back as far as the Yarlung Dynasty (second century B.C.E. to 842 C.E.). Most have either been completely lost or have only survived as fragments, though there are still many texts scattered among various collections that have not been studied or evaluated, and very few of the works have been published. In addition, a philological tradition that would have supported a criti-cal approach to texts and their transmission never arose in Tibet, and Rinpoche hopes to begin to fill in these gaps. One of his primary goals is to ensure the preservation of the Tibetan language itself, understanding that language is the very bedrock of a culture. In occupied Tibet, where the Tibetan people have become a minority in their own homeland, the Tibetan language is at risk—even more so among those in exile—of fall-ing out of use. Yet its conservation is indispensable for the preservation and continuation of Tibetan culture and of Tibetan Buddhism itself.

When he is studying rare texts Rinpoche collects expressions that are unknown or forgotten, or have fallen into disuse. For example, the meanings of certain metaphors in Buddhist texts have been largely lost because the terms used for places, plants, or animals are no longer known. Parables were intended to clarify what was being said, but now many have the opposite effect, as no one knows for certain what they were originally intended to impart; shedding light on such obscure passages would increase the illumination of the Dharma. One of Rinpoche's goals is to create a commentary that makes the interpretation of such passages easier, and another long-term goal is the revision of quotations from the works of the Buddha in Tibetan commentarial texts. Many of the Buddha's statements are quoted correctly in terms of their meaning, but they lack source citations and they are not worded exactly as the original is given in the Kangyur. Rinpoche wants to produce annotated editions of the texts that meet modern scholarly standards, which, given the sheer abundance of material, seems an endless task, but this does not discourage him.

He is also engaged in the reformation of the Tibetan language itself. In particular, standard Tibetan grammar is in need of fundamental revision and clarification. For example, many words have multiple variant forms, which leads to numerous errors and misunderstandings that could be avoided through careful standardization. The preservation of a people's language as an expression of their wealth of cultural, intellectual, and spiritual achievements cannot be separated from the preservation of their material cultural heritage. At the same time, a language's flexibility must be exercised in a world caught up in rapid transformation. In Rinpoche's view, it is vitally necessary to find expressions in one's mother tongue to refer to the new objects, experiences, and achievements of the modern world. Perhaps he feels the urgency of this matter more strongly than most people in the Western world, who have been slowly absorbing English words and expressions without question, because the Tibetans have been subjected to such radical transformation in a very short time. What the West has experienced as a gradual and voluntary transition in cultural values is for Tibetans a rapid, externally imposed reorientation, in the midst of which Chinese expressions are beginning to permeate the language.

One of the most important sources for Rinpoche's intellectual archeology is the huge treasury of manuscripts discovered in the caves of Dunhuang on the Silk Road. Dating from the fourth to the eleventh centuries, these manuscripts are written in Chinese, Khotanese, Kharoshti, Uighur, and Tibetan. The Tibetan corpus includes thousands of manuscripts and manuscript fragments ranging in subject matter from bilingual glossaries to discourses on military affairs, the political and economic history of the Tibetan empire, the pre-Buddhist Bön religion,

Chetsang Rinpoche studying in his private library in Dehra Dun, India.

ancient legends and rituals, geography and neighboring peoples, medicine, and Buddhism. There are also numerous sketches, diagrams, and paintings, including the earliest known Tibetan medical drawing. Thus these ancient texts provide the researcher with a vast array of information on the earliest period, lasting more than two hundred years, of a Tibetan realm united under a dynasty of emperors. The unification of the high Tibetan plateau during the first century, and the following burst of expansion that went beyond the snowy ranges in all directions, exposed the Tibetans to a wide variety of peoples and languages, as well as systems of writing, thought, and government. They acquired new techniques in art and architecture, medicine, and animal husbandry. They adopted new customs, learned new languages, and created their own script and grammatical treatises. The Dunhuang materials provide us with contemporary information on this important historical process, and Rinpoche is in a position to study these texts in depth thanks to his knowledge of both Tibetan and classical Chinese.

The energy and enthusiasm that Rinpoche inspires in those who come in contact with him—whether as spiritual seekers or researchers involved in cultural, linguistic, or historical studies of the Himalayas—

is explained in the Vajrayana as the generation of a mandala. Ordinary human activity is erratic, conditioned by the complex interplay of mental poisons and karmic defilements according to the laws of dependent arising.[1] In contrast to this is the generation of a mandala, the enlightened activity that creates a higher level of order, and thus a more powerful energy and effectiveness, in the world. A mandala arises when access to the secret primordial ground has been gained and a continual unfolding from this center manifests itself as an incessant creative spiritual intelligence: the flawless expression of the buddha nature. The dual manifestation of what is in fact the indivisible mandala is expressed in a Nyingma tantra in the following words:

> Nonmistakenness is the center, nonartificiality is the
>   periphery.
> Energy is the center, the coming-into-presence is the
>   periphery.
> Invariance is the center, nonartificiality is the periphery.
> Unorigination is the center, noncessation is the periphery.
> Indivisibility is the center, presence-*cum*-interpretation is
>   the periphery.[2]

The mandala is a configuration in which the highest wisdom, proceeding from self-existent pristine awareness,[3] becomes manifest through its own immanent dynamism. The tangible forms that a mandala takes, whether that of a realized master (tulku) in his embodiment of spiritual qualities or those created through his enlightened activity, are all manifested in order to help beings come closer to the mystery of being itself in its very meaningfulness.

One such tangible form, the physical heart of the new Drikung Mandala that Rinpoche is developing in Dehra Dun, became the Songtsen Library, a building that embodies the essence of his vision in content, function, and form. It is not a lifeless, dust-covered archive, but rather a treasury and living laboratory of the cultural and spiritual identity of the Himalayan peoples and, in particular, of the Drikung lineage.

Not far from his monastery Rinpoche found a wonderful piece of land on top of a cliff overlooking the wide valley of the Baldi Nadi river. To the east there is a magnificent view of the Himalayan foothills; to the south the eye follows the Baldi Nadi into the distance, where the river

Songtsen Library with statue of Songtsen Gampo in Dehra Dun, India.

flows into the Ganges between the holy cities of Rishikesh and Harid-war; and to the west there is level scrubland before a hill on which long lines of prayer flags flutter in the wind.

This became the site of the Songtsen Library, named for King Songtsen Gampo, seen as the father of Tibetan culture. It was to be no ordinary building, as its outward appearance was intended to reflect its function of preserving and transmitting Tibetan tradition. The building's archi-tectural form has its origin in Tibet's oldest known building (said to predate even Songtsen Gampo), the Yumbu Lagang, a stronghold im-posingly seated atop a sheer cliff.[4] Rinpoche designed the library's plan by conforming to the proportions of the Yumbu Lagang, and an architect worked according to his specifications. Their original plan, which con-tained an additional level, was denied authorization by the city plan-ning department, so the building is not an exact copy of the original. The tower-like construction at the back, which houses a shrine to Avalo-kiteshvara, was added after the plans were approved, and was built at night because according to Indian law, once the roof is tiled a building cannot be torn down. Nevertheless, the planning department was very pleased with the results, and the elegant and impressive building in its prominent location has added to the prestige of the Uttaranchal's capital city and is set to become a local landmark.

Chetsang Thrinle Lhundrup also planned the Songtsen Library's interior design. The paintings were originally intended to represent the diversity of styles in the oldest Tibetan paintings found in various locations on the Himalayan plateau, reflecting influences that range from Persia to China. However, the painters copied the Chinese styles found in the caves of Dunhuang rather than the more specifically Tibetan style of the ancient paintings from Purang and Guge. Rinpoche was satisfied nonetheless, as the paintings provide an artistic antidote to the narrow-mindedness of a political perspective intent on preserving its own cultural heritage exclusively. These artworks are extraordinarily graceful and have the bright coloring characteristic of the Drikung style of thangka painting. On the ceiling of the great reading room opposite the entrance, Shakyamuni Buddha greets the visitor. To his right is King Nyatri Tsenpo,[5] the first monarch of the Yarlung Dynasty, to his left Thonmi Sambhota (seventh century), the first translator of Buddhist texts and creator of the Tibetan script, and above the entrance, the image of Chenrezig.

At the far end of the reading room, between the magnificent editions of the Kangyur and Tengyur in beautiful lockable bookcases, is a pedestal of green marble that holds the three Dharma kings, similar to those in the Chögyalkhang, the shrine room in Rinpoche's parental home in Lhasa. In the Tsarong mansion they were gilded statues with a wealth of jeweled ornamentation, in display cases with intricately carved frames, while in the Songtsen Library they are fine sculptures made of Indian sandstone in a simple glass showcase. Their commanding presence seems to keep watch over the treasury of written knowledge that includes texts on all aspects of the Himalayan region—works on Tibetan culture and traditions, on history, geography, social studies, and economy—and of course, the texts of all Buddhist schools. There is a significant collection of documents from the Dunhuang Caves, and a separate bookcase contains Anagarika Govinda's private library, with many of his personal books bearing his handwritten notes. Everything in the library is cataloged on computer.

Only a few Dharma treasures have survived and found their way to the lineage's new center in Dehra Dun. There is a statue of the lineage founder, Jigten Sumgön, made during his lifetime in his likeness, and the root text of the *Chamchö Denga* (*The Five Treatises of Maitreya*), with handwritten notes by the First Chungtsang Rigzin Chödrak. Another treasure is a little book with wood covers, the lacquer ornamentation worn away through much use, that contains the daily prayers in Shiwe Lodrö's handwriting—tiny letters on small pages, so that he could carry them with him at all times. There are also three malas that belonged to Chetsang Rinpoche's earlier incarnations—one from the Second Chetsang, Thrinle Sangpo, two from the Fourth Chetsang, Peme Gyaltsen—and two very old Drikung seals, one with an archaic, now indecipherable inscription conjecturally ascribed either to Manchurian or Minyak characters.[6] There isn't much, compared to the myriad of precious objects that used to furnish the temples and fill the storerooms of the great monasteries in Drikung.

In the tower shrine there is another Chenrezig, an enchantingly beautiful life-sized statue of the thousand-armed Avalokiteshvara, made of fragrant agarwood. Beautifully embellished Drikung-style tormas, butter sculptures with delicately chased ornaments and figures in vibrant colors, have been placed before it, and there are a couple of cushions for visitors who wish to meditate in the quiet room.

The American Nyima Drolma, a professional sculptor, former college professor, and Drikung *khenmo* (a newly coined monastic title, "female khenpo"), created the equestrian statue of Songtsen Gampo that stands in the large courtyard before the entrance. She was inspired by famous works in the history of art, the statue of Colleoni in Venice and that of Marcus Aurelius on the Capitol in Rome, and her Songtsen Gampo is reminiscent of the sculptures of Gandhara, where contact between the cultures of Asia and the West generated a magnificent aesthetic symbiosis. The bronze statue was set up just before the Dalai Lama's inauguration of the Songtsen Library in 2003. When it was finally resting majestically on its pedestal, the Indian workers started to dismantle their makeshift pulley apparatus and everyone seemed satisfied, except the Kyabgön Rinpoche. He ordered the workers to rebuild their device to lift the statue and turn it around on its axis so that now Songtsen Gampo raises the vajra, the symbol of the indestructible nature, in a gesture of victory toward the peaks of the Himalayas; toward his homeland, the Land of Snows, cradle of the Vajrayana Dharma now scattered in the diaspora. The great Dharma king had once brought the teachings to flower in Tibet, and his memorial stands as a monument and an image of hope against repression of religion, imperialist politics, ideological indoctrination, and cultural genocide.

The artist was shocked when she saw that her creation had been turned around to face in the opposite direction. In keeping with Western conceptions of art, she had placed the statue so that Songtsen Gampo would welcome visitors by riding toward them, but now the horse presents the visitor with its hindquarters. But Rinpoche's decision became clear to Nyima Drolma after she realized that it had nothing to do with European notions of art, its appreciation, and its functions. Here, rather, art was following the deeper logic of the mandala.

The Songtsen Library has been formally recognized by the Hemwati Nandan Bahugana Gharwal University in Srinagar as a research resource center for Tibetan and Himalayan Studies, and has become the venue of biennial international conferences and a destination for individual students and researchers. There are excellent guest quarters for visitors, and the stillness of the place is conducive to both study and retreat.

The Kyabgön Rinpoche's residence lies next to the library. A flourishing garden, where he raises a great variety of plants, blooms before the windows of the audience room, and early in the morning he goes out to enjoy his bushes and perennials. He had a story to tell about each flower and shrub, and even about the little bees that buzzed about the magenta-colored foliage over the stone table where we sat one morning. He remembered the shrine room located on one side of the roof terrace in front of his room in Yangrigar, where bees very similar to those circling around our heads had built their hives under the roof beams. As they flew in and out through countless holes in the walls their buzzing provided background music while he sat on the terrace poring over his texts.

Once, while riding past a wooded lot behind Dehra Dun, he spied champaka flowers blooming on a long tree branch, although his sister Namlha and his driver were convinced that it would have been impossible to identify them in the thick tangle of boughs as they sped past. Nevertheless they turned around and all trudged through the underbrush, and found the flowers. Chetsang Rinpoche took a sapling of this tree, which is highly esteemed in Buddhism, but unfortunately the

*Kagyu College with the Songtsen Library complex in the
background, Dehra Dun.*

sapling did not take root next to his monastery. But when Rinpoche later
built his residence, three lovely champaka trees were already growing
right in front of his house site.

After the library was completed, an area beside it was cleared for construction, and a major new school of higher Buddhist studies (*shedra*),
the Kagyu College, was soon built, with an impressive temple in its center. Inside the Lhakhang an enormous statue of Shakyamuni Buddha is
flanked by Nagarjuna and Asanga, the representatives of the two great
paths deriving from the Buddha: the lineage of the Profound View
through Nagarjuna, the main exponent of the Madhyamaka doctrine
("the Middle Way"); and the lineage of the Vast Conduct, the path of the
bodhisattva, through Asanga. Now the Drikung monks and nuns would
have the opportunity to receive a complete education—from elemen-
tary training to the highest teachings—all in one location.

Rinpoche was very particular about designing and ornamenting the
buildings of Jangchubling, the Songtsen Library, and the Kagyu College
as part of the task of preserving the tradition. He deplored the fact that
the ornamentation of religious buildings no longer conformed to traditional patterns, since temple ornamentation was originally intended to
serve a symbolic, rather than a purely aesthetic function, and was not

to be altered at will. During the construction of the Kagyu College, he had a series of patterns redone because they did not properly correspond to the classical design. The pillars were to be decorated with three very special lines signifying the three collections of the Buddha's teachings: Sutra, Vinaya, and Abhidharma. In their ignorance of the symbolism, the painters had merely painted three short lines, completely missing the intent of the design.

While the Kagyu College was being built, Rinpoche also had a great stupa erected in Lumbini, the birthplace of the Buddha in southern Nepal and one of the most important sacred sites for all Buddhist pilgrims. Years passed before the project could be realized because the Lumbini Development Trust, the agency in charge of the archeological heritage and the development of the site, was riddled with corruption. Drubpön Sönam Jorphel, already directing a monastery in Nepal, was in charge of the project, which finally resulted in a majestic structure that rises thirty meters above the surrounding park that contains ponds, houses for the Kyabgön Rinpoches, lamas, and khenpos, and a retreat center. The unique design features of the Lotus Stupa derive from the writings of the First Chungtsang Rigzin Chödrak. The interior contains a magnificent statue of Vajradhara in union with his consort in the center of an imposing shrine that also holds exquisitely worked statues of the eighty-four Mahasiddhas. The mandala of Chakrasamvara covers the ceiling, and a separate room holds a three-dimensional mandala containing a relic of the Buddha. Many religious dignitaries from Tibet and visitors from all over the world came for the stupa's consecration in 2004. It was a Monkey Year, and the traditional Monkey Year Teachings were given immediately after the opening. This time Chungtsang Chökyi Nangwa could not obtain permission to leave Tibet, but as a result, for the first time in forty-eight years a throne holder was able to conduct the Monkey Year Teachings in Drikung. The Chinese authorities ordered that the teachings take place on a field below Drikung Thil so they could control the expected ten thousand visitors. But the crowd reportedly grew to well over one hundred thousand people, and they were compelled to relocate the event to a place higher up the valley where there was enough room for everyone seeking the phowa blessing of the Drikung lineage.

. . .

Since the establishment of Jangchubling, the reconstruction of the monasteries in Tibet has become an important part of Rinpoche's work for the preservation of Tibet's cultural heritage. The Drikung area lies within the Tibet Autonomous Region, where monasteries do not have strong support from the local population and where the bureaucratic hurdles are considerably higher than in Kham. (Large areas of Kham are located outside the Tibet Autonomous Region in the provinces of Qinghai, Sichuan, and Yunnan, where the administrative authorities grant more freedom to rebuild monasteries than those inside the TAR. Also, the inhabitants of Kham have stronger emotional bonds to their monasteries than do the people in central Tibet, thus they support preservation with more energy.) Despite repeated efforts at reconstruction, not much remains of the former glory of the monasteries. To the east of Yangrigar a new monastery is being built to replace the magnificent old one that was destroyed, but the project has stalled at one small building due to a lack of funds, and the monastery of Yamari has not yet undergone any restoration. Only a small portion of Drikung Dzong has been rebuilt; the once imposing stronghold can no longer be reconstructed, just the residences of the two Kyabgöns and a smaller version of the original assembly hall. Only three monks, who see to it that it does not fall into decay again, live there. After Terdrom Nunnery was repaired, a road into the valley was constructed and many high-ranking Chinese officials travel there now, not for the sake of the unbroken Buddhist tradition, but for the hot springs.

Extensive restoration work on a considerable number of buildings has only taken place in the main monastery of Drikung Thil. The monastery's temples have been renovated and once again house many statues and texts. About two hundred monks live there, and they continue the traditional rituals, chants, lama dances, and butter sculpture, and withdraw to meditation huts for retreats. What they lack, however, are well-trained teachers.

Even the region's natural environment has undergone a marked transformation. There are scarcely any trees or bushes where dense forests once stood, and the once-abundant fauna has all but disappeared. In an especially drastic transformation, Tibet's largest dam has been built south of the confluence of the Shorong and the Lungshö, and the turbines of the hydroelectric plant run straight through the mountain opposite Drikung Dzong. Many families living in the valley had to be resettled, as the open river valley where there had once been villages and fields, and where Chetsang Rinpoche's grandfather had built a suspension bridge a long time ago, has been flooded to become a huge reservoir. Rinpoche follows these developments without rancor, let alone outrage; change is an intrinsic property of all things whether one likes it or not. The power plant will provide many households with electricity, as far away as Shigatse, Lhasa, and Nagchu, and Rinpoche is pleased at the prospect of a wonderful view onto the lake from Drikung Dzong. The Chinese government plans to erect a brand-new city on the southwest bank of the reservoir; fortunately, most of the Drikung monasteries are located on mountain slopes and have not been affected. Only the former site of the Nyima Changra philosophy school, which had already been completely destroyed anyway, is now entirely under water.

Rinpoche has been working on the restoration of Densa Thil, the rundown main monastery of the Phagmodrupa, forefather of many Kagyu lineages, for many years now. This project requires extraordinary diplomatic tact. China has recognized the enormous potential of the monasteries and temples as tourist attractions, and that tourism as a source of income can only be assured if the monuments to Tibet's cultural history are preserved. However, the PRC would prefer to keep them as lifeless museums and as photogenic backdrops for tourists' snapshots, while the Tibetans want to revive them as places of spiritual teachings and practice. Thanks to the loosening of political control in recent decades, more Chinese have been traveling to Tibet as Buddhist pilgrims, and among the Chinese population there is growing interest in maintaining the original use of these sites. But at present, the government remains fixed on the goal of developing Tibet as a kind of "Buddhist Disneyland," an entertaining simulation of Buddhism that exploits the Western fantasies about the legendary paradise of Shangri-La that have shaped the romantic image of Tibet ever since the publication of James Hilton's utopian novel *Lost Horizon* in 1933. No one has ever discovered this fictional land, but now resourceful investors have solved the problem by constructing it in a lovely region in the province of Yunnan, where the district of Zhongdian has summarily been renamed "Shangri-La." New buildings catering to the tourist trade are built to resemble those in old images from the Norbulingka and the Potala purportedly depicting Shangri-La.

An old monastery in the area has been renovated, and additional monastery museums are being built according to old models. The result is a surreal commercial "paradise" pretending to be the genuine paradisiacal Tibet that had never existed in the first place, celebrating the victory of image over authenticity, and of commerce over contemplation.

Meanwhile, as Rinpoche engages in the genuine preservation and renovation of the natural and cultural resources in the region of Phagdru Densa Thil, he must both overcome resistance to his projects and fend off attempts to exploit them in the manner of "Shangri-La." Two very rare species of deer have been discovered in the neighborhood of Densa Thil Monastery, and a small game sanctuary has been set up for the animals. Rinpoche is now working with the help of intermediaries in Tibet, such as relatives in government agencies and monks with family connections in the area, to have the entire region around Phagdru Monastery turned into a conservation area. This is the only hope of preserving the ecosystem of this lovely stretch of land, as there are already plans to lay power lines from the new hydroelectric plant in Drikung through this region. A monk from the province of Yunnan who lived for a long time in Jangchubling Monastery in Dehra Dun is a member of the Nature Conservancy in Beijing, and he has been instrumental in supporting Rinpoche's efforts. The local farmers have been largely convinced of the importance of the project and donated thirty-five fields, and Rinpoche has obtained a permit for reforestation. In this way, the land is being gradually closed off to environmentally harmful development on the local level, and the growing awareness of the importance of nature conservation in Chinese government agencies may secure the project's full realization in the future.

Rinpoche started work on his Phagdru project soon after the construction of his monastery in Dehra Dun was completed, inspired to act by a passage in a historical work. After the death of Phagmodrupa in 1170, his closest disciples discussed where the stupa containing his relics should be erected, and Jigten Sumgön said that if the stupa were built in a place named Mangkhargang the Dharma would blossom throughout the entire world. The eldest monk, Taklung Thangpa Tashi Pel (1142–1210), rejected Jigten Sumgön's proposal and the stupa was built in Phagmodrupa's retreat house, along with a great temple and a second magnificent stupa incorporating some twenty-five hundred statues.

After its destruction in the chaos of the Cultural Revolution, these works of art were dispersed throughout the entire world.

Rinpoche did not view the dispute about Phagmodrupa's stupa as a long-forgotten event; he sees history, especially the Dharma history of his lineage, not as a fossilized chronology of facts, but rather as a living continuum. The lineage founder surely had a definite purpose in mind, perhaps even a visionary insight, when he argued to have his teacher's stupa erected in Mangkhargang, and because it was built elsewhere, the flowering prophesized for the Phagmodrupa did not take place; rather, the lineage soon died out. What others might have seen as an insignificant footnote in the annals of history, Rinpoche took as a sign and a challenge, as if Jigten Sumgön were speaking directly to him.

For Jigten Sumgön, Mangkhargang must have been the geomantically suitable power place, and this alone was decisive for Rinpoche. Although more than eight hundred years had passed, he made every effort to have the destroyed stupa rebuilt on the right location. The undertaking was not easy. The steep terrain near the monastery ruins is difficult to access, and the main problem was finding Mangkhargang in the first place. The *Blue Annals,*[7] in which the event is described, yield no information as to its location, and hardly anyone was left who still knew the old place names. For years, Rinpoche sent out various assistants in vain, searching for clues that might lead to the spot, until he finally entrusted the task to an intelligent monk returning to Tibet for training in traditional medicine. This monk succeeded in locating the site precisely, and sent Rinpoche photos and a detailed description; Mangkhargang is a narrow plateau on an outcropping on the slope below the monastery ruins, with a spectacular view out onto the Yarlung Valley, the cradle of Tibetan culture.

While Rinpoche was sounding out the possibility of erecting the stupa, an inquiry from the department of religious affairs in Lhokha arrived at Chungtsang Rinpoche's desk in the main office in Lhasa, asking whether the Drikungpa could take over responsibility for the reconstruction of Phagdru Monastery, and Phagdru Monastery was officially placed in the hands of the Drikungpa. This type of "coincidence" is not uncommon when Rinpoche makes a heartfelt aspiration. Through intricate and indirect means Rinpoche was able to transfer funds donated by a sponsor to Angon Rinpoche in Drikung Thil, who was officially responsible for the reconstruction, and in a short time, a beautiful stupa arose thanks to the energetic labors of young Drikung monks. It is enclosed in a small red temple covered with a highly polished golden metal roof that shines like a beacon from the dark juniper woods of Phagdru Densa Thil, sending blessings across the Yarlung Valley and out into the world. As soon as the stupa was erected, the Drikung lineage experienced a powerful expansion, as Rinpoche found support for his ideas everywhere and was able to complete many projects without impediments; Jigten Sumgön's prophecy has come true.

The ancient Drikung monasteries in Ladakh were also still urgently in need of renovations, so Edoardo Zentner founded the Achi Association in Switzerland, with Chetsang Rinpoche as its president. With help from international experts in historic preservation, the Achi Association searches for ways to arrest the progressive decay of the old buildings, a problem afflicting all ancient monasteries in the Himalayan region. Tibetans have always been very concerned about keeping their monasteries, temples, stupas, palaces, and dzongs looking bright and freshly painted, but they have made little effort toward the conservation, in the modern sense of historic preservation, of old structures and cultural artifacts. Buildings are given a whitewashing or are provisionally repaired, without addressing the underlying sources of the damage. If something had outlived its usefulness or was in a state of disrepair, it was just considered an example of the fundamental insight of the Buddha—that all that exists is subject to change and decay. If important buildings deteriorated, the ruined parts were simply rebuilt or the images were painted over, and as long as the tradition was being followed, the repairs were neither better nor worse than the originals they had replaced, since continuity was being maintained. However, the issue of preservation of the originals has now become urgent, as knowledge of traditional building methods, materials, forms, colors, architectural structure, and so on, is gradually disappearing. Fewer and fewer people possess sufficient expertise to make appropriate repairs, and even fewer still have the necessary skills to bring such edifices and works of art into existence.

The preliminary measures of experts in historic preservation have already saved a shrine room in Phyang and some badly damaged temples in Wanla and Kanji from ruin, but too many buildings are endangered.

Chetsang Rinpoche is urging the specialists to train monks to undertake appropriate conservation measures that make use of traditional materials. Time is pressing in Phyang Monastery, and Rinpoche must find a middle way between his wish for professional conservation and immediate intervention that will stabilize the temple and allow it to continue to function as a place of religious practice. Above all, some of the wall paintings are in an advanced state of decay. Rinpoche requested the old monk Yeshe Jamyang—one of the few remaining masters of the art of painting in the Drikung tradition, and painter of the young Chetsang Rinpoche's residence in Drikung Dzong shortly after his enthronement—to at least patch them up, but the Indian Agency for Historic Preservation refused to give permission for the work. In response Rinpoche wrote to the agency, "This is not a museum, this is our prayer room, and the Dharma paintings must be restored. If a statue in a museum is missing its nose, its originality is not compromised in any way and it can be left as it is. But we wish to continue using this prayer room in coming generations as well, and the paintings must be maintained accordingly." Delhi gave in and the necessary restoration work was begun.

In ancient Tibet, pilgrimages provided integration into social and economic networks, as well as personal spiritual integration, and the exchange of ideas and goods was often as important as the transformative experiences people had while listening to teachings or taking part in ritual activities at sacred places. Tibet's sacred places are, for the most part, no longer accessible to the majority of exiles, so pilgrimages have lost some basic aspects of their original significance, but this old tradition is beginning to flower again with the emergence of traditional structures abroad. Beyond their significance for ordinary pilgrims, a master's pilgrimages and activities enhance and renew the spiritual energy that exists at sacred locations.

Lapchi is one such place that is closely bound up with the history of the Drikungpa, and Rinpoche often goes on retreat there. Lapchi is not only the speech mandala of Chakrasamvara, it is a sacred place that has been blessed by the practices of siddhas and masters through the centuries. Before Milarepa, the Mahasiddha Saraha and Padmasambhava (Guru Rinpoche) meditated in the caves of Lapchi. Milarepa left his mark in many places as footprints and sacred springs. It is said that through Jigten Sumgön, who sent so many retreatants to Lapchi, the

Chetsang Rinpoche in retreat in Lapchi, Nepal.

Dharma radiated in this holy place like the rays of the sun shining on the snow-covered mountain.

The retreat houses and temples in Lapchi were in a sorry state, and Rinpoche stayed in dilapidated buildings that weren't much more comfortable than caves, with crooked and damp walls ready to collapse. Thanks to the energetic efforts of Nubpa Rinpoche, Chetsang Rinpoche's playmate from childhood days in Lhasa whom he appointed as Lapchi's dorzin, the buildings and the decaying little temple are being restored. Another concern was a famous stupa built by disciples of Shabkar Tsogdrug Rangdol (1781–1851) at a place sacred to Vajrayogini. (The story has it that so many of his followers were present on the day he had the vision of constructing the stupa that, by bringing only one stone each, they raised the stupa in a single day.) Through time it had become dilapidated and was in imminent danger of caving in. Chetsang Rinpoche sent a specialist from Ladakh to construct a new stupa to cover the ancient one without altering it, so that the original stones were preserved inside the new structure and protected against further disturbance from the elements.

Chetsang Rinpoche cares for the animals in Lapchi as well as the buildings. After their second calving, *dzomos*, the female offspring between yak and cow, yield hardly any milk and the farmers neglect them, so many die in winter when feed is short and others fall into ravines, leaving their helpless calves behind. Rinpoche had the calves collected and had a stable built where they now spend the winter. A Nepali was hired to care for them, and they will be distributed among the farmers when they are bigger and stronger.

Seen from a Buddhist perspective, Rinpoche's activity in building new monasteries and institutions and preserving ancient buildings is an expression of the aspect of body. His work in editing, analyzing, and publishing texts on the Tibetan language and religion and the cultural history of the Himalayan region expresses the aspect of speech. The aspect of mind is expressed through the practice retreats that Rinpoche supports in traditional areas such as Lapchi and in the lineage's numerous retreat sites in Ladakh, elsewhere in India, and in Nepal.

Body, speech, and mind are three dimensions of an essential unity. Of them, Rinpoche places the greatest emphasis on the third aspect, spiritual insight, to counter the contemporary fixation on the intellect and discursive thought, and he himself often seeks the seclusion of isolated retreat places. His thinking, speech, and action proceed from this practice—Kalön Tripa Samdhong Rinpoche addressed him as "the vital axis of the practice lineage" at the celebration of Chetsang Rinpoche's sixtieth birthday.

It is said that the actions of a bodhisattva for the benefit of all beings proceed from his realization. In India such a "perfected master" was called a *siddha,* one who has attained *siddhi*s. Siddhi in fact means "success," and originally indicated the successful accomplishment of the practices of yoga, but later this term came to refer to paranormal abilities, as these were regarded as the indications of such mastery. Reports of miracles or inexplicable events in the life of a rinpoche are a delicate matter in many respects, but to simply not mention the subject would be to ignore an important aspect of his existence. Biographies of Tibetan masters are hagiographies filled with remarkable narrations of miraculous events, but their purpose was to inspire faith and devotion to the path through the exemplary lives of extraordinary persons, comparable to the legends of the saints in the Catholic Church. There are, of course, narratives of miraculous events about Rinpoche, and to this day one may be shown a footprint he is said to have left in a stone near Lake Dartso when playing as a ten-year-old.

If one does not wish to perpetuate the rumors of mystical powers and magic that are often associated with Tibetan masters, it is important to sift out what is tenable from what is not. A master never speaks about his own siddhis, so reliance on the reports of third parties is necessary, and a report stands or falls on the reliability of the witnesses. There is an abundance of extraordinary and inexplicable events in Rinpoche's life, which have been witnessed by several reliable persons independently of each other, and which have therefore been elevated to the rank of empirical facts; only a few of them will be mentioned here as examples.

Time and again, *ringsel,* relics in the form of shining, whitish spheroids like tiny pearls, have appeared in Rinpoche's presence. They are often found in the ashes of cremated bodies of deceased rinpoches, in rare cases they are secreted by sacred statues, and, even more rarely, they appear during rituals. The latter occurred in 1985, when he conducted a *Chenrezig Drubchen* in the temple of the Buddhist Society in Leh, Ladakh. The drubchen is a ritual in which the Mani Mantra (OM MANI PEME HUNG) is recited continually, day and night, a hundred million times collectively, over a period of about two weeks.

The traditional three-level mandala representing the palace of the deity was constructed, complete with many religious objects, statues, and vases, as well as the offering cakes. The meditation master from Phyang Monastery had also brought a round mandala, painted on cloth and stretched onto a wooden board, that had been kept in the monastery. Its meaning had been lost, and at the time, Rinpoche himself did not know that it was a Chenrezig mandala in the tradition of Songtsen Gampo. The outside temperature was freezing cold but a charcoal fire kept the temple warm, and drops of the tormas' melting butter ornaments began to fall onto the board. When Sönam Jorphel tried to wipe the butter from the board, he noticed small, round, white globules and immediately wondered if ringsel had appeared. Excitedly, he looked more closely and found an entire row of the pearl-like globules. He tried to bite through one of them, but it did not break—an infallible indication for ringsel. After a while, Rinpoche noticed the excitement that had taken hold of Sönam Jorphel and the other monks near him around the mandala, and he descended from his throne and instantly saw that they were indeed the highly prized relics. Rinpoche ordered the monks back to their places to avoid any commotion or distraction from the ritual, and only at the end of the drubchen, when the mandala was being purified, did Rinpoche collect about five ringsel, which he gave to Phyang Monastery to preserve. They are very small, oval in shape.

For years Rinpoche wished to visit a cave in Zanskar where Naropa had meditated that was also the site of a famous sky-burial ground, a place sacred to Chakrasamvara. A statue of Naropa revered throughout the region is kept there in the Sane Gompa, the local Drukpa Kagyu monastery. The figure, made of clay mixed with medicinal substances and with a heart said to contain Naropa's hair, is kept in a permanently sealed glass shrine. In the summer of 2004 Rinpoche consecrated the statue, with only Stakna Rinpoche, who runs the monastery, and a few monks present during the ceremony. Afterwards, he had turned his attention to the exquisite old wall paintings when Stakna Rinpoche came over and excitedly pulled him back to the statue, where some ringsel had appeared directly in front of the glass case. Stakna Rinpoche was overjoyed; relics had appeared during a visit by the Dalai Lama some time ago, and now they had appeared again, this time in the presence of the Drikung Kyabgön. Some of the ringsel were collected and two were given to him, who had them put into a clay statue of Naropa that was copied from the figure in Zanskar and now has a special place in his personal shrine room.

In 1997, Kyabgön Rinpoche's disciples in Malaysia requested a rain ceremony, as the region had been suffering from a long period of drought. The monks in Chetsang Rinpoche's entourage were upset that their master had actually promised to bring rain, since it would be a terrible embarrassment if he failed. They drove to the sea in five Jeeps, where Rinpoche made offerings to the nagas according to the ancient rituals. The weather remained dry until evening, and as there was no sign that a rain shower was coming, Lama Tsulwang, one of Chetsang

Rinpoche's attendants, became very nervous, fearing a public humiliation; but when he woke the next morning, there was a torrential downpour, followed by a series of heavy rainstorms throughout the day.

Two years later, Rinpoche guided two German book publishers, Angelika Binczik and Carolina von Gravenreuth, and a photographer, Roland Fischer, through the Drikung monasteries in Ladakh, so they could document the extraordinary old wall paintings in the slowly decaying shrine rooms, and the rare antique statues, thangkas, and other religious objects.[8] It was early summer and Ladakh was suffering from a cruel drought, and a delegation of farmers led by the village headman came to Phyang Monastery to request a rain-making ritual. Rinpoche agreed and went up to the monastery's roof terrace with a few monks to perform the chants and rituals. Roland Fischer made fun of this shamanistic hocus-pocus, but appreciated it as a form of impressive and colorful folklore. After hours of ritual a broad band of clouds appeared, the heavens opened, and a mighty rainstorm drenched the land. It was still raining the next day and Rinpoche's German guests were upset because the old mud brick houses in which they were staying were leaking, and the photographer was afraid he would not be able to keep his equipment dry. Now they asked him to stop the inundation. The Drikung Kyabgön was amused and asked them to be patient for a little while longer, as it had not yet rained enough to quench the drought. After another night, the rains stopped.

Rinpoche's direct insight into circumstances and interrelatedness—what is generally termed intuition in the West—is striking. A group of Drikung monks toured the United States in 1999 giving performances of Dharma dances, and one night one of the group tragically drowned in a swimming pool in Boston. At that moment Chetsang Rinpoche, who was in West Virginia, suddenly woke up with a sharp toothache; he knew immediately that this could only be a sign of a completely different kind of event. He sat down and without delay performed a short phowa for the transference of consciousness at the moment of death.

In 1997 the Kyabgön Rinpoche was in Charlestown, West Virginia, to give the entire cycle of empowerments of the *Kagyu Ngag Dzö*, with Gyalpo Rinpoche and Garchen Rinpoche also in attendance. During the initiations and teachings Garchen Rinpoche had many visions and dreams, and once, when Rinpoche was sitting on the throne, Garchen Rinpoche saw the throne grow into a gigantic triangular pedestal, far above the world and as high as the heavens. On top, Chetsang Rinpoche changed into the revered old Drikung nun Khachö Wangmo of Tsele Gön Nunnery in Kham; until her passing in the fall of 2007 at the age of 117 years, visitors waited in line in front of her simple monastery lodging every day. The figure that Garchen Rinpoche perceived in his vision was at the same time the manifestation of the naked young deity, Vajrayogini, the symbol of the emptiness of all phenomena and of the primordial wisdom arising from it. Wild and graceful, she danced poised on one leg, and as her head moved from side to side her unbound hair spread out in all directions to cover the entire earth, blessings streaming out from her undulating hair to all parts of the world.

Seemingly insignificant incidents shed more light on Chetsang Rinpoche's intuitive and spontaneous activity. One evening he was strolling along the streets of Taipei, Taiwan, with his disciple Rinchen Dorje, then known as Yen Chen How, and happened to see a set of Chinese chess (*Xiangqi*). He asked his disciple how to play this game, so Rinchen Dorje explained the complicated rules and, excited, the Kyabgön Rinpoche wanted to play right away. At one point in the game, Rinchen Dorje, although experienced at the game, made a poor move and Chetsang Rinpoche immediately seized the chance and won. His stunned disciple was instantly convinced that nothing in the world was too difficult for His Holiness to achieve.

Chetsang Rinpoche often acts, without pausing to reflect, in such a way that adverse circumstances are overcome with ease and favorable coincidences arise. He acts out of an innermost conviction, as if everything need only be done, no matter how impossible it may seem to the rational mind; this is the secret method by which Vajrayana masters participate in the play of forces through which their goals spontaneously manifest, like an invisible intervention in the energetic fabric of the world.

Chetsang Thrinle Lhundrup—his name describes his way of acting. "Thrinle" means enlightened activity and "Lhundrup" spontaneous arising. What he wishes to accomplish occurs naturally, without calculated effort, as it is described in Tilopa's *Mahamudra Instruction:* "When there is no deliberate effort, that is the king of conduct." What arises is the expression of unhindered wisdom, primordial awareness; Rinpoche realizes his goals with joy, releases them into the world, and keeps on working, guiding the Drikung order with circumspection and wisdom.

His heart is always compassionate toward everyone, especially toward the monks in training, whom the lamas and khenpos often treat very strictly. The Kyabgön Rinpoche does not become angry if someone rebels against him or speaks badly about him, but instead treats him with even greater attentiveness and kindness. This behavior often astonishes the monks attending him, but they have witnessed the continual success of his methods. In his youth he was often hot-headed and irascible, like his grandfather, but with his re-entry into monastic life and his acceptance of responsibility for the order, that energy has been transformed into a dynamic force-field of awakened activity.

Once, when tensions arose at Jangchubling Monastery between the young monks from Tibet and those from Ladakh, a few lamas and khenpos began to crack down harshly, but they failed to regain control of the situation. The goal in Tibetan Buddhism is not to eliminate emotion, but rather to utilize it as a powerful source of energy for spiritual practice, and Rinpoche immediately realized that the young men's strong energies needed an appropriate outlet. He had the students spend several months together in the great hall of the temple performing the preliminary practices. Their unbridled energy was channeled into prostrations, recitation, Chakrasamvara practice, and fire rituals, and the common ground provided by the experience strengthened their feelings of humility and equality, of being no different from anyone else, and their animosities vanished.

It is said that Jigten Sumgön was a master of dependent arising; because he had fathomed the mechanisms of dependent origination to their depths, he knew how to bring about auspicious situations with a passing remark or action. Similarly able to generate favorable circumstances naturally, Chetsang Rinpoche is also a master of dependent arising.

For years the Kyabgön Rinpoche has made numerous journeys around the globe in the service of the Dharma, and he has strengthened people's connections to the Dharma in many countries. He has established an especially strong Drikung presence in Taiwan, where Rinpoche teaches in Chinese. His first visit was at the end of 1988, when he bestowed the

*Chetsang Rinpoche
in Taiwan.*

Kagyu Ngag Dzö over a period of two weeks. Just one year later the first Drikung Kagyu center, Drikung Kagyu Mahayana and Tantra Vihara, was established in Taipei with the strong support of his Taiwanese disciple Yen Chen How (Rinchen Dorje Rinpoche), who continuously helps to sponsor and support the lineage's projects not only in Taiwan, but also in Tibet, India, and in other parts of the world. In 1993, another Drikung Center was established in Nehu, and in 1997 Chetsang Rinpoche assigned Yen Chen How the task of founding the Glorious Jewel Buddhist Center, which is the main center of the Drikung Kagyu lineage in Taipei.

After years of intensive study and performing retreats under the guidance of the Drikung Kyabgön, Yen was recognized as one of two Han Chinese Ngakpa Rinpoches in the Drikung Kagyu lineage.[9] After completing a three-month retreat in 2007 with Chetsang Rinpoche at the holy place of Lapchi, Yen received the name Rinchen Dorje Rinpoche.

Thanks to the activities of Rinchen Dorje, the Drikung Kagyu order is strongly represented in Taiwan and Chetsang Rinpoche visits the country often to give empowerments and teachings. The other Chinese Ngakpa Rinpoche of the Drikung lineage is Huang Yin Jie, popularly known as Acharya Jack Huang, who holds a PhD in religious studies from Taiwan's Hua Fan University and is a long-time translator for many rinpoches, including the Dalai Lama, Sakya Trizin, and Kyabgön Chetsang Rinpoche. In 2005, Chetsang Rinpoche officially recognized him as the third reincarnation of Palme Khyentse Rinpoche.

Chetsang Rinpoche makes use of his travels around the globe to enhance and expand his research, and he is especially quick to perceive the underlying connections and relationships that link seemingly diverse phenomena. He spent hours in the Anthropological Museum in Mexico City, but his anthropological studies had actually begun outside in the museum's great park, where a large number of young people were waiting in line. He studied their physiognomy carefully, noting that some had facial features similar to those of the people of Ladakh, while others had the same features as another ethnic group in Tibet. Chetsang Rinpoche found this remarkable and interesting, and he later studied the research on the migrations of hunting tribes over the Bering Strait during the Paleolithic era. In South America he visited indigenous communities where people live in sod houses, and he also studied the cultural history of the Andean peoples, whose textile designs bear striking similarities to Tibetan weaving patterns.

A Lebanese disciple, Daoud Matta, invited Chetsang Rinpoche to Lebanon, and it was the first visit of a Tibetan lama to that country. Matta made a translation of Shantideva's *The Way of the Bodhisattva* into Arabic, and Rinpoche wrote the introduction, but it hasn't been published because arguments against the concept of an omnipotent creator god are presented in the chapter on wisdom, and this issue would most likely generate controversy and hostility in the Muslim community. Even though Rinpoche's visit to Lebanon had to remain unofficial, a surprising number of people came to his Avalokiteshvara initiation and teachings on bodhicitta. Most of them were from a Christian background, but a few Muslims also took part.

In the ruins of Baalbek, Rinpoche found remarkable similarities to the ornamentation in Tibetan monasteries, including circulating relief borders with ovoid forms. In both cases the symbol of the egg appears to derive from comparable cosmogonic myths in which the world arose from an egg. Rinpoche was certain that their resemblance was not coincidental but came about as a result of trade and the exchange of ideas along the Silk Road.

Vajrayana masters perceive the world on different levels, and landscapes convey meanings to them that remain hidden from the sense perceptions of ordinary life. In his youth, experts in geomancy revealed the secrets of identifying sacred places to him, and wherever Chetsang Rinpoche goes, he scrutinizes the terrain for hidden realities. On one of his Dharma tours Chetsang Rinpoche gave teachings at Dhyani Ywahoo's Sunray Meditation Center in Vermont. Dhyani Ywahoo is the woman chieftain of the Green Mountain Ani Yuniwa, a Native American Cherokee tribe, and she is closely connected with the Drikung lineage; in 1986 her son was recognized as the reincarnation of the Changlochen Rinpoche. Near the center Rinpoche was struck by an unusual topographical conjunction in which river courses, together with the shape of a mountain, create an extraordinarily radiant image of two triangles crossed over each other. He asked Golden True, Dhyani Ywahoo's husband, about the mountain and was told that it was a holy place for Native Americans, and that it contains a sacred cave. Rinpoche inquired about the exact location of the cave, which is right next to Bartlett Falls, and wanted to know whether there were stones there that gave off yellow dust.

In the Tibetan tradition, certain mountains and rivers that create crossed triangles are regarded as the mandala of Vajryogini. They are called *chöjung* (triangles of arising), and are the source of existence, the well-springs of the feminine principle. Sacred caves at these locations contain *sindhura*, a kind of yellow earth or sand.[10] Sindhura is the secret essence of Vajryogini and is utilized in tantric rituals for the Vajrayogini mandala. It is used to draw two crossed triangles on a silver platter, and a little is placed on the foreheads of the participants.

Chetsang Rinpoche was eager to visit the cave at the sacred place of the Cherokee, even though the snow was deep and it was freezing cold. The next day Rick Piche, a friend of Golden True, brought climbing ropes and snowshoes to cross the deep snow. Rinpoche wore lay clothes for this adventure and set off with Gyalpo Rinpoche, Lama Tenzin and his assistant Konchog, guided by Golden True and Rick Piche. As Rinpoche got out of the Jeep, he was still gripping the doorframe when Tenzin slammed the door shut. Rinpoche immediately plunged his bruised and bleeding fingers in the snow and tried to calm Tenzin, who was beside himself with fear and shame. It was no big deal, Rinpoche said, obviously just an attempt by a local deity to put obstacles in their way, but he would not be deterred.

The shaken Tenzin waited by the car while the others stamped through the snow so he could go for help in case of emergency, as they would have to rappel down over the ice-covered cliffs to access the cave entrance. Gyalpo Rinpoche decided that he was too heavily built for such a feat, and stayed up on top of the precipice, as did Konchog. The sun was shining on the cliffs, and meltwater dripped into his eyes as Rinpoche made the perilous descent. There were hardly any footholds on the slippery cliff face, and the waterfall next to them was frozen into a pillar of ice, with only a thin trickle flowing through an opening in the layer of ice that covered the river. Rinpoche was a bit concerned about how they were going to get back up, but rappelled down to the cave entrance. Inside the cave he found a very beautiful, reddish sindhura that he knocked from the cave walls. He packed as much as he could carry into plastic bags.

On his way back up, Chetsang Rinpoche was handicapped by his wounded hand, which he had to use to pull himself up the rope. The hand didn't hurt—he seems to be impervious to most physical pain—but he had trouble keeping a tight grip with it. He had never felt heavier than he did then, and the return climb seemed hopeless; he considered climbing up sideways along splits in the rock face but everything was covered with ice, and the only way back was straight up with the rope, so he breathed calmly and began to haul himself up with sheer muscle power. He had almost reached the top when his strength began to fail, but with one final effort he was able to grasp Rick Piche's hand.

In 2001 the Drikung Kyabgön blessed and named the Vajra Dakini Nunnery, to be established on the land of the Sunray Meditation Center. It became the first Drikung Kagyu monastic community founded for Westerners, to preserve the traditions of the Buddha in forms accessible to them. Nyima Drolma, the nun who had created the statue of Songtsen Gampo for the Songtsen Library was installed as its khenmo. At an assembly of the entire lineage in Lumbini in 2004, Chetsang Rinpoche took the historic step of installing her as the first Western, and first female, abbot, and assigning her the responsibility of establishing Vajra Dakini Nunnery.

Rinpoche's visit in 1993 to the remote valley of Limi in the Humla region of Nepal, on the border with Tibet, was a very special pilgrimage. Chenga Sherab Jungne had brought the Drikung tradition to that exquisitely beautiful but very remote valley in the early days of the order. Because of its isolation, Tibetan culture and the Drikung tradition has survived there intact up to the present. Roads cannot be built in the area and it is a three-day ride on horseback to the nearest helicopter landing site. A river winds its way through the valley with the three villages of Zang, Weltse, and Til and their respective monasteries Zang Phelgye Ling, Weltse Rinchen Ling, and Til Kunzom Dho Ngag Ling. The inhabitants of Limi, many of them astute businesspeople who have accumulated considerable wealth, prepared a truly royal welcoming feast for Chetsang Rinpoche; the last time they had celebrated in such a way was seventy years earlier, to celebrate Shiwe Lodrö's visit. Rinpoche met one very old woman who had encountered Shiwe Lodrö in her youth. They performed the traditional monastic *Cham* dances with masks and ornamented costumes, the masks somewhat different from those used in Tibet, and a Tibetan opera in opulent costumes completed the celebration. People from the neighboring region of Purang in Tibet swarmed to the teachings and initiations.

Limi is like a miniature version of old Tibet, as it has preserved numerous unique cultural artifacts and traditions. During the great exodus from Tibet in 1959, the local people acquired many sacred artifacts from exiles in Kathmandu, and their temples and monasteries now possess superb and carefully guarded collections. Only the simplest objects are publicly exhibited, while the very old, rare, and precious thangkas and statues remain under lock and key, guarded by the most trustworthy members of the community, and not even the monks know where they are kept. When Chetsang Rinpoche came to visit, all of the treasures were brought out of their vaults for consecration, and the old inventories listing the objects for inspection. The Drikungpas' inventories were always flawless, with exact descriptions of the origin, appearance, materials, size, and meaning of the objects, and these lists were no exception.

Chetsang Rinpoche was astonished by their detail and precision, and all entries corresponded exactly to the objects that were in fact presented to him.[11]

One cold morning, a small group of dignitaries, protected by a police escort, set off for the Tibetan border on horseback with the Drikung Kyabgön. When they reached the border the wind died down, and from their elevated position they had a clear view far into Tibet. In the foreground below them Lake Manasarovar shimmered in front of mountains among which the distinctive snow-covered peak of Mt. Kailash rose like a shining jewel. In the distance they could even recognize Gyangdrag Gön, the main Drikung monastery at Mt. Kailash. The sacred landscape emanted the blessings of a Buddha-paradise, suffused with transcendent radiance, removed from all earthly adversities.

18

The Music of Awakening

AMONG CHETSANG RINPOCHE'S many projects is a guide-book for pilgrims to the sacred places of Buddhism, especially of Tibetan Buddhism. He remembers with enthusiasm and affection the chagchen who had introduced him to the visionary interpretation of the sacred places in Drikung, and he has managed to locate the aged chagchen in Tibet and has requested him to commit his knowledge to writing. He also sent emissaries to other chagchens and had their contributions recorded on tape, and he intends to someday collate all of them and produce a comprehensive pilgrimage guide; this is only one of the countless projects he is currently working on with tireless creativity. The Kyabgön Rinpoche often arises at three in the morning to be able to complete his extensive activities, and he frequently withdraws to his simple retreat house in Samtenling—often to dedicate himself to spiritual contemplation, but just as often to be able to work on a project without being disturbed. He has so many works in progress simultaneously that it is hard to imagine how he finds time for the constant stream of visitors lining up at his door to request guidance or blessing, but he receives them with consideration and attentiveness, as if he had all the time in the world.

Encountering Chetsang Rinpoche is like a fireworks display of ideas and projects in constant movement. He still deals with the world with joyful discovery, like a carefree child who seeks to test the limits of reality with every new day. Today, these limits for him no longer lie in the wild regions of Tibet's mountain slopes, but instead in the pathless terrain of his homeland's cultural heritage. They lie on the ridges and in the canyons of history, where remembrance loses its way and the wise begin to read what is unwritten in the darkness of collective memory; in that unfathomable ground out of which the identity of the Tibetan people has unfolded.

During one of my many visits with Rinpoche in his private chambers, his parents, sisters, and younger brother Paljor were all present. Rinpoche was in high spirits, and was eager to play a video he had been sent from Tibet, but there was a problem with the wiring. Undisturbed, he played original, old Tibetan music on a small tape recorder instead, some very rare melodies and songs reserved for the Dalai Lama and the Kashag. Rinpoche observed that the manner in which this music was performed was no longer original, since young Tibetan singers are sent to Beijing for training, and now sing with an unmistakable Chinese coloration; their pitch was higher and the rhythm had been adapted to Chinese prototypes. His parents agreed, and his mother said that the high-pitched voices give her cold shivers. Chetsang Rinpoche sent for his laptop, and we heard more rare Tibetan songs from a CD. Music, too, is part of the cultural heritage he has set out to preserve and he is considering having traditional music documented and archived; his father also has a few rare recordings on old magnetic audio tape.

Rinpoche then asked me to play a DVD about the discoveries along the Silk Road, but unfortunately, the program installed on his laptop did not accept that format. Still untroubled, Rinpoche charged up the stairs to his offices and returned with his treasures for the "scholars"—as he laughingly called Paljor, his father, and myself—handing each of us a mighty folio volume on the Dunhuang Caves. Full of enthusiasm for his topic, he explained in detail the meaning of certain texts to us and then sprang up again to fetch additional documents from upstairs. His mother joked that she was glad that he was moving about so much, since this kept him fit and slim. He returned with two volumes that the Songtsen Library had published on Tibetan manuscripts from Dunhuang from between the sixth and eighth centuries. At that time there was no uniform alphabet or regular system of writing in Tibet, and it is difficult to read the letters and decipher the words. Without a tradition of scientific philology—let alone complementary historical sciences—in Tibet, there are no specialists who have mastered archaic Tibetan sufficiently well to be able to decipher the documents, so research in this area is still in its infancy, but the Songtsen Library's publications, with excellent-quality facsimiles of the Tibetan manuscripts, represent a significant contribution to its development. In March 2007, an international conference under the direction of Heather Stoddard, of the Institut National des Langues et Civilisations Orientales in Paris, brought Dunhuang experts from around the world together in the Songtsen Library in Dehra Dun.

A discussion developed about certain meanings in ancient Tibetan, focusing on a particular syllable that according to Rinpoche was repeatedly used in poetry, in order to lend the contents a special emphasis or accent, but his family was not completely in agreement with this interpretation. His father pointed out that the syllable only underscored a certain content that had already been addressed and offered a few examples in English. Namlha was not so sure, and Rinpoche's mother joined in the discussion as well. Namlha told me not to be surprised, that was just the way the family members were—stubborn, each in his or her own way. Rinpoche's style of stubbornness is very engaging and sparkles with alert intelligence; his father's is reflective, unassuming, and free of intolerance and narrow-mindedness.

Rinpoche was up and about again, and brought two copies of *Songtsen Tsangyang,* the biannual journal of Songtsen Library. In this issue he had published a poem in which the syllable occurs, and then translated it into modern Tibetan. The poem was composed by Songtsen Gampo or one of his ministers and had been recited on the occasion of a victory. Rinpoche then recited the original and his modern version to his father, verse for verse, and his astounded father had to agree with Rinpoche's interpretation.

Rinpoche reviewed for us his progress in collecting and evaluating early, original documents on Tibetan history. His assistants are in the process of cataloging and digitalizing them, as well as making them accessible in print. The Tibetan manuscripts from Dunhuang constitute a significant part of this material, but Rinpoche is also collecting the many ancient inscriptions on rocks and stone pillars scattered throughout Tibet. In this way, the most comprehensive database of source materials on Tibetan history in existence is being created, step by step.

Rinpoche publishes numerous articles in *Songtsen Tsangyang,* mostly on historical topics, under changing pseudonyms. In addition, every issue contains an article he writes on Tibetan linguistics, in which he

Chetsang Rinpoche with the Fourteenth Dalai Lama.

presents ten forgotten Tibetan words, and ten expressions for innovations from contemporary life, all with explanations. The Kyabgön Rinpoche has mastered the uncommon art of successfully combining preservation and innovation.

The Dalai Lama holds Chetsang Rinpoche in high esteem, and consults with him on important issues; there is not much that can really impress the Dalai Lama, but the Drikung Kyabgön's activities impress him. Many Rinpoches attend to the progress of their schools and lineages, but Chetsang Rinpoche, the Dalai Lama notes, came very late from Tibet; without a solid foundation in Buddhist studies and without resources, however, in a very short time he has developed an astounding array of activities for the benefit of Tibetan Buddhism and for the culture of the peoples of the Himalayas as a whole. Kalön Tripa Samdhong expressed a similar idea when he said, "Thanks to Chetsang Rinpoche the Drikung lineage is now complete and flawless, as if he has refined its substance." The Kyabgön Rinpoche maintains that this is not due to him—it all depends on Achi alone.

Within a few years, Rinpoche has breathed new life into the Drikung order, firmly establishing it in exile as well as promoting its restoration in its homeland. Today, the Drikung lineage has more than two hundred monasteries and retreat centers in Tibet, Nepal, and India, and over eighty centers throughout the world. The order is especially strong in the United States, Germany, and Taiwan.

This firm rooting is not solely due to the lineage holder's judicious management and the establishment of the study center in Dehra Dun as a physical base, but also—and above all—to his renewal of the lineage's spiritual foundations. Many among the Drikungpa did not even know the works of their founder, Jigten Sumgön, and even fewer the writings of Rigzin Chödrak. They had been kept locked away as precious secrets, with a transmission given only every few years, and the books wrapped up and sealed again after each one. Rinpoche has done away with such useless secrecy, and Jigten Sumgön's complete works in twelve volumes have been edited and revised a total of five times and assigned new subdivisions; they have now been published once again in their final version, and Rinpoche is also having them translated into English and Chinese. The collected works of Chenga Drakpa Jungne and Chenga Sherab Jungne have also been published, and the hundred and fifty volumes of the Drikung tradition in Angon Rinpoche's safekeeping are currently being revised, but this is a difficult undertaking, as they are full of errors.

Rinpoche had already begun when he was living in the States to supplement Peme Gyaltsen's text with chronicles of the later Drikung throne holders, and during the construction of Jangchubling he published several important Drikung texts, among them the *Drikung Kagyu Sea of Song,* which contains the complete songs of spiritual realization of the masters of the Kagyu lineage from Vajradhara to the great Drikung Kagyu masters, including an extensive appendix on "Pure Vision" by Konchog Rinchen. Chetsang Rinpoche has published his own new prayers for the prospering of the Kagyu lineage complete with explanations and a short, scientifically documented history of the Kagyu lineage, and he has compiled a volume of the fifty authoritative empowerments of the Drikung Kagyu, including precise practice instructions for the special meditative exercises (sadhanas), detailed elucidation of the empowerments themselves, and exhaustive discussion of the difficult points relating to their performance. Teachings by the Kyabgön Rinpoche on the *Fivefold Path of Mahamudra* have been published in English and German, and he has written an explanation to Jigten Sumgön's *Tantric Seven-Limb Prayer* from the viewpoint of Mahamudra.

A thangka with a very unusual and expressive portrait of Marpa Chökyi Lodrö hangs in the room where Rinpoche sleeps and meditates. It is no accident that the portrait radiates immeasurable presence in this particular room. The tradition of the great translator, Marpa, has been neglected in all Kagyu schools, although for the Kagyupa he is the most important connecting link in the transmission from India to Tibet. Many of his teachings are in danger of being lost, and with them goes the central pillar that upholds the spiritual edifice of the schools. Marpa is wrongly considered to have been relatively uneducated, and therefore of lesser significance, but Marpa represents the main trunk of the Kagyupa, from which many schools branched off. Marpa had four main disciples who are known as the "Four Pillars": Milarepa, Ngog Chöku Dorje, Metön Tsonpo, and Tsurtön Wanggi Dorje. Milarepa practiced primarily in retreat while Ngog Chöku Dorje and Metön Tsonpo focused mainly on composing tantric commentaries. Tsurtön Wanggi Dorje upheld the Guhyasamaja tradition that was later passed on to the Gelugpa.

The main line of transmission of the Drikungpa follows the lineage from Milarepa through Gampopa to Phagmodrupa and Jigten Sumgön. However, Marpa transmitted a series of tantras to Ngog Chöku Dorje that were known as the *Seven Mandalas of Ngog*. This tradition, with its own transmissions and initiations, but without special commentaries and teachings, lasted for seven generations. The transmission of the seven mandalas was also primarily upheld by the Drikung Kagyu lineage, and to save them from oblivion, Jamgön Kongtrul combined them with other teachings of Marpa to form the *Kagyu Ngag Dzö*. Today, Marpa's teachings have been scattered, and only parts of their transmissions are preserved by a few lamas. Rinpoche has long been actively seeking out holders of these transmissions to receive the teachings from them. From Khenchen Petse, a Nyingma master from Kham, he received the *Manjushri Nama Samgiti,* one of the *Seven Mandalas of Ngog,* and from the Dalai Lama he received the Marpa tradition of the *Guhyasamaja Tantra*.[1]

Chetsang Rinpoche during an empowerment in Dehra Dun, India.

Another of the *Seven Mandalas of Ngog* is the *Hevajra Tantra,* also known as the "King of Tantras." It is a special transmission that in earlier times was primarily passed on in the Sakya lineage, and through Marpa in the Mar-ngog lineage (Marpa and Ngog). The Indian source texts were translated by Drogmi Lotsawa (993–1050) for the Sakya, and by Marpa for the Kagyu. Dezhung Ajam transmitted a combination of Sakya and Kagyu Hevajra teachings to Khenpo Ape, an outstanding scholar and founder of the Sakya College in Dehra Dun and of the International Buddhist College in Kathmandu, and Rinpoche received the Hevajra transmission from Khenpo Ape in Kathmandu. During this transmission Rinpoche relied on a commentary from the Marpa tradition that Gene Smith had discovered in a private collection in Japan, and since then he has published this text.

Tantric practice consists of two stages, the generation stage and the completion stage. The process of generation (*kyerim*) contains visualizations and recitations, and the completion stage (*dzogrim*) encompasses work with subtle energies and the Path of Mahamudra. Today the Kagyupa mainly rely on the Chakrasamvara Tantra for the generation phase and the *Six Yogas of Naropa* for the completion stage, although the process of generation was originally based on the Hevajra Tantra. One may, of course, make use of any Anuttara Yoga Tantra,[2] but if one takes the force of history into account, the transmission originated with Marpa and he taught the Hevajra Tantra for the generation stage, so Rinpoche has made it his mission to revive this original tradition and reestablish it in all Drikung monasteries. In the course of his studies, he has discovered additional remarkable commentarial works that he is examining and revising. He received a previously unknown text by Marpa on the Hevajra Tantra from a man from eastern Tibet who had worked for a long time in the archives of the Potala, where numerous works were simply jumbled together, but at least they were preserved. He discovered the unknown work by Marpa among them and instantly recognized the work's significance, but because he was unable to take anything out of the Potala, he carefully copied the text and added his copy to a collection of Taklung Kagyu texts. Rinpoche had access to that collection, and thus to the copy of Marpa's text, because he actively supports the currently weak Taklung Kagyu lineage and is personally supervising the education of the young Taklung Shabdrung in Dehra Dun.[3] He has painstakingly revised this previously unknown work containing unique teachings of Marpa and published it in a special edition containing the root text, Marpa's commentary, and Rinpoche's own notes, with his explanations of concepts that Marpa left unexplained or that are difficult to interpret. In addition, Marpa's collected works are in the process of being edited by four monks at the Songtsen Library. Thanks to Chetsang Rinpoche's efforts, Marpa is being returned to his proper place of honor in the lineage.

In Tantrayana, when taking refuge, one visualizes a tree of buddhas, bodhisattvas, lamas, Dharma texts, and other objects of refuge; this is called the "Field of Accumulation." The trunk of the tree stands upright, straight as a pillar. It consists of the lineage lamas and represents the transmission of teaching and experience. Only if this unbroken continuity is maintained is the further transmission of blessing and inspiration guaranteed. With the retrieval of Marpa's teachings, Rinpoche has returned the source of the Kagyu tradition's inner stability to the lineage. This stability is essential; not only does the transmission's connection to its historical roots depend upon it, but because the transmission of the

Chetsang Rinpoche blessing the Peace Stupa in Zalaszanto, Hungary.

lineage arises from the formless enlightened experience of the Dharma-kaya, the lineage lama who holds the transmission thereby becomes inseparable from the transmission's origin. As he is identical with the ultimate level of enlightened being, he is able to make the blessing power available to his disciples so that their minds are increasingly turned toward the Dharma.

This profound energy is like a resonance that is passed on in reincarnation and transmission lineages as if from one sounding box to another. A realized master brings a special resonance into the world that can permeate those who come under its influence, resonating in and through them. It can strike a chord with those waiting to be moved by the right sound, a chord that assists in unfolding that core of higher potential immanent in them.

This is why the sound of authentic Dharma is so fragile and so precious, and why its continuity through the manifestation of great masters is so critically important for the uninterrupted resonance of transmission, sounding onward unceasingly.

Every tone of the music of awakening will diminish and fade away unless it resonates without obstruction in the one who receives the master's transmission. Surrendering to the resonance of the masters transforms perception and transforms knowledge into insight beyond thought, thus transforming the perceiver himself. Surrendering to the resonance of the masters means surrendering to one's own mind.

> All of one's activities become spiritual,
> Regardless of how they conventionally appear;
> And every sound that one makes
> Becomes part of a great Vajra song.
>
> —GEDUN GYATSO, the Second Dalai Lama,
>   *Song of Tantric Experience*

ACKNOWLEDGMENTS

I OWE PROFOUND THANKS TO His Holiness Drikung Kyabgön Chetsang Rinpoche as my root lama, who has given me many priceless teachings, not only verbally, but also through his actions and simply through his presence. My encounters with him are a continual source of inspiration and joy. It has been my great good fortune to have been entrusted by him with the task of writing his biography and that he has made himself available to me tirelessly for many long conversations throughout the years. He has provided me with a spectrum of insights that reaches far beyond the framework of a biography through his admirable memory, his compassionate presence, and his special way of seeing things.

Tulkus and rinpoches of the Drikung lineage kindly made themselves available to me for interviews, and allowed me to share in their memories of their lives in Tibet and in exile, and in their many-faceted reminiscences of Kyabgön Chetsang Rinpoche. Without the different perspectives they contributed, a presentation of the circumstances and events in Rinpoche's life that is both exact and lively would not have been possible. First and foremost, my thanks go to His Holiness Drikung Kyabgön Chungtsang Rinpoche, His Eminence Garchen Rinpoche, His Eminence Togden Rinpoche, Venerable Gyalpo Rinpoche, Venerable Khenchen Konchog Gyaltshen Rinpoche, and Venerable Drubpön Sönam Jorphel Rinpoche.

I have obtained an abundance of valuable information from many lamas, khenpos, and monks. The older ones among them even provided detailed descriptions of the times of the previous Chetsang Rinpoche and the circumstances of the discovery of his reincarnation. My heartfelt thanks go to Khenpo Konchog Sangye, Bugpa Konchog Chönyi, Drubpön Konchog Tenzin, Chagdzö Tsulwang, Lama Chödzong, Lama Yeshe Jamyang, Khenpo Konchog Rangdrol, Nyerpa Konchog Sempa, and Kangyur Lama Jampa Wangchug for their enthusiasm and support.

The conversations that I had with members of Rinpoche's family were of special importance for my task. Through his work for the Tibetan government, Rinpoche's father, Dundul Namgyal Tsarong, provided me with deep insights into political contexts and the family's history with his unassuming manner. I am grateful to his wife, Yangchen Dolkar, for access to the manuscript of her autobiography. Rinpoche's brothers and sisters, Namgyal Lhamo Taklha, Norzin Shakabpa, Dr. Jigme Tsarong, and Dr. Paljor Tsarong, also allowed me to share in their memories. I owe special thanks to Namgyal Lhamo, who always answered my endless questions about details of the family's history and of their more distant relatives with a patience that was equaled only by her thoroughness.

I was able to rely on the active support of many people while I was collecting information in Dehra Dun and elsewhere: I wish to thank Dr. Tashi Samphel, director of the Songtsen Library, and his secretary Norbu Wangchug; Acharya Konchog Jamyang, Rinpoche's private secretary, and his assistant Yeshe Dorje; Lama Konchog Tsering, the resident lama of the Garchen Dharma Institute in Munich, Germany; Lama Konchog Sangye, the resident lama of the Drikung Ratna Shri Center in Tallinn, Estonia; and Khenpo Tenzin Nyima and Jampal Dorje.

Companions and disciples of Rinpoche in all parts of the world have helped me to gain a more complete understanding of the personality and activity of Rinpoche through accounts and anecdotes they shared with me. I wish to thank Dr. Heather Stoddard, Heinrich Harrer, Tenor Taring, Pema Lhamo Ponritsang, Angelika Binczik, Carolina von Gravenreuth, Armin Ackermann, Gita Gaupp-Berghausen, Florian Lauda, Swami Shambhavananda and Faith Stone, Zabrina Leung, Peeter Vaehi, Verónika Tupayachi, Daoud Matta, Venerable Rinchen Dorje Rinpoche, Venerable Dhyani Ywahoo, and Khenmo Nyima Drolma.

Inka Jochum takes a special place among these companions. This book would never have been written without her, as I have her to thank for my first encounter with Rinpoche. In addition, she shared her decadeslong acquaintance with Rinpoche with me.

My thanks go to André Alexander of the Tibet Heritage Fund, Reinhold Messner, Phil Borack, Dr. Remo F. Roth, Thomas Roth, Ani Konchog Tsecho (Sabine Tsering), Lama Konchog Samten, Dr. Jan-Ulrich Sobisch, and Rudolf Schratter, director of the Harrer Museum in Hüttenberg, for supplementary information, documents, film material, and discussions on specific topics dealt with in the book.

Ani Konchog Palmo of Samtenling Nunnery translated an important Tibetan text for me with great dedication.

I deeply miss the astute and perceptive advice of Dr. Petra Eisele, the former director of my German publisher O.W. Barth, whose untimely death is a painful loss for all who knew her, and who supported this project with great enthusiasm from the beginning.

My wife, Dagmar, and Susanne Kahn-Ackermann read the manuscript in various stages of completion, and they contributed to its improvement through their sensitive understanding and appreciation of content and style and with their numerous critical observations. I could always rely on their suggestions for changes. Furthermore, Dagmar has continually supported me with her generosity and warm-hearted sincerity, not only during this time-consuming project. My projects have benefited immeasurably from her loving presence.

Ani Jinpa Lhamo (Edith C. Watts) did a wonderful job of translating this book. In addition, her special understanding of the subject matter helped me clarify some passages that had been unclear in my original manuscript. I am deeply indebted to Meghan Howard, who offered me sound advice and incessantly helped at every stage to get the book published in English. The English edition of this book would not have been possible without the competent assistance of Kay Candler, who graciously contributed her excellent editing skills, and Emily Bower from Shambhala Publications, who patiently provided thoughtful suggestions throughout the editing process.

Nevertheless, this book could never have appeared in this form without the tireless support of Tsering Geleg Pangri, Kyabgön Chetsang Rinpoche's long-standing private secretary. Thanks to his excellent command of German and English, Geleg served as a superb translator during many lengthy interviews with Tibetan dialog partners. His gift for communication and his friendly nature caused all doors to open. Geleg is a wonderful friend. Always charming and full of enthusiasm, he also translated numerous Tibetan texts for me that I used as source material and patiently explained the complex interconnections of Tibetan terms. He accompanied my work from beginning to end with dedication and enthusiasm, and was indispensable for it not only for his knowledge, his contacts, and his identification with the project, but also for his refreshing repartee and his great sense of humor.

APPENDIX

The Throne Holders of the Drikung Kagyu Order of Tibetan Buddhism

THRONE HOLDER *Wylie transcription*	DATES OF BIRTH AND DEATH	HOLDING THE LINEAGE
1. Kyobpa Jigten Sumgön *skyob pa 'jig rten gsum mgon*	1143–1217	1179–1217
2. Khenchen Tsultrim Dorje *mkhan chen tshul khrims rdo rje*	1154–1221	1217–1221
3. On Sönam Drakpa *dbon bsod nams grags pa*	1187–1235	1221–1235
4. Chenga Drakpa Jungne *spyan snga grags pa 'byung gnas*	1175–1255	1235–1255
5. Chung Dorje Drakpa *gcung rdo rje grags pa*	1210–1278	1255–1278
6. Thogkhawa Rinchen Senge *thog kha ba rin chen seng ge*	1226–1284	1278–1284
7. Tsamche Drakpa Sönam *mtshams bcad grags pa bsod nams*	1238–1286	1284–1286
8. Nub Chögo Dorje Yeshe *snubs chos sgo rdo rje ye shes*	1223–1293	1286–1293
9. Chunyi Dorje Rinchen *gcu gnyis rdo rje rin chen*	1278–1314	1293–1314
10. Nyergyepa Dorje Gyalpo *nyer brgyad pa rdo rje rgyal po*	1284–1350	1314–1350

THRONE HOLDER Wylie transcription	DATES OF BIRTH AND DEATH	HOLDING THE LINEAGE
11. Chenga Chökyi Gyalpo *spyan snga chos kyi rgyal po*	1335–1407	1351–1395
12. Goshri Döndrup Gyalpo *go shri don grub rgyal po*	1369–1427	1395–1427
13. Dhakpowang Rinchen Wangyal *bdag po wang rin chen dbang rgyal*	1395–?	1427–1428
Khenpo, Lopön, Chöpön [regents] *mkhan po slob dpon chos dpon*		1429–1435
14. Chögyal Rinchen Palsang *chos rgyal rin chen dpal bzang*	1421–1469	1435–1469
15. Rinchen Chökyi Gyaltsen *rin chen chos kyi rgyal mtshan*	1449–1484	1469–1484
16. Gyalwang Kunga Rinchen *rgyal dbang kun dga' rin chen*	1475–1527	1484–1527
17. Gyalwang Rinchen Phuntsog *rgyal dbang rin chen phun tshogs*	1509–1557	1527–1534
18. Phagmo Rinchen Namgyal *phag mo rin chen rnam rgyal*	1519–1576	1534–1565
19. Panchen Sönam Gyatso *pan chen bsod nams rgya mtsho*	1527–1570	1565–1570
20. Chögle Namgyal *phyogs las rnam rgyal*	1557–1579	1570–1579
21. Chögyal Rinchen Phuntsog *chos rgyal rin chen phun tshogs*	1547–1602	1579–1602
22. Naro Tashi Phuntsog *na ro bkra shis phun tshogs*	1574–1628	1603–1615
23. Gyalwang Konchog Rinchen [first Chetsang] *rgyal dbang dkon mchog rin chen*	1590–1654	1615–1626
24. Kunkhyen Rigzin Chödrak [first Chungtsang] *kun mkhyen rig 'dzin chos grags*	1595–1659	1626–1659
25. Konchog Thrinle Sangpo [second Chetsang] *dkon mchog 'phrin las bzang po*	1656–1718	1661–1718
26. Thrinle Döndrup Chögyal [second Chungtsang] *'phrin las don grub chos rgyal*	1704–1754	1718–1747

THRONE HOLDER Wylie transcription	DATES OF BIRTH AND DEATH	HOLDING THE LINEAGE
27. Konchog Tenzin Drodul [third Chetsang] *dkon mchog bstan 'dzin 'gro 'dul*	1724–1766	1747–1766
28. Tenzin Chökyi Nyima [third Chungtsang] *bstan 'dzin chos kyi nyi ma*	1755–1792	1766–1788
29. Tenzin Peme Gyaltsen [fourth Chetsang] *bstan 'dzin pad ma'i rgyal mtshan*	1770–1826	1788–1810
30. Tenzin Chökyi Gyaltsen [fourth Chungtsang] *bstan 'dzin chos kyi rgyal mtshan*	1793–1826	1810–1826
Lhochen Chökyi Lodrö [regent] *lho chen chos kyi blo gros*	1801–1859	1827–1832
31. Konchog Chönyi Norbu [fifth Chungtsang] *dkon mchog chos nyid nor bu*	1827–1865	1832–1865
32. Konchog Thukje Nyima [fifth Chetsang] *dkon mchog thugs rje nyi ma*	1828–1885	1865–1871
33. Tenzin Chökyi Lodrö [sixth Chungtsang] *bstan 'dzin chos kyi blo gros*	1868–1906	1871–1906
34. Tenzin Shiwe Lodrö [sixth Chetsang] *bstan 'dzin zhi ba'i blo gros*	1886–1943	1906–1943
35. Tenzin Chökyi Jungne [seventh Chungtsang] *bstan 'dzin chos kyi 'byung gnas*	1909–1940	1927–1940
Tritsab Gyabra Tenzin Thubten [regent] *khri tshab bstan 'dzin thub bstan*	1924–1979	1943–1955
36. Tenzin Chökyi Nangwa [eighth Chungtsang] *bstan 'dzin chos kyi snang ba*	1942–	1955–
37. Tenzin Thrinle Lhundrub [seventh Chetsang] *bstan 'dzin 'phrin las lhun grub*	1946–	1958–

The official websites of the Drikung Kagyu Order of Tibetan Buddhism are www.drikung.org and www.drikung-kagyu.org.

NOTES

PROLOGUE

1. The four maras (Tib. dü shi *bdud bzhi*) designate four types of obstructions or negative influences that create obstacles for Buddhist practitioners.
2. The Tibetan concept of lama (*bla ma*) corresponds to that of the Indian guru and refers to a spiritual teacher.

CHAPTER 1. IN SEARCH OF THE PRECIOUS JEWEL

1. Tsampa (*tsam pa*) is roasted barley meal, usually mixed with Tibetan butter tea. This is Tibet's staple food. *Chang* is Tibetan barley beer.
2. Rinpoche (*rin po che*, "the precious one") is the title of incarnate lamas (tulkus) and, in rare cases, of extraordinary spiritual masters who are not tulkus.
3. Bodhicitta ("mind of enlightenment" or "awakened state of mind," Tib. jangchub kyi sem, *byang chub kyi sems*) refers on the relative level to the altruistic aspirations of love and compassion, and on the absolute level to insight into the true nature of reality and the innate wakefulness of mind.
4. A stupa (Tib. chörten, *mchod rten*) is a building or a specially formed urn for preserving relics. The stupa form has multiple levels of symbolic meaning.
5. The chagdzö (*phyag mdzod*) is the administrator of the estate of an incarnate lama.
6. A labrang (*bla brang*) is an estate of a tulku, his household. The labrang is run by a hierarchy of managers, secretaries, and servants. Labrangs are run like businesses that generate the income of the tulku and his employees. A labrang can also have the function of a business or trading house, depending on its influence and wealth.
7. Vajra (Tib. dorje, *rdo rje*): a ritual implement that is symbolic of the indestructible nature; bell (Tib. drilbu, *dril bu*); mala (Tib. trengwa, *phreng*

ba): a string of prayer beads; hand drum (Tib. damaru, *da ma ru*); ritual dagger (Tib. phurba, *phur ba*).

8. Dharmakaya ("body of the great order," Tib. chöku, *chos ku*) is the true essence of a buddha and is identical with the essence of the universe. Sambhogakaya ("body of bliss," Tib. longku, *longs ku*) is the manner of existence of a buddha, expressing the joy of incarnated truth. Nirmanakaya ("body of appearance," Tib. tulku, *sprul ku*) is the manner of existence on the form level in which a buddha appears to human beings in a human body, in order to guide all beings to liberation.

9. At present, Tibetan Buddhism recognizes four main schools: Nyingma (*rnying ma*), Sakya (*sa skya*), Kagyu (*bka' brgyud*), and Gelug (*dge lugs*). Adherents of the schools are mostly denoted by the suffix *pa*, for example, Nyingmapa. The Kagyu tradition is divided into different schools, one of which is the Drikung Kagyu.

10. This practice sometimes led to suspicion and controversy over genuine attempts at finding tulkus. The entire system of leadership through uninterrupted lineages of reborn masters depends upon the integrity of those who implement it. At the end of the eighteenth century, the Manchu Emperor Ch'ien-lung (1736–1795) attempted to put a stop to the increasingly common cases of nepotism and deliberate jockeying for advantage by issuing a decree that prohibited preferential treatment of children of the aristocracy in the selection of tulkus. He presented the Gelugpa with the famous golden urn that was to serve as a nonpartisan instrument for the selection of their high incarnations, as the candidates' names were to be drawn from the urn in a manner similar to the dough-ball procedure. Although the *amban*s, the delegates of the permanent Chinese mission that had been installed in Lhasa in 1727, did not always succeed in monitoring adherence to this directive, it was a step toward restricting the circumference of power and political privilege of the monasteries.

Chapter 2. Family and Childhood in Lhasa

1. The Kashag (*bka' shag*) is the Council of Ministers or cabinet, the highest authority after the Dalai Lama. It consists of three laymen from the Tibetan aristocracy and one minister from the clergy. The cabinet ministers are called kalön (*bka' blon*) or shape (*zhabs pad*, "lotus foot").

2. The Tibetan system of government has seven ranks, and the Dalai Lama holds the first rank.

3. Tara ("Savior," Tib. Dolma, *sgrol ma*), the female bodhisattva of limitless compassion, she appears in twenty-one forms, of which the most popular are Green Tara (Tib. Doljang, *sgrol ljang*) and White Tara (Tib. Dolkar, *sgrol dkar*).

4. The Tibetan calendar consists of twelve animals, each assigned to a year. Five elements are combined with the animals so that five repetitions of the twelve-year series produce a cycle of sixty years, called a rabjung (*rab byung*). This method of counting was introduced in the year that the Kalachakra Tantra, on which it is based, was translated from Sanskrit. Thus, the Tibetan calendar begins with the first rabjung in the Fire-Rabbit Year, corresponding to 1027 C.E.

CHAPTER 3. ON THE THRONE IN DRIKUNG

1. A khatag (*kha btags*) is a ceremonial white scarf.
2. A solpön (*gsol dpon*) is a servant in the household with the rank of a personal assistant or head cook.
3. It is often claimed that the term *hotogthu* is of Mongolian origin. The Mongolian Geshe Ngawang Nyima has shown that it in fact derives from Manchurian. Translated into Tibetan, the title is Phagpa Tsunpa (*'phags pa btsun pa*), *phagpa* meaning "wise," "sacred," or "noble," and *tsunpa*, "strictly following the discipline" or "honorable."
4. In Tibetan samsara is called khorwa (*'khor ba*). It is the cycle of death and rebirth within the six domains of existence, characterized by ignorance, suffering, and impermanence. Samsara also refers to conventional reality and the condition of ordinary sentient beings, trapped in delusion, dualistic perception, disturbing emotions, and karma.
5. According to the historical chronicle *Gyalrab Selwai Melong* (*rgyal rabs gsal ba'i me long*, "Mirror of Royal Genealogies") by the Sakya scholar Lama Dampa Sönam Gyaltsen (1312–1375).
6. A statue made in the likeness of a person is termed a kudra (*sku 'dra*) and a "speaking statue" is termed sungjonma (*gsung byon ma*).
7. Yeshe Gonpo (*ye shes mgon po*) is an aspect of Mahakala.
8. To produce these especially valuable manuscripts, a mixture of wheat beer, salt, and black ink was applied to the indigo-colored paper and smoothed with a pumice stone after it had dried. Sutras are the discourses of the Buddha, and the tantras (Tib. *rgyud*, "continuum," "stream of being," "mind-stream") are the foundational works of Vajrayana and its meditation techniques.

CHAPTER 4. TUTORS AND STORYTELLERS

1. Yongzin (*yongs 'dzin*): Tutor of a high incarnate lama, an honorific title for a virtuous spiritual friend.
2. In the threefold structure of the Buddhist practice of ground, path, and fruit, an empowerment brings about maturation on the path of practice, while the pith instructions, if applied, lead to liberation. The person who

guides one on this path is considered one's root lama. If he provides empowerment, transmission, and pith instructions, he is called "the lama who grants the three kindnesses."

3. The term Kundun (*sku mdun*) means "presence" and refers to the presence of a spiritually high-ranking person.

4. Nomads lived in the northern part of Drikung, semi-nomads in the south. As they were poor, they were unable to provide the monasteries with additional food. They had hardly any vegetables, only *droma* (the sweet roots of silverweed, *Potentilla anserina*) and radishes, but sufficient meat, yoghurt, dried cheese, and butter. In Drikung, raw meat was put in ice to preserve it during the winter. A very bitter type of radish was crushed, mixed with tsampa and chopped meat, and seasoned with some hot peppers and salt. Now and again droma or stinging nettle soup with tsampa was provided.

5. Ro Dung (*ro sgrung*, "Tales of the Corpse") is a collection of stories deriving from the ancient Indian compilation of texts *Vetalapancavimsati* ("The Twenty-Five Tales of the Corpse-Demon"), regarded as the model for the *Thousand and One Nights*.

6. The Tibetan government also sent a delegation of monks to the sacred lake every year to make an offering of a silver urn filled with medicinal substances. The lake is bound up with a tragedy in the Drikung lineage. During a severe drought in 1938, the Seventh Chungtsang Chökyi Jungne (1909–1940) had gone there to perform a rain ritual. He brought a very revered, magical horn filled with mantras made by the First Chungtsang Rigzin Chödrak, who had been regarded as a great sorcerer. Chökyi Jungne was to drive the horn into the ground on the riverbank during the ritual. Thereupon an unusually powerful rain began to fall, and quickly developed into a wild snowstorm. The wind and snow were so severe that none of his attendants were able to reach the riverbank and retrieve the precious horn, which sank into the waters and disappeared. Chökyi Jungne soon fell ill, and died in 1940 at the young age of thirty-one.

7. Drubwang (*grub dbang*, "Great Siddha"), title of a meditation master.

8. Yogis work with the inner winds (*lung*) that flow through the channels (*tsa*) of the subtle body and the drops (*tigle*) located in them. These drops are both the seed forms of the elements as well as points of concentrated spiritual energy potential. It is said that the subtle winds are not separate from consciousness. During their retreats yogis "distill" the wind of primordial awareness from the very winds that serve as the bearers of obscured conventional consciousness and direct it into the central channel that leads from the navel to the crown. In this way they gain control over the drops, and the mind can be guided back to its original essence of clarity and insight. In Tibetan, yoga is termed *naljor* (*rnal 'byor*), "attaining the fundamental state." Opening the subtle energy channels enables the

practitioner to make rapid progress in meditation and is a precondition for attaining higher levels of tantric practice.

CHAPTER 5. INSIDE THE MANDALA

1. The Vajrayana ("Diamond Vehicle," also called Tantrayana or Mantrayana) developed in India in the middle of the first millennium from the Mahayana ("Great Vehicle"). Elements of yoga and the ancient Indian nature religions were combined with Buddhist thought into an esoteric system. Its classical form developed in Tibet as a method of spiritual training with a pronounced emphasis on ritual.

2. So-called "mind-treasures" (Tib. gongter, *dgongs gter*) also exist. They were not concealed in the external world and are revealed through direct spiritual insight.

3. A dakini (Tib. khandro or khandroma, *mkha' 'gro ma*; "female spacefarer") is a female enlightened being who assists tantric practitioners.

4. The time for the baths in Terdrom hot springs was calculated astrologically. To be most effective, the bath would take place when the star Canopus shone in the heavens. Called Karma Rikyi in Tibetan, this star is closely associated with water because in Indian astrology, which is a major source of Tibetan astrology, it is said to have been a sage named Agastya who swallowed all of the water on earth before transforming into this star. Thus, Karma Rikyi was said to have the power to purify water.

5. Yogis and yoginis perform this ritual in both real and visionary burial grounds; it is a meditative practice in which the yogi offers the local demons and spirits his own body to eat, thus gradually relinquishing his self-attachment.

6. The Eight Great Caves are Yangdzong Phuk (*yang rdzong phug*), Chimphu Phuk (*mchims phu phug*), Kharchu Phuk (*mkhar chu phug*), Sheldrak Phuk (*shel brag phug*), Senge Dzong Phuk (*seng ge rdzong phug*), Yerpa Phuk (*yer pa phug*), Yama Lungphuk (*g.ya' ma lung phug*), and Namkha Ding Phuk (*nam mkha' lding phug*).

7. *Khandro Nyingtig* (*mkha' 'gro snying thig*). A collection of profound Dzogchen teachings.

8. Dzogchen (*rdzogs chen*, "Great Perfection," Atiyoga). The highest teaching of the Nyingma tradition, in which the master directly introduces the disciple into the ultimate nature of mind.

9. An object that has arisen miraculously or appeared spontaneously, in and of itself, is referred to as rangjung (*rang byung*), in contrast to that which has arisen dependently, i.e., conditionally (*gzhan byung*).

10. Khenpo (*mkhan po*). A title for the graduates of higher Buddhist studies in the Kagyu tradition. "Khenpo" is also used to designate the abbot of a monastery.

11. The CIA spotted an opportunity to undermine international Communism, and began to organize secret operations inside Tibet with Khampas who had fled the country. Thubten Norbu, the brother of the Dalai Lama who escaped to India in 1956, served as one of the CIA's middlemen with the activists.

12. Bongtrul Rinpoche had very long hair that he usually wore tied in a knot on his head. One of his former reincarnations had applied a razor to his hair after a retreat in order to cut it, but it spewed sparks and could not be cut. Since that time the long hair of the Bongtrul Rinpoches was held in reverence. When giving teachings he let it hang loose.

13. Dorje Phurba (*rdor rje phur pa,* Skt. Vajrakilaya), a wrathful male meditation deity.

14. Phowa (*'pho ba*) literally means "transference." One of the *Six Yogas of Naropa,* it is a yoga practice in which, at the time of death, one's consciousness is transferred from the body and projected into a buddha field. For those who feel they are not able to study and master difficult meditation techniques, the essence of consciousness is safely transferred into Dewachen, the Pure Land of Great Bliss of Buddha Amitabha. The basis of the phowa commonly practiced in the Drikung lineage is a text, entitled *Planting the Stalk,* from a treasure text of Guru Rinpoche that was discovered in southern Tibet in the fourteenth century by Nyinda Sangye. According to one tradition, Nyinda Sangye was the father of Karma Lingpa, the famous terton who discovered the renowned *Tibetan Book of the Dead* (Tib. Bardo Thödol, *bar do thos grol,* literally "Liberation through Hearing in the Intermediate State").

15. Oddiyana was the country where Padmasambhava was born, Zahor was an ancient Indian kingdom associated with the early transmission of tantra; it was Shantarakshita's homeland, among other things.

16. Gongchig (*dgongs gcig*). A collection of commentaries on Jigten Sumgön's Pith Instructions on Buddhist philosophy that his heart disciple Chenga Sherab Jungne (1187–1241) had received from him in private instructions. It is considered to be the most profound philosophical work of the Drikung Kagyu school.

Chapter 6. Tibet at the Abyss

1. Melvyn C. Goldstein, *A History of Modern Tibet, 1913–1951. The Demise of the Lamaist State* (Berkeley: University of California Press, 1989), 204.

2. Chushi Gangdrung (*chu zhi gang drung*). This ancient name for Kham refers to the four rivers Drichu, Machu, Gyalmo Ngulchu, and Dachu, and the six mountain ranges Damo Gang, Tsawa Gang, Markham Gang, Pobor Gang, Mardza Gang, and Minyak Rab Gang.

3. Khenpo Shenpen Chökyi Nangwa (*mkhan po gzhan phan chos kyi snang ba* 1871–1927), also known as Gyakung Khenpo Zhenga (*rgya bskung mkhan po gzhan dga'*), studied for thirteen years with Ön Urgyen Tendzin Norbu (*dbon u rgyan bstan 'dzin nor bu*). Based on these teachings, he wrote his famous "annotation commentary" (*mchan 'grel*) on the *Thirteen Great Treatises* (*gzhung chen bcu gsum*) of Indian origin. These philosophical textbooks, together with Chökyi Nangwa's commentary, traditionally constitute the basic works studied in colleges for higher Buddhist studies.

4. Madhyamaka is the doctrine of the Middle Way, a philosophical system in Mahayana Buddhism expounded by Nagarjuna (second and third centuries) and Aryadeva (third century) on the basis of the teachings of the historical Buddha. Among the main exponents were Buddhapalita (fifth century), Bhavaviveka (sixth century), Chandrakirti, Shantirakshita, and Kamalashila (eighth century), who exerted significant influence on the development of the Madhyamaka doctrine as the philosophical basis of Tibetan Buddhism.

5. *The Way of the Bodhisattva* (*Bodhicharyavatara*, Tib. *byang chub sems dpa'i spyod pa la 'jug pa*) was written by Shantideva (eighth century) and the *Thirty-Seven Practices of a Bodhisattva* (*rgyal sras lag len so bdun ma*) by Ngulchu Thogme Sangpo (1295–1369). Both are highly revered texts in Tibetan Buddhism.

6. The three mental poisons (*dug gsum*): desire/attachment (*'dod chags*), anger/hatred (*zhe sdang*), and ignorance/delusion (*gti mug*).

7. The Eight Practice Lineages (*sgrub brgyud brgyad*) or the eight independent schools of Buddhism that flourished in Tibet: Nyingma (*rnying ma*), Kadampa (*bka' gdams*), Marpa Kagyu (*mar pa bka' brgyud*), Shangpa Kagyu (*shangs pa bka' brgyud*), Sakya (*sa skya*) or Lamdre (*lam 'bras*), Jordruk (*sbyor drug*) or Kalachakra, Shije (*zhi byed*) or Choyul (*gcod yul*), and Nyendrub (*o rgyan rdo rje bsnyen sgrub*).

8. Thu is a type of soft cheese kneaded with butter that becomes hard when dried. The nomads made several products from milk. The flakes were sieved from buttermilk with a cloth and the whey was squeezed out. After being dried in the sun, a hard, dry cheese resulted that had a long shelf life and therefore served as food in winter and on journeys. The remaining whey was simmered down further until it congealed into a thick mass that the women rubbed on their faces as protection against the weather.

9. Gochok Rinpoche sponsored the production of new wooden printing blocks for the Kangyur (*bka' 'gyur*), the comprehensive canon of the "written teaching" of the Buddha. It took fifteen years to complete this task. He originally intended to have them brought to Yangrigar, but the government requested that they be left in Shol at the foot of the Potala. They are now known as the "Shol printing blocks," and numerous historians have

wrongly asserted that they were commissioned by the Thirteenth Dalai Lama.

10. For thirty-five years, the *Seventy Thousand Character Petition* was only available in Chinese Communist Party circles. In 1996, the *Tibet Information Network* obtained a copy of the Chinese version and published an English translation two years later.

CHAPTER 9. THEATER OF CRUELTY

1. The central committees of the CCP are in session for periods of time and are numbered consecutively. The Eighth Central Committee was in session from 1956 to 1969 and held twelve plenary sessions.
2. Chenrezig (*spyan ras gzigs,* Skt. Avalokiteshvara), the Bodhisattva of limitless compassion.

CHAPTER 12. THE BURDEN OF FREEDOM

1. Kushok Bakula Rinpoche (1917–2003), from Ladakh, was deeply engaged in a number of welfare and minorities' rights issues from remote places like Ladakh to the vast areas of Scheduled Casts and Tribes in India. His commitment played a decisive role in the preservation of Buddhist religion and culture in the politically disputed region of the state of Jammu and Kashmir, for which he was called the "Architect of Modern Ladakh." He was the Indian ambassador to Mongolia for more than ten years. In November 2002, near the end of his life, he visited London as a guest of Queen Elizabeth II.

CHAPTER 13. SPIRITUAL GENEALOGY

1. In Vajrayana, Vajradhara (*rdo rje 'chang,* "Diamond Holder") is regarded as the "Primordial Buddha," the primordial ground of all buddhas and Buddhist teachings.
2. Yidams (*yi dam*) are deities embodying the qualities of buddhahood that the practitioner visualizes in meditation. Chakrasamvara ("The Wheel of Highest Bliss," *'khor lo bde mchog*) is a meditation deity and a tantra of the Anuttara Yoga. This practice is cultivated primarily, but not exclusively, by the Kagyu School.
3. Ripa (*ri pa*) are practitioners who carry out their retreats in the seclusion of the mountains.
4. Hulagu was a grandson of Genghis Khan. He conquered southwestern Persia, destroyed the powerful Caliphate of the Abbasids in Baghdad, and founded the empire of the Ilkhans that extended over the eastern part of

Asia Minor, Persia, present-day Afghanistan and Pakistan, and up to the Indian Ocean.

5. The teachings of Tibetan Buddhism are divided into four ascending levels: outer, inner, secret, and ultimate. These correspond to the levels of meaning of the four bodies of a buddha: nirmanakaya, sambhogakaya, dharmakaya, and svabhavikakaya (as the "essence body" that describes the three bodies' unity).

6. Sönam Gyatso became the Third Dalai Lama because the two predecessors in his reincarnation line were given the title of Dalai Lama posthumously.

7. He was a close disciple of the Ninth Karmapa Wangchug Dorje (1555–1603), gave teachings to the emperor of China and the king of Nepal, and enthroned the Tenth Karmapa, Chöying Dorje (1604–1674). The tulku lineage of the Shamarpas is the most important lineage of the Karma Kagyu, apart from that of the Karmapas.

8. Champaka is a type of magnolia (*Magnolia champaca*) with an intensive fragrance. It is used for secret tantric rituals and plays an important role in the Buddhist tradition.

9. The most important Drikung incarnation lineages aside from the Chetsang Rinpoche and Chungtsang Rinpoches come from the three monasteries of Lho, Gar, and Nyidzong in Kham: Lhochen, Garchen, and Nyidzong Tripa, respectively. The Drikung lineage was led jointly by three high dignitaries as regents for the first time between 1429 and 1435—by a khenpo, a lopön (*slob pon*, "spiritual master"), and a chöpön (*chos dpon*, "ritual master").

CHAPTER 14. A NOBLE BEING'S PROMISE

1. There is an old, chronologically untenable oral tradition, which was also narrated to me by Drikung lamas from Ladakh, associating Denma Kunga Drakpa with King Jamyang Namgyal (ca. 1590–1616), as the former was said to have healed this king of leprosy.

2. Chöje (*chos rje*) is a Dharma master, religious teacher; a title of high-ranking lamas and oracles.

CHAPTER 15. ABSORPTION AND WITHDRAWAL

1. Dorzin is the abbreviated form of Dorje Dzinpa (*rdo rje 'dzin pa*, "vajra-holder"), a respectful title for a realized master who guides practitioners at special retreat locations. In the Drikung tradition, there were dorzin at Mt. Kailash, Tsari, and Lapchi, while the meditation master at the main monastery of Drikung Thil bore the title of tripön (*khri dpon*, "master of

the throne"). The tripön always selected his successor himself. The most recent tripöns in Drikung Thil were the great yogi Pachung Rinpoche (1901–1988), followed by Gelong Tenzin Nyima (1924–2006). The present tripön is Gelong Tashi Rabten, one of Gelong Tenzin Nyima's most accomplished disciples.

2. The *Thegchen Tenpe Nyingpo* (*theg chen btsan pa'i snying po'i gsal ba zhes bya ba*) was written by Ngoje Repa (*ngo rje ras pa,* also called Shedang Dorje, *zhe sdang rdo rje,* twelfth century), a disciple of Jigten Sumgön. It presents the entire Graduated Path of the Mahayana, including one of the oldest commentaries on the profound Fivefold Path of Mahamudra.

3. Ngöndro (*sngon 'gro*), "preliminaries."

4. Calm abiding (Tib. shine, *zhi gnas,* Skt. shamatha). Special insight (Tib. *lagthong, lhag mthong,* Skt. *vipashyana*).

5. Heinrich Harrer, *Rinpotsche von Ladakh* (Innsbruck, Frankfurt: Pinguin, 1981). Unfortunately, the short summary of Chetsang Rinpoche Thrinle Lhundrup's biography contained in the book is full of errors.

6. Siddhis are extraordinary and paranormal abilities attained in the course of spiritual progress. The Vajrayana recognizes eight ordinary and one supreme or sublime siddhi. The eight ordinary siddhis are: (1) the sword of invincibility (*ral gri'i dngos grub*), (2) the eye-potion enabling one to see the gods (*mig sman gyi dngos grub*), (3) swift-footedness—the ability to walk extremely fast (*rkang mgyogs kyi dngos grub*), (4) invisibility or the power of becoming nonapparent (*mi snang ba'i dngos grub*), (5) the art of extracting the essence, meaning the ability of practicing rejuvenation (*bcud len gyi dngos grub*), (6) becoming a "sky-traveler" by achieving the ability to fly (*mkha' spyod kyi dngos grub*), (7) the capacity to make certain medicinal pills (*ril bu'i dngos grub*), and (8) the power of perceiving treasures under the earth (*sa 'og gi dngos grub*). Distinguished from these ordinary siddhis is the supreme or sublime siddhi—the state of complete enlightenment (*mchog gi dngos grub*).

7. Jamgön Kongtrul Lodrö Thaye (1813–1899) opposed the sectarian fragmentation of the teachings and composed over one hundred volumes of writings. His compilation of transmissions from all of the Tibetan schools, *The Five Treasures,* achieved renown: Dam Ngag Dzö (*gdams ngag mdzod,* "Treasury of Oral Instructions," the pith instructions of the Eight Practice Lineages), *Kagyu Ngag Dzö* (*bka' brgyud sngags mdzod,* the most important Kagyu transmissions), *Rinchen Terdzö* (*rin chen gter mdzod,* "The Great Treasury of Precious Termas," the collection of Nyingma treasure texts in 63 volumes), *Sheja Kunkhyab Dzö* (*shes bya kun khyab mdzod,* an encyclopedia of Buddhism and Buddhist culture), and the *Gyachen Kadzö* (*rgya chen bka' mdzod,* Jamgön Kongtrul's own collected writings).

8. The Mani Kabum (*ma ni bka' 'bum*) contains the comprehensive teachings on Chenrezig deriving from Songtsen Gampo.

9. Dorje Phagmo (*rdo rje phag mo,* Skt. Vajravarahi, "Diamond Sow") is a sambhogakaya manifestation of the female Buddha Samantabhadri, also a wisdom dakini.

10. The *Nyingtig Yashi* (*snying thig ya bzhi,* "Four Heart Essences") unites all the nyingtig ("Heart Essence") teachings of Padmasambhava and Vimala-mitra, and is a fundamental work for all Dzogchen practitioners. It was compiled by Longchen Rabjam (1308–1363), an important master of the Nyingma school.

CHAPTER 16. CONCENTRATION AND DEVELOPMENT

1. The practice lineage (Drubgyu, *sgrub brgyud*) is distinguished from the scholastic lineage (Shegyu, *bshad brgyud*), which focuses on the explication and exposition of texts.

CHAPTER 17. MASTER OF DEPENDENT ARISING

1. Dependent arising, or dependent origination (Tib. *rten cing 'brel bar 'byung ba,* Skt. *Pratityasamutpada*) consists of twelve links and explains the process of rebirth. Every phenomenon of ordinary, everyday life is also subject to the same process.

2. Quotation summarized following Herbert V. Guenther, *Matrix of Mystery: Scientific and Humanistic Aspects of rDzogs-chen Thought* (Boulder, London: Shambhala, 1984), 42–44.

3. "Self-existent pristine cognitiveness" is the interpretation of the Tibetan term rangjung yeshe (*rang byung gi ye shes*) by Herbert V. Guenther, *Matrix of Mystery: Scientific and Humanistic Aspects of rDzogs-chen Thought* (Boulder, London: Shambhala, 1984), 44.

4. Yumbu Lagang (*yum bu bla sgang*) is also known as Yumbu Lhakar (*yum bu lha mkhar*).

5. The lifetime of Nyatri Tsenpo is generally placed in the second century B.C.E., but according to some researchers he lived from 417–345 B.C.E.

6. Minyak is the Tibetan term for the Tanguts, a nomadic people that lived in the north of the country and spoke a now-extinct Tibeto-Burmese language. During Jigten Sumgön's times, the Drikungpa had close contacts with the king of the Minyak.

7. The *Blue Annals* (*deb ther sngon po*) were written by Gos Lotsawa Gzhon Nu Pal (*'gos klo tsa ba gzhon nu dpal,* 1392–1481) between 1476 and 1478.

8. Angelika Binczik and Roland Fischer, *Verborgene Schatze aus Ladakh. Hidden Treasures from Ladakh* (Munich: Otter, 2002).

9. A Ngakpa (*sngags pa*) is a lay tantric practitioner.

10. Sindhura (*sin dhu ra*) is often translated as cinnabar or minium, but is also a synonym for limonite (*rgya mtso'i dreg pa*) and blood (*khrag*). It

consists of mineral deposits that have formed in water. The kind that is found at sacred places is the most valuable kind and has a sweetish taste.

11. During a later visit of Chetsang Rinpoche to Limi in 2008, the sealed entrance of a very ancient temple inside Til Kunzom Dho Ngag Ling was discovered and opened. On the walls inside, Rinpoche and his entourage encountered a considerable number of outstanding paintings in vivid colors.

Chapter 18. The Music of Awakening

1. Manjushri Nama Samgiti (Tib. *'jam dpal mtshan brjod,* "Reciting the Names of Manjushri"). Guhyasamaja Tantra (Tib. *gsang ba 'dus pa,* "The Secret Union").

2. The Anuttara Yoga Tantra (Tib. *bla med rnal 'byor rgyud,* "Unsurpassed Yoga Tantra") is the highest of the four tantra classes, and is subdivided into Father, Mother, and Non-dual Tantra.

3. The Taklung Shabdrung is the great-nephew of Yangchen Dolkar, Chetsang Rinpoche's mother.

BIBLIOGRAPHY

Andrugtsang, Gonpo Tashi. *Four Rivers, Six Ranges: Reminiscences of the Resistance Movement in Tibet.* Dharamsala: Information and Publicity Office of H. H. The Dalai Lama, 1973.

Aziz, Barbara M., and Matthew Kapstein (eds.). *Soundings in Tibetan Civilization.* New Delhi: Manohar, 1985.

Barnett, Robert (ed.). *A Poisoned Arrow: The Secret Report of the Panchen Lama.* London: Tibet Information Network, 1998.

Benson, Sandra. *Tales of the Golden Corpse: Tibetan Folk Tales.* Northampton, MA: Interlink, 2007.

Binczik, Angelika, and Roland Fischer. *Verborgene Schätze aus Ladakh. Hidden Treasures from Ladakh.* Munich: Otter, 2002.

Bell, Sir Charles. *Portrait of a Dalai Lama: The Life and Times of the Great Thirteenth.* Boston: Wisdom, 2005.

Brauen, Martin (ed.). *Peter Aufschnaiter: Sein Leben in Tibet.* Innsbruck: Steiger, 1983.

Cabezón, José E., and Roger R. Jackson (ed.): *Tibetan Literature: Studies in Genre.* Ithaca, NY: Snow Lion, 1996.

Butön. *The History of Buddhism by Bu-ston,* edited and translated by Eugéne Obermiller. Heidelberg: Harrassowitz, 1932.

Chan, Victor. *Tibet Handbook: A Pilgrimage Guide.* Chico, CA: Moon Publications, 1994.

Chapman, F. Spencer. *Lhasa: The Holy City.* London: Chatto & Windus, 1938.

Dalai Lama, H. H. the. *My Land and My People.* New York: McGraw-Hill, 1962.

Dalai Lama, H. H. the. *Freedom in Exile.* New York: HarperCollins, 1990.

Dawa Norbu. *Red Star over Tibet.* New Delhi: Sterling, 1987.

Dowman, Keith. *The Power Places of Central Tibet: The Pilgrim's Guide.* London: Routledge & Kegan Paul, 1988.

Drikung Bhande Dharmaradza. *The Jewel Treasury of Advice: A Hundred Teachings from the Heart.* Translated by Khenchen Konchog Gyaltshen Rinpoche. Frederick, MD: Vajra, 1997.

Drikung Kyabgön Chetsang Rinpoche. "Survival, Escape, Revival: Drikung Kyabgon Chetsang Rinpoche's Story." *Chö Yang: The Voice of Tibetan Religion and Culture* 6 (1994): 20–27.

Drikung Kyabgön Chetsang Rinpoche. *Head of the Drikung Kagyu Order.* Malaysia, 1998.

Drikung Kyabgön Chetsang Rinpoche. *The Practice of Mahamudra.* Ithaca, NY: Snow Lion, 1999.

Drikung Kyobpa Jigten Sumgön. *Introduction to Mahamudra: The Co-emergent Unification.* Translated by Khenpo Konchog Tamphel. Dehra Dun, Songtsen Library, 2006.

Everding, Karl-Heinz. "The Mongol States and Their Struggle for Dominance over Tibet in the 13th Century." In *Tibet, Past and Present: Tibetan Studies I,* edited by Henk Blezer, 109–128. Leiden, Boston, Cologne: Brill, 2002.

Ferrari, Alfonsa, and Luciano Petech. *Mk'yen brtse's Guide to the Holy Places of Central Tibet.* Rome: Istituto Italiano per il Medio ed Estremo Oriente, 1958.

Goldstein, Melvyn C. *A History of Modern Tibet, 1913–1951: The Demise of the Lamaist State.* Berkeley: University of California Press, 1989.

Goldstein, Melvyn C., and Matthew T. Kapstein (eds.). *Buddhism in Contemporary Tibet: Religious Revival and Cultural Identity.* Berkeley: University of California Press, 1998.

Goldstein, Melvyn C., Ben Jiao, and Tanzen Lhundrup. *On the Cultural Revolution in Tibet: The Nyemo Incident of 1969.* Berkeley: University of California Press, 2009.

Grunfeld, A. Tom. *The Making of Modern Tibet.* Armonk, NY: M. E. Sharpe, 1996.

Guenther, Herbert V. *Matrix of Mystery: Scientific and Humanistic Aspects of rDzogs-chen Thought.* Boulder, CO: Shambhala, 1984.

Guenther, Herbert V. *Meditation Differently: Phenomenological-Psychological Aspects of Tibetan Buddhist (Mahāmudrā and sNying-thig) Practices from Original Tibetan Sources.* Delhi: Motilal Banarsidass, 1992.

Harrer, Heinrich. *Rinpotsche von Ladakh.* Innsbruck, Frankfurt: Penguin, 1981.

Harrer, Heinrich. *Erinnerungen an Tibet.* Frankfurt: Ullstein, 1993.

Huber, Toni (ed.). *Sacred Spaces and Powerful Places in Tibetan Culture: A Collection of Essays.* Dharamsala: Library of Tibetan Works and Archives, 1999.

Huber, Toni. "Guide to the La-phyi Mandala: History, Landscape, and Ritual in Western Tibet." In *Mandala and Landscape,* edited by A. W. Macdonald, 233–286. Delhi: D.K. Printworld, 1997.

Jamgön Kongtrul Lodrö Taye. *Enthronement: The Recognition of the Re-incarnate Masters of Tibet and the Himalayas.* Ithaca, NY: Snow Lion, 1997.

Jackson, David P. "Lama Yeshe Jamyang of Nyurla, Ladakh: The Last Painter of the 'Bri gung Tradition." *The Tibet Journal* 27 (2002): 153–176.

Jackson, David P. *A Saint in Seattle: The Life of the Tibetan Mystic Dezhung Rinpoche.* Boston: Wisdom, 2003.

Kapstein, Matthew T. "A Pilgrimage of Rebirth Reborn: The 1992 Celebration of the Drigung Powa Chenmo." In *Buddhism in Contemporary Tibet: Religious Revival and Cultural Identity,* edited by Goldstein, Melvyn C., and Matthew T. Kapstein, 95–119, 178–83. Berkeley: University of California Press, 1998.

Khétsun, Tubten. *Memories of Life in Lhasa Under Chinese Rule.* Translated and with an introduction by Matthew Akester. New York: Columbia University Press, 2008.

Konchog Gyaltshen Rinpoche. *In Search of the Stainless Ambrosia.* Ithaca, NY: Snow Lion, 1988.

Konchog Gyaltshen Rinpoche. *Great Kagyu Masters: The Golden Lineage Treasury.* Ithaca, NY: Snow Lion, 1991.

Konchog Gyaltshen Rinpoche. *Prayer Flags: The Life and Spiritual Teachings of Jigten Sumgön.* Ithaca, NY: Snow Lion, 1986.

Kunga Rinchen. *The Garland of Mahamudra Practices: A Translation of Kunga Rinchen's Clarifying the Jewel Rosary of the Profound Fivefold Path.* Translated and edited by Khenchen Konchog Gyaltshen Rinpoche and Katherine Rogers. Ithaca, NY: Snow Lion, 1986.

La Question du Tibet et la Primauté du Droit. Geneva: Commission internationale de juristes, 1959.

Le Tibet et la République Populaire de Chine: Rapport présenté à la Commission internationale de Juristes par le Comité juridique d'enquête sur la question du Tibet. Geneva: Commission internationale de juristes, 1960.

Lopez, Donald S. (ed.). *Religions of Tibet in Practice.* Princeton NJ: Princeton University Press, 1997.

Michael, Franz H. *Rule by Incarnation: Tibetan Buddhism and its Role in Society and State.* Boulder: Westview Press, 1982.

Mullin, Glenn H. *Readings on the Six Yogas of Naropa.* Ithaca, NY: Snow Lion, 1997.

Mullin, Glenn H. *Mystical Verses of a Mad Dalai Lama.* Wheaton: Quest Books, 1996.

Nebesky-Wojkowitz, René de. *Oracles and Demons of Tibet: The Cult and Iconography of the Tibetan Protective Deities.* Den Haag: Mouton, 1956.

Petech, Luciano. *Central Tibet and the Mongols: The Yuan-Sa-Skya Period of Tibetan History.* Rome: Istituto Italiano per il Medio ed Estremo Oriente, 1990.

Petech, Luciano. *Aristocracy and Government in Tibet, 1728–1959*. Rome: Istituto Italiano per il Medio ed Estremo Oriente, 1973.

Petech, Luciano. "The 'Bri-gung-pa Sect in Western Tibet and Ladakh." In *Proceedings of the Csoma de Körös Memorial Symposium*, edited by Louis Ligeti, 313–325. Budapest: Akadémiai Kiadó, 1978.

Richardson, Hugh E. *Tibet and Its History*. Boston, London: Shambhala, 1984.

The Blue Annals, translated by George N. Roerich. Delhi: Motilal Banarsidass, 1988.

Shakabpa, Wangchug Deden. *Tibet: A Political History*. New Haven, London: Yale University Press, 1967.

Shakya, Tsering. *The Dragon in the Land of Snows: A History of Modern Tibet Since 1947*. New York: Columbia University Press, 1999.

Snellgrove, David, and Hugh Richardson. *A Cultural History of Tibet*. Boston, London: Shambhala, 1980.

Sørensen, Per K. *Tibetan Buddhist Historiography: The Mirror Illuminating the Royal Genealogies. An Annotated Translation of the XIVth Century Chronicle rGyal-rabs gsal-ba'i me-long*. Asiatische Forschungen 128. Wiesbaden: Harrassowitz, 1994.

Südkamp, Horst. *Breviarium der tibetischen Geschichte*. Opuscula Tibetana. Rikon: Tibet-Institut, 1998.

Surkhang, Wangchen Gelek. "Tibet in the Early 20th Century." *Tibetan Studies Internet Newsletter*, 1, no. 2 (January 12, 1999), www.case.edu/affil/tibet/moreCenterInfo/tsin/tsinjan99.html.

Taklha, Namgyal Lhamo. *Born in Lhasa*. Ithaca, NY: Snow Lion, 2001.

Taring, Rinchen Dolma. *Daughter of Tibet*. London: John Murray, 1970.

Tibet under Chinese Communist Rule: A Compilation of Refugee Statements 1958–1975. Dharamsala: Information and Publicity Office of H. H. The Dalai Lama, 1976.

Tilopa. *Mahāmudrā. Die Große Gegenwart am Gangesstrom*. Christoph Klonk (trans.) and Angelika Binczik (ed.). Mit einem Kommentar von S. H. Drikung Kyabgon Chetsang Rinpoche. Munich: Otter, 2003.

Tilopa. *Mahāmudrā Upadeśa. Essentielle Mahāmudrā-Unterweisungen am Ganges*. Karl Brunnhölzl (trans.). Munich: Otter, 2006.

Tsarong, Dundul Namgyal. *Le Tibet tel qu'il était. What Tibet was*. Nancy: Anako Editions, 1995.

Tsarong, Dundul Namgyal. *In the Service of His Country: The Biography of Dasang Damdul Tsarong, Commander General of Tibet*. Ithaca NY: Snow Lion, 2000.

Tucci, Giuseppe. *Preliminary Report on Two Scientific Expeditions in Nepal*. Rome: Istituto Italiano per il Medio ed Estremo Oriente, 1956.

Tucci, Giuseppe. *Tibetan Painted Scrolls*. Rome: Libreria dello Stato, 1949.

Tibetan Works

dpal mgon 'phags pa klu sgrub kyis mdzad pa'i ro langs gser 'gyur gyi chos sgrung nyer gcig pa rgyas par phye ba bzhugs so. Lhasa: bod ljongs mi dmangs dpe skrun khang, 1980.

bstan 'dzin pad ma'i rgyal mtshan. *nges don bstan pa'i snying po 'bri gung pa chen po'i gdan rabs chos kyi byung tshul gser gyi phreng ba zhes bya ba bzhugs so.* Dehra Dun: 'bri gun bka' brgyud gsung rab nyams gso khang, 2000.

dkon mchog ratna phrin las rnam rgyal. "gdan sa chen po dpal gyi 'bri gung mthil la bstod pa dad pa'i gsal byed." *bod ljongs nang bstan* 14 (1995) 1: 3–7.

'bri gung pa bstan 'dzin chos kyi blo gros. "la phyi gangs kyi ra ba'i gnas yig." *bod ljongs nang bstan* 10 (1991) 2: 78–111.

'bri gung dkon mchog rgya mtsho. *'bri gung gi gnas spyi dang sprel lo 'pho ba chen mo'i ngo sprod.* Lhasa: bod ljongs mi dmangs dpe skrun khang, 2004.

'bri gun dkon mchog rgya mtsho. *'bri gung chos 'byung.* Lhasa: bod ljongs mi dmangs dpe skrun khang, 2004.

dkon mchog 'phel rgyas. "'bri gung gzhu stod gter sgrom gyi gnas yig." *bod ljongs nang bstan* 10 (1991) 2: 3–57.

dkon mchog 'phel rgyas. "mnyam med 'bri gung bka' brgyud kyi phag lo bka' chos chen mo'i byung rim mdor bsdus su brjod pa thar pa'i sgo 'byed." *bod ljongs nang bstan* 14 (1995) 1: 8–28.

'bri gung phyag mdzod dkon mchog bsam gtan. *dpal 'bri gung bka' brgyud kyi gdan sa'i lo rgyus gtso bor brjod pa dang kho bo ngon grub khang gsar gyi mi tsho'i lo rgyus spyi'i gyung ba brjong pa lugs gnyis 'bel gtam rna ba'i dga' ston.* Dehra Dun: 'bri gun bka' brgyud gsung rab nyams gso khang, 2002.

bstan 'dzin thar lam. "'bri gung bka' brgyud kyi gtsug rgyan skyob pa 'jig rten mgon po'i mdzad rjes rags tsam ngo sprod byas pa." *bod ljongs nang bstan* 3 (1987) 2: 18–30.

'phrin las rgyal mtshan. "'bri gung yang sgar thub bstan sde bzhi rab rgyas gling gi lo rgyus mdo tsam bkod pa." *bod ljongs nang bstan* 4 (1988) 2: 28–35, 36.

tsha rong dbyangs can sgrol dkar gyis brtsams. *sde dpon mi drag gi sras mo gzhon nu ma zhig gis sge'u khung nas mthong ba'i bod kyi rgyal sa lha sa'i snang tshul mdor bsdus.* Dharamsala: Amnye Machen Institute, 2006.

PHOTOGRAPHY
CREDITS

Page xiv. Courtesy of Drikung Labrang. Photographer unknown. About 1995.

Page 6. Courtesy of Drikung Labrang. Photographer unknown. About 1940.

Page 9. Dundul Namgyal Tsarong, 1950.

Page 16. Courtesy of Pitt Rivers Museum, University of Oxford, 1998.131.473.1 (photographer Frederick Spencer Chapman), 1937.

Page 18. Dundul Namgyal Tsarong, 1945.

Page 22. Dundul Namgyal Tsarong, 1946.

Page 23. Dundul Namgyal Tsarong, 1946.

Page 27. Dundul Namgyal Tsarong, 1950.

Page 27. Dundul Namgyal Tsarong, 1950.

Page 28. Dundul Namgyal Tsarong, 1950.

Page 29. Dundul Namgyal Tsarong, 1950.

Page 30. Dundul Namgyal Tsarong, 1950.

Page 31. Dundul Namgyal Tsarong, 1950.

Page 33. Dundul Namgyal Tsarong, 1950.

Page 34. Courtesy of Pitt Rivers Museum, University of Oxford, 2001.59.15.30.1 (photographer Hugh Richardson), 1948.

Page 37. Dundul Namgyal Tsarong, 1950.

Page 43. Dundul Namgyal Tsarong, 1951.

Page 47. Courtesy of Pitt Rivers Museum, University of Oxford, 2001.59.15.14.1 (photographer Hugh Richardson), 1948.

Page 55. Courtesy of Pitt Rivers Museum, University of Oxford 1998.131.473.1 (photographer Hugh Richardson), 1948.

Page 57. Dundul Namgyal Tsarong, 1953.

Page 58. Dundul Namgyal Tsarong, 1956.

Page 62. Courtesy of Drikung Labrang. Photographer unknown. 2004.

Page 64. Dundul Namgyal Tsarong, 1953.

Page 75. Dundul Namgyal Tsarong, 1956.

Page 78. Dundul Namgyal Tsarong, 1956.

Page 82. Dundul Namgyal Tsarong, 1956.

Page 85. Dundul Namgyal Tsarong, 1958.

Page 89. Courtesy of Pitt Rivers Museum, University of Oxford, 2001.59.15.17.1 (photographer Hugh Richardson), 1948.

Page 116. Courtesy of Drikung Labrang. Photographer unknown. 1965.

Page 167. Courtesy of Drikung Labrang. Photographer unknown. 1975.

Page 172. Courtesy of Drikung Labrang. Photographer unknown. 1975.

Page 174. Courtesy of Drikung Labrang. Photographer unknown. 1975.

Page 179. Dundul Namgyal Tsarong, 1976.

Page 185. Courtesy of Drikung Labrang. Photographer unknown. 2005.

Page 204. Courtesy of Drikung Labrang. Photographer unknown. 1978.

Page 215. Courtesy of Drikung Labrang. Photographer unknown. 1978.

Page 221. Courtesy of Drikung Labrang. Photographer Heinrich Harrer. 1979.

Page 222. Courtesy of Drikung Labrang. Photographer unknown. 1984.

Page 224. Courtesy of Drikung Labrang. Photographer unknown. 1985.

Page 236. Elmar R. Gruber. 2003.

Page 238. Courtesy of Drikung Labrang. Photographer unknown. 1992.

Page 241. Courtesy of Drikung Labrang. Photographer unknown. 1996.

Page 246. Courtesy of Drikung Labrang. Photographer unknown. 2000.

Page 248. Courtesy of Drikung Labrang. Photographer unknown. 2002.

Page 252. Courtesy of Drikung Labrang. Photographer unknown. 2005.

Page 260. Elmar R. Gruber. 2003.

Page 267. Elmar R. Gruber. 2006.

Page 276. Courtesy of Drikung Labrang. Photographer unknown. 2003.

Page 279. Elmar R. Gruber. 2007.

Page 281. Elmar R. Gruber. 2006.

INDEX OF NAMES
AND PLACES

Names of places are in italic type.